MW01054905

Thomas Aquinas's Earliest Treatment of the Divine Essence:

Scriptum super libros Sententiarum, Book I, Distinction 8

TRANSLATED INTO ENGLISH WITH FACING LATIN TEXT, INTRODUCTION, GLOSSARY, AND SELECT BIBLIOGRAPHY

by

E. M. MACIEROWSKI
Department of Philosophy
Benedictine College
Atchison, Kansas

with a Foreword by

JOSEPH OWENS, C.SS.R.
Pontifical Institute of Mediaeval Studies

Center for Medieval and Renaissance Studies
and
Institute for Global Cultural Studies

Binghamton University (State University of New York)
Binghamton, NY
1998

IMPRIMATUR:
✝James Patrick Keleher
Archbishop of Kansas City in Kansas

The research for this book was partially funded by
a 1995 summer study grant for college teachers from
the National Endowment for the Humanities.

ISBN 1–883–058–22–8

Medieval Studies Worldwide

EPISTEME

Classical Greek and Latin Texts with English Translation

Sponsors

Binghamton University and Brigham Young University

Publisher and Distributor

Global Publications. Binghamton University
Binghamton. New York 13902-6000
Tel: (607) 777-4495: Fax (607) 777-6132

Thomas Aquinas's Earliest Treatment of the Divine Essence:

Scriptum super libros Sententiarum, Book I, Distinction 8

by

E. M. MACIEROWSKI

Binghamton University (State University of New York)
Binghamton, NY
1998

Foreword

Today, more appreciatively perhaps than ever, the philosophical importance of explanations given to metaphysical themes in Aquinas' youthful work on the *Sentences* of Peter Lombard keeps coming to the fore. Those chronologically earlier discussions by the great thirteenth-century Dominican thinker exhibit a freshness and a vigor often unmatched in the settled and more complacent spirit of his own later works. This importance of the earlier coverages emerges sharply enough in recent studies about the differing meanings of existence in Scholastic treatises or about the varying notions of creation when that term is applied respectively to Aristotle and to Aquinas.

In accord with that background Professor Macierowski in the present book has undertaken a searching study on the Scholastically important topic of essence. Problems regarding essence play a crucial role in discussions today about the respective merits of the metaphysics of Aquinas vis-à-vis the metaphysics of Duns Scotus and of Suarez. From that significant angle, as well as from the viewpoints of the numerous philosophical concerns thereby involved, a careful reading of Macierowski's book will amply repay the time and attention demanded.

J. Owens, C. Ss. R.
Pontifical Institute of Mediaeval Studies

Contents

Introduction

"Contemplare et contemplata aliis tradere"—Summa Theologiae, II–II, q. 188, a. 6.

The body of this book provides scholars and students of medieval philosophy and theology a readable and accurate American-English version of St. Thomas Aquinas's earliest major treatment of God's simplicity along with about half a dozen other themes characteristic of his metaphysics (the *Scriptum super libros Sententiarum,* Book I, Distinction VIII) face-to-face with the original Latin text; it is followed by a glossary of technical terms, indications of sources cited, and a select annotated bibliography.

As to the Latin text, Pierre Mandonnet began to put out an improved Latin text in 1929, which I have used as the base for this translation. Aquinas's discussion of Distinction VIII of Book I occupies about 50 out of the 1116 pages of the first volume of this long out-of-print, rare, and inaccessible text. There is still no critical edition available of this very important text, and consequently even scholars—especially those at some distance from a major research library—may appreciate having at least this portion available in Latin. It goes without saying that Distinction VIII of Book I would have been a doubly closed book for most modern students of St. Thomas, since, even if they were able to lay their hands on the rare text in Latin, the Latin itself would have been another obstacle. Further, until the critical edition of the Leonine text does come out (comparing all the different groups of manuscript readings for the past 700 years and more, and tracking down all sources, implicit and explicit), this interim partial text, keyed as it is to the pagination of Mandonnet's edition which has been standard amongst scholars for three generations, will, I hope, enable readers to

follow citations to it in the scholarly literature bearing on St. Thomas Aquinas's *Scriptum super libros Sententiarum,* Book I, Distinction VIII.

My motive, then, is two-fold: first, to let English readers for the first time into Aquinas's workshop (for this is a key passage from his first major scholarly publication); second, quite frankly, to recruit intellectually ambitious students to philosophy (especially its highest branch—metaphysics), to medieval studies, and to the thought of one of the wisest thinkers of the Western world.

I aim to make the translation stand alone, as much as possible uncluttered by learned notes. On the other hand, the more ambitious student may wish to enter into the deeper by using the glossary of technical terms and the annotated select bibliography.

Accordingly, in the glossary of technical terms and citations, I include (a) the most important English rendering of key Thomistic terms, (b) the original Latin term as it would be found in a standard dictionary entry, (c) the location of at least the first occurrence of each term in the section of Mandonnet's Latin text, and (d) a notation of major differences of meaning for any word that is likely to be a source of confusion. Such terms will be marked in the text of my translation with an asterisk (*). In addition, I put all explicit citations to authors in this glossary in the order in which they are cited in the text, and use the author's name (marked in the text of the translation also with an asterisk) as the key-word to the glossary; for ease of reference, I first cite the page of Mandonnet's Latin text and then, in parentheses, give the internal reference to the question, article, and further subdivision of Aquinas's discussion proper.

The Annotated Select Bibliography is constructed in three parts: 1.0 Bibliographical Tools; 2.0 Historical, Geographical and Philological Background; 3.0 Aquinas Proper. The first part consists of two divisions: 1.1 Works of Orientation, which are intended to guide students in their initial entry to research in philosophy in general and Thomism in particular and 1.2 Major Bibliographical Series. The second part consists of five divisions: 2.1 Chronology; 2.2 Historical Geography; 2.3 Historical Surveys; 2.4 Technical Vocabulary (Latin, Greek, Arabic); 2.5 Composition and Transmission of Manuscripts and the Work of the Leonine Commission. The third part has three main divisions: 3.1 Aquinas's Works and Translations of Them into English; 3.2 Ancient and Medieval Sources Cited; 3.3 Select Modern Works on Being, God, and Thomism, and other works mentioned incidentally.

Explanations of these last two divisions are called for. The Ancient and Medieval Sources Cited (division 3.2) contains three sections: 3.21 An Index to Authorities Cited by Peter Lombard Himself, on Mandonnet pages 187–193 accompanied by the citation data; 3.22 An Index to Sources Cited by Aquinas, again giving the Mandonnet pagination and the references; 3.23 A Bibliography of Ancient and Medieval Sources Cited in sections 3.21 and 3.22. As to this last division (3.3), in the case of literature cited in Ingardia's bibliography (described in division 1.1), I have attempted to mention at least one item from each author publishing in English who has been most frequently cited, as well as the authors whom I know to have written on topics most closely related to the themes of the present text. In this way students may come to know at least some of the most important scholars and institutions involved in Thomistic studies today.

Life and chief works of Aquinas in their historical setting

Following James A. Weisheipl's *Friar Thomas d'Aquino* (2nd ed. 1983) and Jean-Pierre Torrell's more recent *Saint Thomas Aquinas: The Person and His Work* (1996), we can sketch the essential elements of Thomas's life as follows:

Thomas Aquinas (1224/5–1274) lived in the second and third quarters of the 13th century. He was born at Roccasecca in Southern Italy at almost the same time as his king Frederick the Second (1194–1250) decreed the founding of the University of Naples, a secular institution designed to shape the minds of young men into loyal instruments of the State. Aquinas lived under eight Popes and in what today are three countries (Italy, France, and Germany). For geographical precision, of course, it will be necessary to examine a historical atlas, but we can distribute the highlights of Aquinas's life according to where and when he was.

What we call Italy was then divided roughly into three major zones of control. Northern Italy fell under the Holy Roman Empire extending north through modern Germany. The Patrimony of Peter served as a belt across the middle of the Italian boot cutting off circulation to the lower leg and foot. The Kingdom of Sicily comprised Southern Italy and the island of Sicily proper.

Lying athwart the Mediterranean Sea, the Italian boot and its Sicilian football constitute the chief geo-political crossroads of European history. The Kingdom of Sicily contained Muslims, Christians (both Roman and Byzantine) and Jews, not to mention its most recent conquerors, the Norman French, descended from Viking ancestors. One could expect to hear Italian dialects, as well as Greek, Arabic, and the other languages of trade. Aside from these religious and linguistic tensions, there was one important historical problem: Frederick the Second not only ruled the Kingdom of Sicily, but also (22 Nov. 1220) was ruler of the Holy Roman Empire. Accordingly, the emperor's great political objective was to unite northern and southern Italy. On the other hand the popes, who were not only spiritual leaders of Christendom but also political rulers over the Patrimony of Peter, felt none too comfortable lying between the southern hammer and the northern anvil; they wanted to keep them apart, so that their territory would remain uncrushed and under papal control.

As a child of about five Aquinas was sent as an oblate to the Benedictine Abbey of Monte Cassino (1230), where he lived until it was occupied by troops of Frederick II (1239). He then left to study the liberal arts at the University of Naples.

Amongst the most powerful motives for obedience is fear, and, of fears, the fear of poverty is especially well adapted to motivate subjects to obey their king or employees to behave according to the will of their boss. This fear is even more effective if the boss can create a monopoly or near-monopoly on access to the ways of making a living. Frederick Hohenstaufen exploited this fear of poverty as a master-craftsman, blending fear with hope by rewarding the obedient and punishing the opponent. Two groups of religious, however, actually were embracing poverty voluntarily—the Order of Preachers (founded by St. Dominic, d. 1221) and the Order of Friars Minor (founded by St. Francis of Assisi, d. 1226). These mendicant or "begging" friars attracted some men from exactly the same talent pool as that which Frederick wanted—the lesser nobility, and fished in the same economic waters as the secular clergy.

The Aquino family, as lesser nobility under Frederick the Second, seem to have been his loyal and pliable dependents (See Ernst Kantorowicz, *Frederick the Second 1194–1250,* tr. E. O. Lorimer [New York: Frederick Ungar, 1957; orig. London: Constable, 1931], p. 313). Thus, when young Thomas Aquinas received the Dominican habit in 1244 and

left for Paris to study with the Preachers, his brothers waylaid him, imprisoned him in the family castle at Roccasecca, and attempted unsuccessfully to distract him by means of a lady of the night. Also in 1244 Innocent IV fled Frederick and went to Lyons, at that time not quite in French territory. On 17 July 1245 Frederick was excommunicated and formally deposed by the Council of Lyons, but, unintimidated by spiritual powers, continued to rely on military methods to stay on top. In July or August of the same year Aquinas was freed. He returned to the Dominicans—who, true to their status as beggars, preferred walking to riding—and marched over 900 miles to Paris.

Aquinas went to study in Paris at Saint-Jacques under Albert the Great (ca. 1200–1280). Within a year (1246), one of the Aquino brothers who had abducted Thomas was executed, having been implicated in a plot to assassinate Frederick.

From Paris Aquinas walked another 350 miles or so to study theology and to become Albert's protégé in the *studium generale* at Cologne (1248), where he was ordained a priest (1250/51). Frederick II Hohenstaufen died on 13 December 1250, succeeded by his son Conrad IV.

In 1252 Thomas walked back to Paris for advanced studies, lecturing on Peter Lombard's (c. 1095–1160) textbook of authoritative theological opinions (*sententiae*) from 1252–1256. Among the important shorter works dating from this period are *On being and essence,* an exposition on Boethius's *De Trinitate* (unfinished), and probably the one on Boethius's *De Hebdomadibus.* His completion of the 4–volume *Scriptum super libros Sententiarum* (an important piece of which is translated here) marked his eligibility for assuming a professoriate as *magister regens* (1256–1259) at Paris. (This eligibility required Papal intervention backed by royal archers to keep anti-mendicants at bay as Thomas and Bonaventure, his co-mendicant from the Franciscans, actually took office.) There, according to Weisheipl, Thomas disputed the last 21 questions of his series *On truth.* In June of 1259 he attended the Dominican General Chapter meeting at Valenciennes and was charged with revising the Dominican curriculum or *ratio studiorum.* He began writing the *Summa contra Gentiles* at Paris and toward the end of 1259 hiked almost 1150 miles to Naples to execute his charge.

At Naples Aquinas continued the *Summa contra Gentiles* (1260–61). He was transferred to lecture 80 miles north of Rome at Orvieto (1261–65) just before it came to be the seat of the Papal court under the

Frenchman Urban IV (who was crowned on 29 August 1261 and, leaving Orvieto amid attack and riots, died in Perugia on 2 October 1264). Thomas completed the *Summa contra Gentiles* in the fall of 1264.

After Charles of Anjou occupied Rome Aquinas moved there as regent master in the Dominican house of studies Santa Sabina (1265–1267), where he settled a series of disputed questions *On the Power of God* and another *On evil* and, in 1266, began his *Summma Theologiae.* According to Weisheipl "without compelling reasons" (p. 382), Thomas may also have lectured on pseudo-Dionysius the Areopagite's treatise *On the divine names* at this point in his career. In the proem to that work St. Thomas tells us that "the Platonists . . . used to assert one prime <instance> which is the very essence of goodness and unity and *being,* which we call God, and that all others are called good or one or beings through derivation from that prime <instance>. Hence they used to name that prime <instance> 'the Good itself' or 'the good through itself' or 'the principal good' or 'the super-good' or even 'the goodness of all goods' or goodness, essence,and substance as was explained of the separated man. This argument of the Platonists is harmonious neither with the faith nor the truth with respect to what it contains about separated natural species, but with regard to what they used to say about the First Principle of things, their opinion is most true and in harmony with the Christian faith."

A year or so after the consecration of Clement IV on 5 February 1265 in Perugia, the new French Pope moved to Viterbo, where in 1266 he was sent news of trouble brewing in Paris: a renewed and enlarged attack upon the mendicants. Aquinas was assigned to lecture at the priory of Viterbo to be close to the papal curia (1267) where he determined the questions *On spiritual creatures* and finished the first part of the *Summma Theologiae.* Here the Pope offered Thomas the archbishopric of Naples; Thomas declined. Here also Aquinas lived in the same house with William of Moerbeke who finished translating Proclus's *Elementatio Theologica* from Greek into Latin on 18 May 1268; this book provided Thomas the proof he later used to show that the *Liber de Causis* was not by "the Philosopher," as Aristotle was nicknamed, but was rather a pastiche of quotations from the neoplatonic philosopher Proclus. Moerbeke also revised the Latin version of Aristotle's *On the soul* against the original Greek, apparently in 1268. Here, too, on 29 November 1268

Clement died. Friar Thomas was reassigned to Paris. Parts of this trip and probably others, suggests Father Torrell (p. 280), were by boat.

In his second stint as *magister regens* at Paris Aquinas composed the second part of the *Summa Theologiae.* Simultaneously, he began writing a series of hard-to-date commentaries on the works of Aristotle—on *the Physics, De anima, De sensu et sensato, De memoria et reminiscentia, Perihermeneias* (unfinished), *Posterior Analytics, Ethics, Metaphysics, De caelo, De generatione, Meteora* (incomplete), and *Politics* (unfinished), as well as on the non-Aristotelian *Liber de Causis.* He executed a series of "quodlibetal" questions (a daring offer to respond before the whole university to "any question you please," including whether there was a place for beggars in the Church), justifying the role of mendicant communities against the attacks of the secular clergy. Addressing the growing threat of Averroism in the faculty of arts, Aquinas argued a series of *Disputed Questions on the Soul,* demonstrating, on both textual and philosophical grounds, the absurdity of the Averroistic claim that there was only one mind for the whole human race. In a similar vein he wrote a treatise *On the unity of the intellect against the Parisian Averroists.* In the midst of Aquinas's stay (10 December 1270) the bishop of Paris, Stephen Tempier condemned 13 theses of Latin Averroism. Meanwhile, the indefatigable Thomas also wrote a commentary on John's Gospel and those on Paul's letters to the Romans and the first 10 chapters of First Corinthians. His treatise *On Separated Substances,* i.e. angels, also dates from this period (ca. 1270–ca. 1273).

With the election of Tedaldo Visconti as Pope Gregory X on 1 September 1271 the three-year gap in Papal leadership was stopped. To be sure, the coronation was delayed until 27 March of the following year, but this provided opportunity for a regrouping of the Pope's men. Thus, the Dominicans gathered for their General Chapter on Pentecost Sunday (12 June 1272) with Thomas in attendance. That finished, the members of the Roman Province held their local Chapter and charged Aquinas with setting up a school of theology, which he eventually chose to establish at Naples, almost 150 miles to the south.

Thomas returned to Naples and served as Master of Theology in the Dominican house of studies at the Priory of San Domenico and apparently, in addition, was cross-listed in and paid by the secular University of Naples founded by Frederick II Hohenstaufen. Here Aquinas started the Third (unfinished) Part of his *Summa Theologiae* and, with a light

teaching load and the aid of a squad of secretaries, continued his commentaries on Aristotle, most notably that on the *Metaphysics,* which concludes with Book XII. The commentaries on the *De caelo* and the *De generatione,* however, were not finished.

On 6 December 1273, the Feast of St. Nicholas, Thomas reported an experience at Mass which led him to regard all that he had written "as straw." He apparently never wrote again. Summoned to the Council of Lyons, where the Pope was residing, Aquinas suffered a blow to the head in a traveling accident. After a few days' effort to recover at his niece's residence in the castle of Maenza during February, he asked to be transferred to the Cistercian Abbey at Fossanova where, on 7 March 1274, he died, less than fifty years old.

After his death, his story does not end. Piety led his Dominican confrère Reginald of Piperno to remove Thomas's thumb before the funeral, and the monks at Fossanova to exhume, relocate, and decapitate his body, hiding his treasured head so that they would have at least some relic of the great theologian. Eventually on 28 January 1369 Aquinas's remains—head and body—were transferred under papal order from Fossanova to Dominican custody at Toulouse, except of course for tiny fragments reserved for pious veneration the world over.

There were also intellectual divisions. On 7 March 1277 Stephen Tempier, Bishop of Paris, condemned a list of 219 propositions (including some held by Thomas); Robert Kilwardby, the Dominican Archbishop of Canterbury also condemned a batch of propositions, again including Thomistic theses. The General Chapter of the Dominicans defended Thomas's teachings the following year, two years before the death of Albert the Great in 1280. On 17 May 1282 the General Chapter of the Franciscans at Strasbourg restricted the use of Aquinas's *Summa Theologiae:* the only way they would allow it to circulate was if William de la Mare's *Correctorium* was published with it. John Peckham, Archbishop of Canterbury, rejected a number of Thomistic propositions in 1284. On 18 July 1323 Pope John XXII at Avignon canonized Thomas Aquinas as a Saint, and on 14 February a year later Stephen Bourret, Archbishop of Paris, revoked those portions of the Condemnation of 1277 that bore on Aquinas's doctrine. This does not mean, however, that discussion and even controversy about the thought of St. Thomas Aquinas has ceased: from 1977 to 1990 over 4200 items of scholarly literature on his philosophy alone have appeared.

A Remark on Medieval Scholastic Method

The great medieval teachers of philosophy and theology used two principal methods of instruction—reading (*lectio*) and the so-called disputed question. Vestiges of both of these techniques appear in Aquinas's *Scriptum super Sententias*. A word about each of these methods is appropriate, but it is important to bear in mind that each teacher adapted these methods in different ways for different purposes on different occasions. We shall try to say enough about scholastic methods to illustrate how these methods show up in the selection we have translated, to the extent that it is needed to follow the argument correctly.

As a reader of Aristotle, Aquinas's seems to borrowed much from the great commentaries of the Muslim philosopher Averroes (d. 1098). The most noticeable enhancement of this method is Aquinas's employment of the technique of *divisio textûs*. In modern terms, what this amounts to is outlining the whole book, first into its chief components, and subsequently into finer and finer subdivisions until every paragraph or argumentative unit is assigned its place in relation to the whole. A good contemporary adaptation of this scholastic technique of *divisio textûs* is found in the fifteen rules of analytical reading formulated by Mortimer J. Adler and Charles Van Doren in the second edition of *How to Read a Book*. The divisions of the text mentioned in the translation are vestiges of this lecture-method.

Exercises in answering yes-or-no questions constituted the other chief standard technique of the medieval classroom. The object of this intellectual jousting or dialectic was to come up with a true or at least a plausible claim in the course of a disputation. The orchestration for a formal disputation might run something like this. First, the teacher poses a yes-or-no question and assigns students to one side or the other. Their job is to find arguments, as best they can, to justify their position. Next, one side, usually the negative, presents its arguments against the proposed position. Then the other side, usually in the person of an apprentice respondent, presents its arguments and sometimes the true response to the question. Then—almost finally, if need be, the teacher explains the true answer to the question.

But what about all the students' arguments, contra and pro? A good teacher does not uncover a hole and leave it unattended. He reviews all the arguments, both those that agree and those that disagree with his

own conclusion. Sometimes students agree with their teacher, but for inadequate reasons or the wrong reasons; such fallacies must be detected and pointed out; if the conclusion is properly justified, the teacher can let the argument pass. But what about the arguments presented against the teacher's own position? If the teacher is in fact right, he should be able to show where each of the students' opposing arguments went wrong—either by committing some logical fallacy or by being based upon at least one false premise. Finally, therefore, he answers all the objections against his own position.

Such *quaestiones disputatae* or 'disputed questions' are quite often embedded within literal commentaries, as occasion arises. Sometimes the disputed question style is almost vestigial: 'someone might object that . . .'; 'to this one should reply . . .'. Sometimes a full-dress disputation occurs. Sometimes there is something in between.

That commentaries often contain at least vestigial disputed questions—including disputes between conflicting authorities—betokens the fact that authorities were regarded as instrumental in attaining truth and that students and teachers had to use their own powers of reasoning to make the truth their own. In Aquinas's commentaries, it is always worth asking why he introduces apparent digressions answered with formulas like 'considerandum autem est' (one ought to consider, however . . .), 'attendendum est' (one ought to notice), 'sciendum est' (one ought to know). In such cases, at least, it is plausible that the personal voice of the commentator is breaking through.

Peter Lombard, His *Sentences*, and its Influence

Master Peter Lombard (c.1095–1160) was famous for his collection of authoritative theological texts, composed in 1155–1158, according to the editors of the third critical edition of his *Sententiae in IV Libris Distinctae* (Tom. I, Pars I, Prolegomena, p. 32*) published at Grottaferrata (Rome) in 1971. Here we can pass by his gloss on the Psalms, his gloss on Paul's Epistles, his sermons, and works spuriously attributed to him. That he died as Bishop of Paris, which came to be the most active center of theological study in Christendom, and that his collection of *Sententiae* served as the background text for the advanced professional training of generations of theologians, including Thomas Aquinas, bear more upon the issues at hand.

Basing himself on the Augustinian distinction between things and signs in the *De doctrina christiana,* Peter Lombard assigns the first three books to the former (I. God; II. Creation; III. Christ) and the last (IV. Sacraments) to the latter. The Lombard seems originally to have divided each of the four books into chapters. Thus, Book I contains 210 chapters; Book II, 269; Book III, 164; and Book IV, 290 chapters. Subsequently, probably owing to Alexander of Hales (ca. 1186–1245), a more compendious method of grouping the sub-units of the four books came into use around 1223–1227, namely a division of the books into *Distinctiones* (Prolegomena, pp. 143*-144*). Accordingly, Book I came to be divided into 48 Distinctions; Book II, into 44; Book III, 40; and Book IV, into 50 Distinctions. Further, in Master Alexander of Hales's *Glossa,* the *Divisiones Textûs* were already in use (Prolegomena, p. 144*).

According to P. Glorieux's article concerning the commentaries on the *Sentences,* hundreds were written from the 13th to the 17th centuries, most being one or two large volumes in length, devoted to the key themes of theology. They constituted a highly regulated scholastic exercise in the normal program of studies for professional theologians. Normally, the theologian-in-training would first spend a couple of years reading through, i.e. lecturing on, all of Holy Scripture in a cursory fashion (*cursorie*), i.e. pausing only long enough to clarify the literal meaning, to resolve textual and exegetical difficulties, and to note the standard received opinions of glossators and the Church Fathers. Only after having been certified as a Master Theologian would he be entitled to lecture on Sacred Scripture in his own right (*ordinarie*), adding to his explanation of the text personal thoughts on the problems of advanced theology and speculations arising from the text. Between these two stages of apprentice-theologian and Master Theologian he would need to become acquainted with the chief problems of theology proper; it is here where Peter Lombard's collection of *Sentences* comes into play. Under supervision of already certified Masters, the journeyman-theologian would lecture on the Lombard's handbook, thereby familiarizing himself with the main outlines of the theological tradition; these lectures were apparently taken down in stenographic reports (*reportationes*) that he might, after his promotion to Master Theologian, rework and publish after the appropriate university officials had excercised quality control. It is probably in circumstances such as this that Thomas's lectures on the Sentences came to have been written down (*scriptum*).

Of course, the exact details must await the researches of the Leonine Commission for Thomas's personal effort to show up precisely, but something like this seems to have been normal. There were, however, many liberties that the bachelor of the Sentences might enjoy—the order in which to lecture on the four books, how to divide his lectures, how much he wanted to focus in each lecture on the division of the Lombard's text (*divisio textus*), on the exposition of the text itself (*expositio*), and on the questioning process (the *dubia circa litteram*).

The relative standardization of the scholarly exercise, however, makes the commentaries on the Sentences an important resource for comparing medieval and renaissance scholars' personal intellectual positions on key issues toward the beginning of their careers, normally between 30 and 35 years of age. Thomas Aquinas toward 1265 apparently abandoned his effort to recast his *Scriptum super libros Sententiarum* in favor of an entirely new plan—that of the *Summa Theologiae* (Glorieux, col. 1871).

Approaching God Intellectually with Thomas Aquinas

In his more mature works, like the *Summa contra Gentiles,* Aquinas distinguishes truths that are accessible to human investigation from those that transcend the power of the unaided human mind. Thus, since philosophers have demonstrated that God exists, this truth is not something that belongs to the Faith as such but is, as it were, a preamble to matters proper to the Faith. On the other hand, doctrines like the Trinity of Persons and the Incarnation of the Second Person of the Trinity within a human nature as Jesus Christ exceed the power of reason to prove.

Into which class of propositions do the claims of the Lombard's Book I, Distinction VIII fall? At first glance, it appears that Aquinas appeals both to Scriptural and theological authority, on the one hand, and philosophical arguments and authors, on the other. Accordingly, it seems that Aquinas, at least, behaves as though these issues fall, at least to some degree, within the competence of the philosopher to discuss.

In the history of medieval philosophy, one of the most important themes is the nature of God. Jews, Christians, and Muslims all have claims respecting God, but not all Jews, Christians, and Muslims are philosophers. One of the characteristically philosophical questions, dating from the time of Socrates, is "What is it?"

Among the Muslims, Avicenna (d. 1037) offers a metaphysical analysis of the divine simplicity, but does not offer an explicit Qur'ânic scriptural warrant. Amongst the Jews, Maimonides (d. 1204) stands out in offering a metaphysical interpretation of scripture. Standing in a long line of Christians offering various metaphysical interpretations (such as those of Augustine, pseudo-Dionysius the Areopagite, and John of Damascus) and also depending upon both Avicenna and Maimonides, Aquinas (d. 1274) articulates his personal metaphysics of Exodus 3: 14 here apparently for the first time in his academic career. The same theme shows up again in other major works of Aquinas written later in his life, for example in the *Summa contra Gentiles* (Book I, Chapter 22) and the *Summa Theologiae* (Part I, Question 3, Articles 3 and 4). In those two works, Aquinas closes onto the central issue using a plan of his own; in the *Scriptum on the Sentences* his thought is embedded within an Augustinian structure embellished by Peter Lombard.

A brief glance at Aquinas's later strategy will be useful to set what he is doing here into a more systematic context. After some preliminary remarks that claim everything 'revealable' belongs to the study of the theologian, Aquinas lays claim to certain points demonstratively established by philosophers as belonging to what is revealable. Such truths do not, as such, require divine revelation to be known, but non-philosophers have the benefit of revelation to guide them securely to the 'preambles of faith' proved by philosophers.

Aquinas asks, for example, whether the fact that there is a god is self-evident. If the answer is simply 'Yes', then no proof would be either required nor even possible. Aquinas, drawing a distinction between what is knowable in itself or to experts and what is knowable to us, says that for God, Who qualifies as the supreme expert in knowing Himself, the answer is Yes; but for us, the answer is No. Since immediate knowledge of God is closed to us, we would be inclined to look for proof—some means whereby to get indirect knowledge.

Accordingly, the question arises whether the claim 'there is a god' can occur in the bottom line of a demonstration or proof. Clearly if the answer here is No without qualification, we will have to stop and give up; for if there is no indirect evidence to justify the claim that there is a god and we have already established that there is no direct human insight into it, we would have no knowledge of a god at all. Relying on an Aristotelian distinction between two types of demonstration, how-

ever, Aquinas shows that the answer is Yes to one and No to the other. Aristotle distinguishes between demonstrations that proceed through the very essence of a thing and explain *why* some characteristic belongs to it and demonstrations that do not proceed through the very essence of the thing but one of its effects in order to show *that* something is. Aquinas points out that if god is a first being, there is no way to show *why* he is; i.e., there is no demonstration *propter quid.* But Aquinas admits that there is also proof *that* something is (demonstration *quia*) and thus, in principle, the answer here can be Yes.

At this stage, in *Summa Theologiae* I, q. 2,a. 3, Aquinas can begin to offer his famous five ways to show *that* there is a god.

There are, however, a number of unsettled and unsettling issues left over from Book XII of Aristotle's *Metaphysics.* Aristotle had established that to be a god is to be an intelligence. So far so good. Aristotle was sure that such substances contain no matter, but are pure intelligences. Such intelligences, since they contain no matter, cannot have many instances of any given species. Each intelligence is its own species. Aquinas appreciates the power of this conclusion and appropriates it as his own. The god he has proven to be is identical with his own essence or species. This means that there are beings whose entity is much more concentrated than our own. For example, Aquinas and Avicenna and Maimonides each deserved to be called a human, but none of them deserved to be called humanity. Why? If the whole perfection of human nature or the essence of man were perfectly instantiated in, say, Maimonides, then he would BE humanity and both Aquinas and Avicenna—to say nothing of the rest of the human race—would not be. Unlike essences that contain matter, however, the angel Gabriel (if I may be permitted a biblical example) is its full essence; Gabriel is his Gabrielity, Michael is his Michaelity, etc. Each separate substance is its own essence. The problem is that Aristotle is not quite sure whether separate substances number 47 or 55. There are far too many Aristotelian gods to be congenial to a monotheistic theology. How then can this plurality of separate substances be reduced to unity?

What if one separate entity, which is its own essence, also simply is IS itself? This exploration is the topic of *Summa Theologiae* I, q. 3, a. 4 and the most important metaphysical issue of the passage here translated. Whatever is IS, can only be so essentially. Accordingly, every other essence can only *have* IS; nothing else can *be* IS. Accepting that there are

or can be many substances separate from matter, only one of them can BE God.

Here it would be useful to consider how Aquinas handles the materials he gets from Peter Lombard. The 210 chapters in Book I of Lombard's collection of *Sentences* are distributed into 48 Distinctions (See Appendix). Here only Distinction VIII is immediately at issue. Our English translation of Aquinas incorporates the pagination of Pierre Mandonnet's 1929 Latin edition of St. Thomas's *Scriptum super Sententias* for ease of reference. What Aquinas here calls Distinction VIII comprises Peter Lombard's *Sentences,* Book I, chapters 21–28. These passages from Peter are given in the Mandonnet edition on pages 187–193.

Aquinas divides the text of Peter Lombard into two parts:

Mandonnet pp. 187–189

Ch. 21. The truth and propriety of the divine essence.

Ch. 22. Its incommutability.

Mandonnet, pp. 189–193

Ch. 23. Its simplicity.

Ch. 24. How a bodily or spiritual creature is multiple and not simple.

Ch. 25. That though God is simple, He is spoken of in many ways.

Ch. 26. That God's simplicity is not subject to any of the categories.

Ch. 27. That God is called a substance by abuse of language.

Ch. 28. That there is nothing in God which is not God.

Aquinas's Division of the first part of the text is found on p. 193 of Mandonnet's text. The First Part of the text consists of Lombard's Chapters 21–22. The critical edition of Peter Lombard's Latin text (see Grottaferrata 1971ed., Tomus I, Pars II, pp. 95–98) gives the following headings. The text of ch. 21 (nn. 1–7) is divided into three bold-faced segments at n. 1 (**De proprietate et incommutabilitate et simplicitate Dei essentiae**), n. 4 (**Qualiter intelligenda sint verba Hieronymi quaerendum est**), and n. 6 (**Hic aperit qualiter sint intelligenda**). Chapter 22 (nn. 1–4) is divided into two such segments at n. 1 (**De incommutabilitate hic**) and n. 2 (**Quae sit vera immortalitas quae in solo Creatore est**).

Under the heading of the Division of the First Part of the Text Aquinas poses three questions. Question I contains three articles: (1) Does *being* properly belong to God? (2) Is His *being* the *being* of any creature? (3) Is the name "He Who is" first among the divine names? Question II also contains three articles: (1) Is the definition of eternity posited by Boethius fitting? (2) Does eternity belong only to God? (3) Can temporal words be said of God? Then Aquinas inserts his exposition of the first part of the text, and finally, he continues with Question III, which also contains three articles: (1) Is God in any way mutable? (2) Is every creature mutable? (3) Are the modes of mutation of creatures suitably assigned by Augustine?

Aquinas's Division of the second part of the text is given on p. 217 of the Mandonnet edition. The Second Part of the text deals with Lombard's Chapters 23–28 (see Grottaferrata 1971ed., Tomus I, Pars II, pp. 98–103). Chapter 23 is an undivided unit (**Hic de simplicitate—Quare creatura sit multiplex et non simplex**). Chapter 24 (nn. 1–3) is divided into two units at n. 1 (**Hic de corporali creatura ostendit quare sit multiplex**) and at n. **2** (**Hic de spirituali creatura ostendit quomodo sit multiplex et non simplex**). Chapter 25 consists of an undivided unit (**Qualiter Deus, cum sit simplex, tamen multipliciter dicatur**). Chapter 26 is again an undivided unit (**Tanta est Dei simplicitas quod nulli praedicamentorum subicitur**). Chapter 27 is an undivided section (**Quod Deus non proprie, sed abusive dicitur substantia**). Chapter 28 (nn. 1–3), the last of Distinction 8, is also taken under a single bold-face heading at n. 1 (**Quod non est in Deo aliquid quod non sit Deus**).

Under the heading of the Division of the Second Part of the Text Aquinas poses two more questions. Question IV, addressing the divine simplicity, contains three articles: (1) Is God entirely simple? (2) Is God in the category of substance? (3) Are the other categories said of God? Question V, addressing the simplicity of creatures, also contains three articles: (1) Is any creature simple? (2) Is the soul simple? (3) Is <the soul as> a whole in each part of the body?

Finally, Aquinas offers his exposition of the second part of the text, which completes his discussion of Distinction VIII.

The Base Texts, Style and Mechanics, and a Remark about Aquinas's Philosophical Orientation

This translation contains two texts, that of Peter Lombard's collection (Mandonnet pp. 187–193) and that of St. Thomas writing on issues arising from the Lombard's *Sentences* (Mandonnet pp. 193–236). This translation of Peter Lombard's *Sententiae* in this book is based on the text published in Mandonnet, not that of the 1971 critical edition. My reason for using Mandonnet's provisional text is that, pending the publication of the Leonine critical edition of Aquinas's *Scriptum*, I have no way of telling exactly what textual tradition Aquinas was using. I have, however, supplied in angle brackets indications of how the Mandonnet text lines up with that of the 1971 Quarrachi edition.

The Latin text preserves the pagination of the Mandonnet edition, with the addition of the letter 'a' to indicate the left-hand page (pp. 187a–236a). The facing pages of the English translation will have the same numeration, except that the letter 'b' will be added to mark the right-hand pages (pp. 187b-236b).

Since medieval Latin manuscripts do not employ modern typographical conventions like quotation marks, I have unhesitatingly and silently adjusted Mandonnet's punctuation, wherever necessary, to conform to modern typographical conventions. I have more than once used the help of the Quarrachi editors in adjusting the placement of double quotation marks to note the beginnings and endings of direct quotations from sources. Aside from variations resulting from a difference in base text, the chief reason for my occasionally departing from the Quarrachi editors seems to be a difference of judgment about whether the verbal formulation as such is meant (in which case I use single quotation marks) or whether the reality about which the formulation is made is meant (in which case I have not used quotation marks). Their superb work in identifying quotations and allusions makes their *apparatus fontium* an indispensable tool, which I have relied upon regularly; it should be noted, however, that they also supply a secondary *apparatus fontium*, which I have not included here, pointing out implicit quotations and modern researches, illustrating, for example, Peter Lombard's dependency upon the work of Peter Abelard.

As a final remark, let me say that in my teaching experience I have found that students approaching Aquinas for the first time suffer from two problems.

The first of these problems arises from the fact that most modern thought arises from no-longer examined philosophical presuppositions drawn from the so-called Rationalist position. One way to diagnose whether one suffers from this obstacle is to ask oneself, What is the natural habitat for *ideas*? If our first inclination is to think of *ideas* as pieces of furniture somehow boxed within something called a mind, then we are not untouched by the Rationalist tradition. From this philosophical perspective, our problem is how to get out of the house, that is, How can I get from my mind to reality?

A quick survey of any standard Greek Lexicon (say, Liddell-Scott-Jones) under the headings *eidos* and *idea* suggest a quite refreshing alternative. A physician like Hippocrates, for example, must first look at his patient in order to see what the patient looks like. Only through the patient's own *eidos* or "looks" does the physician acquire something through which he can use his mind's eye to catch sight of the aspect of the disease. In short, the *idea* is first found in things and only derivatively do we have a mental *idea*. Within this orientation, the characteristic modern problem simply disappears, because we *are already* at reality. The fact that there are physicians and the fact they their diagnosis starts from the patient's symptoms suggest that experience somehow must start with things themselves. Thus, Aristotle can reasonably make the extraordinary claim, "The soul somehow *is* all beings" (De anima, III, 8).

It is sometimes extra-ordinarily difficult for students locked within the Rationalist position even to approach classical and medieval philosophy with its strongly realistic orientation. To be sure, not everyone starts from a mind-centered or self-centered preoccupation, but those who do often find themselves entangled in it. Beginners in philosophy may find it helpful to look at Mortimer Adler's helpful little book *Ten Philosophical Mistakes* for more details.

The second of these problems is somewhat deeper. Both modern Rationalism and modern Empiricism seem to agree in curious way with Plato, who, for reasons we need not go into here, seems to have thought that being itself is *eidos* or *idea*. Their disagreements are about how we get it or where we keep it. The position itself that being is *eidos* or *idea* or essence or quiddity has a profound influence throughout Western

philosophy. But is it in fact true that being is ultimately just essence? Thomas Aquinas seems not to have thought so. He speaks of being (*esse*) as "the act of the essence," and indeed as the "actuality of all acts and therefore the perfection of all perfections." For a consideration of Aquinas's position in contrast with that of several others', it is worthwhile to read Étienne Gilson's *Being and Some Philosophers* and to browse through the select bibliography.

There is, however, no substitute for reading Thomas Aquinas himself, and at this point the reader is invited to start.

Acknowledgments

This book is the fruit of a 1995 eight-week summer study under funding from the National Endowment for the Humanities focusing upon the metaphysical notion of the divine simplicity in Avicenna, Maimonides, and Thomas Aquinas. This book presents only the target text from Aquinas and my annotations to that capital text including Aquinas's metaphysical proof that what God is is no other than His "IS" or act of being. Originally the proposal was merely to read these 50 pages and to broaden the perspective to include a consideration of the Biblical and Qur'ânic texts that provide the religious warrant for belief that God is utterly simple, along with a survey of early Greek interpretations of Exodus 3: 14. My reading program was built upon the outline of an anthology of French essays published in *Dieu et l'être: Exégèse d'Exode 3, 14 et de Coran 20, 11–24* (Paris: Études Augustiniennes, 1978). Curiously, it seems that the Qur'ân, unlike Exodus 3: 14 "I am who am," focuses on God's "I" rather than His "IS".

I should also like to thank publicly a number of other contributors to the successful completion of this project: the wise and generous donors who have helped build the philosophical holdings in the Benedictine College Library, particularly the late True Snowden; among the living, Head Librarian Mrs. Anna Cairney and interlibrary loan specialist Mrs. Florine Muelhlenburg must be mentioned at the start, as well as all the cooperating lending institutions. Dr. Parviz Morewedge of Binghamton University persistently but gently demythologized the process of publication, supplied the word-processing program to ensure compatibility with his system, and granted me use of his fine personal philosophical library in Binghamton, a collection especially rich in

Arabic and Persian books. I am grateful to Dr. Sandro Sticca of Binghamton University, for his editorial expertise in improving this manuscript. I also wish to thank Charles Burroughs, Director of CEMERS at Binghamton University, for his support on the publication of this manuscript. Dr. Richard G. Cummings, CPA, generously and inconspicuously granted me uninterrupted use of his office in the Business Department at Benedictine College. Dr. William Hyland of the Department of History kindly read and criticized an early draft of the translation. My stepson Sean Nitz word-processed the Latin text. My diligent and loving wife Carol helped to free me from many distractions, provided an exemplar of determination to get things finished even in the midst of interruptions and a living incentive to virtue. And of course, as the theme of this little book shows, there is One to be thanked Who makes all things and all thinking possible.

28 January 1997

E. M. Macierowski
Benedictine College
Atchison, Kansas

Thomas Aquinas's Earliest Treatment of the Divine Essence

[Mandonnet, p. 187a]

DISTINCTIO VIII

De veritate, et proprietate, et incommutabilitate, et simplicitate essentiae Dei

Nunc de veritate, sive proprietate, et incommutabilitate atque simplicitate divinae naturae vel substantiae sive essentiae, agendum est. "Est itaque Deus," ut ait Augustinus in V lib. *De trinit.*, cap. ii, col. 912, t. VIII, "sine dubitatione substantia, vel si melius hoc appellatur essentia: quam Graeci 'ousian' vocant. Sicut enim ab eo quod est sapere, dicta est sapientia, et ab eo quod est scire, dicta est scientia, ita ab eo quod est 'esse' dicta est essentia. Et quis magis est quam ille qui dixit famulo suo Moysi, Exod., iii, 14: *Ego sum qui sum*; et : *Dices filiis Israel: Qui est misit me ad vos*?" Ipse vere ac proprie dicitur essentia cujus essentia non novit praeteritum vel futurum. Unde Hieronymus, ad Damasum scribens, *Epist.* xv, § 4, col. 357, t. I, ait: "Deus solus, qui exordium non habet, vere essentiae nomen tenet; quia in ejus comparatione qui vere est, quia incommutabilis est, quasi non sunt quae mutabilia sunt. De quo enim dicitur 'fuit', non est; et de quo dicitur 'erit', nondum est; Deus autem tantum est, qui non novit fuisse vel futurum esse. Solus ergo Deus vere est cujus essentiae comparatum nostrum esse non est."

Quaeritur qualiter intelligenda sint verba Hieronymi

Hic diligenter advertendum est quomodo intelligi debeant verba illa Hieronymi, scilicet, Deus tantum est, et non novit fuisse vel futurum esse, tanquam non possit dici de Deo 'fuit', vel 'erit', sed tantum 'est'; cum de Deo frequenter scriptum reperiamus: 'fuit ab aeterno', 'fuit semper', et 'erit in saecula', et hujusmodi. Unde videtur quia non est tantum dicendum de Deo, fuit, est, vel erit. Si enim diceretur tantum 'fuit', putaretur quia desierit esse. Si diceretur tantum 'est', putaretur

[Mandonnet, p. 187b]

BOOK I, DISTINCTION VIII

<Here begins Peter Lombard's Chapter 21.>

On the truth, propriety, unchangeability, and simplicity of God's essence

Now we must treat of the truth or propriety and the unchangeability and simplicity of the divine nature or substance, i.e., essence. "And so God is," as *Augustine says "without doubt a substance, or, if this is a better term, an essence, which the Greeks call 'ousia'. For just as wisdom was named from being wise, and knowledge was named from knowing, so too is essence named from 'esse'—*being* or to be. Indeed who is greater than He who said to his servant Moses: *I AM WHO AM* and *You shall tell the sons of Israel: HE WHO IS sent me to you* (Exodus 3, 14)?" He is truly and properly called Essence whose essence knows neither past nor future This is why *Jerome, writing to Damasus, says: "God alone, Who has no beginning, truly holds the name Essence, since in comparison to Him Who truly is because He is unchangeable the <things> that are changeable almost are not at all. For that of which one says 'it was,' is not; and that of which one says 'it will be' is not yet; God, however, Who knows neither having been nor being about to be, merely is. Hence God alone is truly that in comparison with Whose essence our being is not."

How are the words of Jerome to be understood?

Here we must diligently turn to consider how we ought to understand Jerome's words 'God merely is' and He 'knows neither having been nor being about to be', since it is impossible to say of God He 'was' or 'will be,' but only He 'is,' although we often find it written of God that He 'was from eternity,' 'was always' and 'will be for ever' and such. Hence it seems that one must not say of God merely that He 'was,' 'is' or 'will be'. For if one were to say merely 'He was,' one might think that He would have ceased to be. If one were to say merely 'He is,' one might think that He was not always but rather began to be. If

quod non semper fuerit, sed esse coeperit. Si tantum 'erit', putaretur non esse modo. Dicatur ergo, quia semper /188a/ fuit, est, et erit, ut intelligatur quia nec coepit, nec desiit, nec desinit, nec desinet esse. De hoc Augustinus, *Sup. Joann.*, tract. xcix, §§ 4 et 5, col. 1888, t. III, ita ait: Cum de sempiterna re proprie dicatur 'est', secundum nos bene dicitur 'fuit' et 'erit': 'fuit', quia nunquam desiit; 'erit', quia nunquam deerit; 'est', quia semper est; non praeteriit, quasi quod non maneat; non orietur, quasi quod non erat. Cum ergo nostra locutio per tempora varietur, de eo vere dicuntur verba cujuslibet temporis qui nullo tempore defuit, vel deest, vel deerit. Et ideo non mirum, si de spiritu veritatis, veritas loquens, Joann., xvi, 13, dixit per futurum: *Quaecumque audiet, loquetur*: audiet, scilicet ab eo a quo procedit. Audire illius est scire: idem etiam esse. A quo ergo est illi essentia, ab illo audientia, id est scientia, quae non est aliud quam essentia. Audiet, ergo dixit de eo quod audivit; et audit, id est quod semper scivit, scit et sciet. Ecce hic dicit Augustinus, verba cujuslibet temporis dici de eo, sed tamen proprie, est. Illud ergo quod Hieronymus dicit, ita intelligendum est. Non novit fuisse, vel futurum esse, sed tantum esse; id est, cum dicitur de Deo, quod fuit vel erit, non est intelligendum quod praeterierit vel futurus sit; sed quod existat simpliciter, sine aliquo temporali motu: licet enim verba substantiva diversorum temporum de Deo dicantur, ut fuit, erit, est et erat; non tamen temporales motus esse distinguunt, scilicet praeteritum vel futurum, vel praeteritum imperfectum vel praeteritum perfectum, vel praeteritum plusquam perfectum; sed essentiam, sive existentiam suae divinitatis simpliciter insinuant. Deus ergo solus proprie dicitur essentia vel esse. Unde Hilarius ita ait in VII lib. *De Trinit.*, § 11, col 208; t. II: "Ecce non est accidens Deo, sed subsistens veritas et manens causa, et naturalis generis proprietas."

one were to say merely 'He will be,' one might think that He is not now. Therefore, let it be said that He always /188b/ was, is, and will be, in such fashion that one understand that He did not begin and He did not cease, nor is He ceasing, nor will He cease to be. On this point *Augustine says: "Although 'is' is properly said of a sempiternal thing, it is all right for us to say 'was' and 'will be'. <It is all right to say> 'was,' since He never ceased; 'will be,' since He will never be lacking*; 'is,' since He always is; He has not gone away like something that does not remain, and He will not arise like something that was not. Therefore, since our manner of speaking varies by tenses* (tempora), verbs of any tense may be truly said of Him Who at no time was, is, or will be missing. So it is no wonder that the Truth, speaking of the Spirit of Truth, said, using the future <tense>: *Whatever he shall hear, he shall speak* (John, xvi, 13): <from whom> 'shall He hear'?—From Him from Whom He proceeds. His hearing is knowing; it is also the same as *being*. From Whom then does Essence belong to Him? From the One to Whom hearing, i.e., the knowing which is nothing but Essence belongs. Therefore He said 'He shall hear' about what He has heard and is hearing, i.e., what He always knew, is knowing, and will know." Notice that here Augustine says that verbs of any tense are said of Him, but yet properly He *is*. Hence what Jerome says ('He knows neither having been nor being about to be but merely *being*') is to be undersood in this way: when 'was' or 'will be' is said of God, one must not understand that He will have gone away or is about to be, but rather that He exists simply, without any temporal motion; for although substantive verbs of various* tenses—e.g., 'was,' 'will be,' 'is' and 'used to be'—may be said of God, nevertheless they (the past, future, past imperfect, past perfect, or past pluperfect <tenses>) do not discern there to be temporal motions <in God>, but rather they imply simply the essence or existence of His divinity. Therefore God alone is properly called Essence or *Being*. This is why *Hilary says, "Look, there is nothing accidental to God, just the subsistent truth, the permanent cause, and the propriety of <His> natural genus."

Hic de incommutabilitate

Dei etiam solius essentia proprie incommutabilis dicitur, quia nec mutatur nec mutari potest. Unde Augustinus in V lib. *De Trinit.*, cap. ii, col. 912, t. VIII: "Aliae," inquit, " essentiae, vel substantiae capiunt accidentia, quibus in eis fiat vel magna vel quantacumque mutatio. Deo autem aliquid hujusmodi accidere non potest: et ideo sola substantia, vel essentia, quae est Deus, incommutabilis est. Cui profecto maxime ac verissime competit esse. Quod enim mutatur, non servat ipsum verum esse; et quod mutari potest, etiam si non mutetur, potest quod fuerat non esse. Ideoque illud solum quod non tantum non mutatur, verum etiam omnino mutari non potest, verissime dicitur esse," id est substantia /189a/ Patris, et Filii, et Spiritus sancti. Ideo Apostolus, I ad Tim., vi, 16, de Deo loquens, ait: *Qui solus immortalitatem habet.* Ut enim ait Augustinus in lib. I *De Trinit.*, cap. I, § 2, col. 821, t. VIII, "cum anima quodammodo immortalis esse dicatur et sit, non diceret Apostolus: *Solus habet immortalitatem*: nisi quia vera immortalitas incommutabilitas est, quam nulla potest habere creatura, quoniam solius Creatoris est. Unde Jacobus ait, cap. i, 17: *Apud quem non est transmutatio, nec vicissitudinis obumbratio;* et David, psal. ci, 28: *Mutabis ea, et mutabuntur; tu autem idem ipse es.* Ideo Augustinus, *Super Genes. ad litteram*, lib. VIII, cap. xx, col. 388, t. III, dicit, quod Deus nec per loca nec per tempora movetur; creatura[m] vero per tempora et loca, et per tempora moveri, est per affectiones commutari. Deus autem nec loco nec affectione mutari potest, qui per prophetam Malach., iii, 6, ait: *Ego Deus, et non mutor*: qui est immutabilis solus. Unde recte solus dicitur habere immortalitatem. "In omni enim mutabili natura," ut ait Augustinus, *Contra Maximinum*, lib. II, cap. xii, § 2, col. 768, t. VIII, "nonnulla mors est ipsa mutatio: quia facit aliquid in ea non esse quod erat. Unde et ipsa anima humana, quae ideo dicitur immortalis, quia secundum modum suum nunquam desinit vivere, habet tamen quamdam mortem suam: quia si juste vivebat et peccat, moritur justitiae; si peccatrix erat et justificabitur, moritur peccato: ut alias ejus mutationes taceam, de quibus modo longum est disputare. Et creaturarum natura caelestium mori potuit, quia peccare potuit. Nam et angeli peccaverunt et daemones facti sunt, quorum est diabolus princeps; et qui non peccaverunt, peccare et

<Here begins Peter Lombard's Chapter 22.>

Here <begins the treatment> of unchangeability

The essence of God alone is also said to be unchangeable*, since it is neither changed nor can it be changed. This is why *Augustine says: "Other essences or substances receive accidents, by which change either to a great or to any extent arises in them. Something of this sort, however, cannot be accidental to God: and so only the substance or essence that God is is unchangeable. To this <essence> *being* belongs to the greatest and truest degree. For what is being changed does not itself keep true *being;* and what can be changed, even if it is not changed, can not-be what it had been. So only that which not only is not being changed but also cannot be changed at all is most truly called the *being,"* namely the substance /189b/ of the Father, Son, and Holy Spirit. Thus the *Apostle, speaking of God, *says He Who alone has immortality.* For, as *Augustine says, "since the soul may be said to be and is in a way immortal, the Apostle would not say *He alone has immortality,* for any other reason than that true immortality is unchangeable—<an immortality> which no creature can have, since it belongs to the Creator alone. Hence *James says: *With Whom there is no change nor shadow of a shift;* and *David: *You will change them and they will be changed; but You Yourself are the Same.* So *Augustine says that God is moved neither throught places nor through times, whereas the creature is moved through places and times; and 'to be moved through times' means to be changed through affections. God, however, can be changed neither by place nor by an affection; for He says through the Prophet*: *I am God and I am not changed,* <the One> Who alone is unchangeable. Hence He alone is rightly said to have immortality. "For in every changeable nature," as *Augustine says, "change is itself a sort of death, since it makes something that was in it not-be. Hence even the human soul, which is said to be immortal because in its own way it never ceases to live, nevertheless has a sort of death belonging to it: since if it used to live justly and sins, it dies to justice; if it was sinful and will be justified, it dies to sin—to say nothing of its other changes, which would take a long time to discuss. The nature of celestial creatures, too, was able to die, since it was able to sin. For even the angels sinned and were made demons, the prince of whom is the devil; and those that did not sin

cuicumque creaturae rationali praestatur ut peccare non possit, non est hoc naturae proprie, sed Dei gratiae. Et ideo solus Deus, ut ait Apostolus, loc. cit., habet immortalitatem, qui non cujusquam gratia, sed natura sua nec potuit nec potest aliqua conversione mutari; nec potuit nec poterit aliqua mutatione peccare."—"Proinde," ut ait Augustinus in libro I *De Trinit.*, cap. I, § 3, col. 821, t. VIII, "substantiam Dei sine ulla sui commutatione mutabilia facientem, et sine ullo suo temporali motu temporalia creantem intueri et nosse," licet sit difficile, oportet. Vere ergo ac proprie incommutabilis est sola divinitatis essentia, quae sine sui mutatione cunctas condidit naturas.

Hic de simplicitate

Eadem quoque sola proprie ac vere simplex est, ubi nec partium nec accidentium, seu quarumlibet formarum, ulla /190a/ est diversitas sive variatio vel multitudo. Ut autem scias quomodo simplex sit illa substantia, ut te docet Augustinus in lib. VI *De Trinit.*, cap. vi, col. 928, t. VIII, animadverte primo quare omnis creatura sit multiplex, et nullo modo vere simplex. Et primum de corporali, postea vero de spirituali creatura. Corporalis utique creatura ex partibus constat, ita ut sit sibi alia pars major, alia minor, et majus sit totum quam pars quaelibet: et in unoquoque corpore aliud est magnitudo, aliud color, aliud figura: potest enim, imminuta magnitudine, manere idem color et eadem figura; et, colore mutato, manere eadem figura et eadem magnitudo: ac per hoc multiplex esse convincitur natura corporis, simplex autem nullo modo.

Hic de spirituali creatura ostendit, quomodo sit multiplex et non simplex

Creatura quoque spiritualis, ut est anima, in comparatione quidem corpo^Sris est simplex, sine comparatione vero corporis multiplex est et non simplex: quae ideo simplex dicitur respectu corporis, quia mole non diffunditur per spatium loci, sed in unoquoque corpore et in toto tota est, et in qualibet parte ejus tota est: et ideo cum sit aliquid in qualibet

were able to sin: and to whatever rational creature is granted the power not to sin, this <power> does not belong to the nature properly but to God's grace. So *only God,* as the *Apostle says, *has immortality*—the One Who by nature and not by anyone's grace was not able and is not able to be changed by any conversion and <Who> was not able nor will be able to sin by any change."—"Hence," as *Augustine says, "even though difficult, it must be the case that the divine substance sees and knows the changeable things it makes without any associated change of its own and <sees and knows> the temporal things it creates without any temporal motion." Hence only the essence of divinity, <the essence> that founded all natures without any change of its own, is truly and properly unchangeable.

<Here begins Peter Lombard's Chapter 23.>

Here <begins the treatment> of simplicity

The same <essence> alone is also properly and truly simple, where neither <its> parts nor accidents or any of <its> forms has any /190b/ diversity, variation or multiplicity. Now, to know how simple that substance is, as *Augustine teaches you, "in the first place consider why every creature is manifold and in no way truly simple," and first with respect to the corporeal and then with respect to the spiritual creature. <Here begins Peter Lombard's Chapter 24.> "A corporeal creature consists of parts in such fashion that it has one part greater and another lesser, and the whole is greater than any part: also in each body size is one <feature>, color another, shape another: for, once the size has been reduced, the same color and the same shape can persist; and, if the color has been changed, the same shape and the same size can do so; and hence the nature of a body is bound to be multiple and in no way simple."

Here he shows how a spiritual creature may be manifold and not simple

"A spiritual creature too, e.g., the soul, is simple with respect to the body but is manifold and not simple without relation to the body. It is called simple with respect to the body since it is not diffused by mass throughout an interval of a place but is rather a whole in each bit of body and in the whole; and the whole <soul> is in each part of it: and

particula corporis exigua, quod sentiat anima, quamvis non fiat in toto corpore, illa tamen tota sentit, quia totam non latet. Sed tamen nec in ipsa tota anima vera simplicitas est. Cum enim aliud sit artificiosum esse, aliud inertem, aliud acutum, aliud memorem, aliud cupiditas, aliud timor, aliud laetita, aliud tristitia; possintque haec et alia hujusmodi innumerabilia in animae natura inveniri, et alia sine aliis et alia magis alia minus: manifestum est animae non simplicem, sed multiplicem esse naturam. Nihil enim simplex mutabile est; omnis autem creatura mutabilis est: nulla ergo creatura vere simplex est. Deus vero, etsi multipliciter dicatur, id est multis nominibus significetur, vere tamen et summe simplex est. Dicitur enim magnus, bonus, sapiens, beatus, verus, et quidquid aliud non indigne dici videtur. Sed eadem magnitudo ejus est quae sapientia: non enim mole magnus est, sed virtute: et eadem bonitas ejus quae est sapientia, et magnitudo, et veritas: et non est ibi aliud ipsum beatum esse, et aliud magnum, aliud sapientem, aliud verum aut bonum esse, aut omnino esse.

/191a/ *Qualiter cum Deus sit simplex, multiplex tamen dicatur*

Hic diligenter notandum est, cum dicat Augustinus, solum Deum vere simplicem esse, cur dicat eumdem multipliciter dici. Sed hoc non propter diversitatem accidentium vel partium dicit; immo propter diversitatem ac multitudinem nominum quae de Deo dicuntur: quae licet multiplicia sint, unum tamen significant, scilicet divinam naturam. Haec enim non ita accipiuntur, cum de illa incommutabili aeternaque substantia incomparabiliter simpliciore quam est humanus animus, dicuntur, quemadmodum cum de creaturis dicuntur. Unde Augustinus, in lib. VI *De Trinit.*, cap. iv, col. 927, t. VIII: "Deo," inquit, "hoc est esse quod fortem esse, vel sapientem esse, vel justum esse, et si quid de illa simplici multiplicitate vel multiplici simplicitate dixeris, quo substantia ejus significetur. Humano autem animo non est hoc esse quod est fortem esse, aut prudentem, aut justum: potest enim esse animus, et nullam istarum habere virtutum."

so, since there is something the soul senses in each part of the body, howsoever small, even though it not come about in the whole body, nevertheless <the soul> as a whole does the sensing, since <the bodily part> does not hide from the whole <soul>. But yet neither is it the case that there is true simplicity in the soul itself as a whole. For since to be clever is one thing, lazy another, sharp again another, good at remembering another still <and> cupidity is one thing, fear another, joy and sadness other yet again, and since these and countless other such can be found within the nature of a soul, some without others and some more than others: it is clear that the nature of soul is not simple but manifold. For nothing simple is mutable; but every creature is mutable": hence no creature is truly simple. "But even though God is spoken of in many ways, that is, is signified by many names, nevertheless He is simple truly and to the highest degree. For He is called great, good, wise, happy, true, and whatever else may worthily be said of Him. But His greatness is the same as wisdom: for He is great not in mass but in power; and His goodness is the same as wisdom, greatness, truth: and yonder for Him to be happy is not one thing and to be great or wise or true or good or to be at all something else."

<Here begins Peter Lombard's Chapter 25.>

/191b/ *How it is that although God is simple, He is nevertheless spoken of as manifold.*

Here we must diligently note why Augustine says that God is spoken of in many ways even though he says that He is truly simple. He says this not because of a diversity of accidents or parts <in God Himself> but rather because of the diversity and multitude of the names that are said of God: although these <names> are manifold, nevertheless they signify <something> one, namely the divine nature. For when these <names> are said of that unchangeable and eternal substance incomparably simpler than is the human mind*, they are not to be taken in the same way as when they are said of creatures. Hence *Augustine says: "For God, to-be is the same as to-be-strong or to-be-wise or to-be-just or anything you might say about that simple-multiplicity or multiple-simplicity by which His substance may be signified. For the human mind, however, to-be is not the same as to-be-strong or to-be-prudent or just: for the mind can be and yet have none of these virtues."

Tanta est Dei simplicitas quod nulli praedicamentorum subjicitur

Quod autem in divina natura nulla sit accidentium diversitas, nullaque penitus mutabilitas, sed perfecta simplicitas, ostendit Augustinus in V libro *De Trinit.*, cap. I, col. 912, t. VIII: dicens: "Intelligamus Deum, quantum possumus, sine qualitate bonum, sine quantitate magnum, sine indigentia creatorem, sine situ praesentem, sine habitu omnia continentem, sine loco ubique totum, sine tempore sempiternum, sine ulla sui mutatione mutabilia facientem, nihilque patientem. Quisquis Deum ita cogitat, etsi nondum potest invenire omnino quid sit, ipse pie tamen caveat, quantum potest, aliquid de illo sentire quod non sit." Ecce, si subtiliter intendas, ex his atque praedictis aperitur, illa praedicamenta artis dialecticae Dei naturae minime convenire, quae nullis subjecta est accidentibus.

Quia Deus non proprie, sed abusive dicitur substantia

Unde nec proprie dicitur substantia, ut Augustinus, lib. VII *De Trinit.*, cap. iv, § 9, et cap. v, col. 942, t. VIII, ostendit, dicens: "Sicut ab eo quod est esse, appellatur essentia, ita et ab eo quod est subsistere substantiam dicimus: si tamen dignum est ut Deus dicatur subsistere." Hoc enim de his rebus recte intelligitur in quibus, ut in subjectis, sunt ea quae in aliquo, ut in subjecto, esse dicuntur, sicut in corpore color atque forma. Corpus enim subsistit, et ideo substantia est. Res vero mutabiles neque simplices, proprie dicuntur /192a/ substantiae. Deus autem si subsistit, ut substantia proprie dici possit, inest in eo aliquid tanquam in subjecto, et non est simplex. Nefas autem est dicere, ut subsistat Deus, et subsit bonitatae suae; et illa bonitas non substantia sit vel potius essentia; neque ipse Deus sit bonitas sua, sed in illo sit tanquam in subjecto. Unde manifestum est, Deum abusive substantiam vocari, ut

<Here begins Peter Lombard's Chapter 26.>

God's Simplicity is so great that it is not made subject to any of the categories

But *Augustine show that in the divine nature there is no diversity of accidents nor any mutability at all, but only perfect simplicity, saying: "Let us understand God, to the extent that we are able, <as> good without quality, great without quantity, Creator without need, present apart from location, containing all things without being held, a whole everywhere but without place, sempiternal without time, making all mutable things without any mutation of His own, and passive with repect to nothing. Even though it is not yet possible for anyone who thinks about God in this way to discover what He is at all, still let him, to the extent that he can, be religiously careful about thinking anything about Him that He is not." From this and what was said before, if you look into it with subtlety, it becomes obvious that the categories* of the art of dialectic* do not belong at all to God's nature, which is subject to no accidents.

<Here begins Peter Lombard's Chapter 27.>

That God is called a substance not properly but by abuse of language.

Hence, neither is He properly called a substance, as *Augustine shows saying: "Just as 'essence' is named from *being* (*esse*), so also do we say 'substance' from subsisting, if, at any event, it is fitting to say that God subsists. For this is rightly understood of those things in which, as subjects, those <features> that are in something as a subject are said to be, e.g., color and shape in a body. For a body subsists, and so it is a substance. But the changeable things that are not simple are properly called /192b/ substances. Now if God subsists in suchwise as properly to be able to be called a substance, then something is in Him as in a subject, and He is not simple. But it is wicked to say that God subsists and that He is subject to His goodness; and <that> that goodness is not <His> substance or better <His> essence; and <that> neither is God Himself His own goodness, but <that> it is in Him as in a subject. Hence it is clear that God is called a 'substance' by abuse of

nomine usitatiore intelligatur essentia: quod vere ac proprie dicitur, ita ut fortasse solum Deum dici oporteat essentiam. Est enim vere solus, quia incommutabilis est.

Quod non est in Deo aliquid quod non sit Deus

Hujus autem essentiae simplicitas ac sinceritas tanta est quod non est in ea aliquid quod non sit ipsa; sed idem est habens et quod habetur. Unde Hilarius, in VII lib. *De Trinit.*, § 27, col. 223, t. II, ait: "Non enim ex compositis Deus, qui vita est, subsistit; neque qui virtus est, ex infirmis continetur; nec qui lux est, ex obscuris coaptatur; nec qui spiritus est, ex disparibus formis est; totum quod in eo est, unum est." Item Hilarius, in VIII lib. *De Trinit.*, § 43, col. 269, t. II: "Non humano modo Deus ex compositis est, ut in eo aliud sit quod ab eo habetur, aliud sit ipse qui habeat; sed totum una est natura, scilicet perfecta et infinita; et non ex disparibus constituta, sed vivens ipsa per totum." De hoc eodem Boetius, in I lib. *De Trinit.*, cap. ii, col. 1250, t. II, ait: "Quocirca hoc vere est unum, in quo nullus numerus: nullum in eo aliud praeter id quod in eo est: neque enim subjectum fieri potest." Augustinus quoque, in lib. *De fide et symbol.*, cap. ix, § 20, col. 193, t. VI, dicit: "In Dei substantia non est aliquid quod non sit substantia; quasi aliud sit ibi substantia, aliud quod accidit substantiae: sed quidquid ibi intelligi potest, substantia est. Verum haec dici possunt, et facile credi; videri autem nisi puro corde omnino non possunt." Item Augustinus, in XV lib. *De Trinit.*, cap. xvii, § 28, col. 1080, t. VIII: "Sic habetur in natura uniuscujusque trium, ut qui habet, hoc sit quod habet, sicut immutabilis simplexque substantia." Unde Isidorus, lib. I *De sum. bono*, cap. I, col. 540, t. VI, ait: "Deus simplex dicitur, sive non amittendo quod habet, sive quod aliud non est ipse et aliud quod in ipso est: et cum tantae simplicitatis atque sinceritatis sit natura divina, est tamen in ea personarum Trinitas." Unde Augustinus, in XI lib. *De civitate Dei*, cap. x, col. 325, t. VII, ait: "Non propter hoc naturam summi boni simplicem dicimus, quia Pater est in ea solus, aut Filius in ea solus, /193a/ aut Spiritus sanctus in ea solus; id est, quia est ista nominum Trinitas sine subsistentia personarum, sicut Sabelliani putaverunt. Sed ideo simplex dicitur, quia est hoc quod habet, excepto quod relative quaeque persona ad alteram dicitur, nec est ipsa.

language, so that He may be understood <as> essence by the more usual name: He is truly and properly called this <name> in such fashion that perhaps God alone has to be called Essence. For He alone truly is, since He is unchangeable."

<Here begins Peter Lombard's Chapter 28.>

That there is not anything in God that is not God

Now the simplicity and *authenticity of this essence is so great that there is not anything in it that is not itself; but the haver and the had are the same. Hence *Hilary says: "For God, Who is life, does not subsist out of composites; nor is <the One> Who is power, held together from <things that are> weak; nor is He Who is light fitted together out of <things that are> shadowy; nor is He Who is spirit <derived> out of unequal forms; the whole that is in Him is one." Again, *Hilary: "God is not out of composites in human fashion in such wise that what is had by Him is one thing and He Who has it is another; rather the whole is one nature, perfect and infinite, and it is not constituted out of unequals but is itself living throughout the whole." On this same point *Boethius: "Thus that is truly one in which <there is> no number: nothing else <is> in it aside from that which is in it; for neither can it become a subject." *Augustine also says: "In God's substance there is not anything that is not substance, as though substance there were one thing and that which is accidental to substance another: but whatever can there be understood is substance. But there things can be said and easily believed, but they cannot at all be seen except with a pure heart." Again *Augustine: "The nature of each of the three is so related that He Who has is that which He has as an unchangeable and simple substance." Hence *Isidore: "God is said to be simple either by not losing what He has or because He is Himself no other than what is in Him: and though the divine nature is of such simplicity and authenticity, there is nevertheless a Trinity of Persons within it." Hence *Augustine says: "We call the nature of the highest good simple not because the Father alone is in it, <nor because> the Son alone is in it, /193b/ <nor because> the Holy Spiriti alone is in it; i.e., because it is a Trinity of names without being a subsistence of Persons, as the Sabellians thought. No, it is called simple because it is what it has—except what each Person is called

Nam utique Pater habet Filium, ad quem relative dicitur, nec tamen ipse est Filius; et Filius habet Patrem, nec tamen ipse est Pater. In quo vero ad semetipsum dicitur, non ad alterum, hoc est quod habet; sicut ad semetipsum dicitur vivus, habendo vitam, et eadem vita ipse est. Propter hoc utique natura haec dicitur simplex, quod non sit aliud habens et aliud id quod habet, sicut in caeteris rebus est. Non enim habens liquorem liquor est, nec corpus color, nec anima sapientia est." Ecce quanta est identitas, quanta est unitas et immutabilitas, simplicitas, puritas divinae substantiae, juxta infirmitatis nostrae valetudinem assignavimus.

DIVISIO PRIMAE PARTIS TEXTÛS

Ostensa Trinitate personarum in unitate essentiae, hic incipit prosequi determinationem suam de his quae pertinent ad utrumque. Sunt autem in divinis tria, scilicet essentia communis, persona distincta, proprietas distinguens. Dividitur ergo haec pars in duas: in prima determinat de istis secundum se; in secunda, quomodo ad invicem comparantur, XXXIII dist., ibi: "Post supradicta, interius considerari, atque subtiliter inquiri oportet." Prima in tres: in prima determinat de essentia: in secunda de personis, IX dist., ibi: "Nunc ad trium personarum distinctionem accedamus"; in tertia determinat de proprietatibus, XXVI dist., ibi: "Nunc de proprietatibus personarum... aliquid loqui nos oportet."

Prima in tres, secundum tria attributa essentiae, quae prosequitur:

relatively to another and itself is not. For the Father does indeed have the Son, to Whom He is spoken of relatively but is not Himself the Son; and the Son has the Father, but is yet not Himself the Father. In what is said in His own right, however, and not to another, He is what He has; e.g., He is called 'living' in His own right, by having life, and He is that self-same life. This nature is called simple because the one having and that which it has are not other than each other, as is the case in other things. For what holds liquid is not liquid, nor is a body color, nor is a soul wisdom." Thus we have assigned, as the strength of our weakness will allow, how great is the identity, how great is the unity and unchangeability, the simplicity, the purity of the divine substance.

<The text of Peter Lombard ends here;
what Saint Thomas himself has to say begins as follows:>

DIVISION* OF THE FIRST PART* OF THE TEXT*

After the Trinity of Persons in a unity of essence* has been shown<Book I, Distinctions* 2–7>, here <at Distinction 8, the Master*> begins to pursue his determination* about the things that pertain to both. In divine things there are three <topics to be considered>: the common essence, the person distinguished, and the distinguishing property*. This part, however, is divided into two <divisions>: in the first <Distinctions 8–32>, he determines about them in their own right; in the second <Distinctions 33–48>, how they are related to each other, at <the words> "After the aforesaid it must be considered interiorly and must be subtly subjected to inquiry."

The first <division, comprising Distinctions 8–32, in turn is divided> into three <subdivisions>: in the first <beginning here, at Distinction 8>, he determines* about the essence; in the second <Distinctions 9–25>, about the Persons, at <the words> "Now let us proceed to the distinction of the three Persons"; in the third <Distinctions 26–32>, he determines about the properties*, at <the words> "Now it is necessary for us to say something about the properties of the Persons."

The first <subdivision, namely, Distinction 8, is divided> into three <sections> according to the three attributes of the essence that he pursues: for <in the> first <place, at Chapter 21 the Master*> determines*

primo enim determinat de essentiae, unitate; secundo de incommutabilitate, ibi: "Dei etiam solius essentia incommutabilis dicitur proprie"; tertio de simplicitate, ibi: "Eademque sola proprie ac vere simplex est." Circa primum duo facit: primo ostendit veritatem divinae essentiae; secundo removet dubitationem, ibi: "Hic diligenter advertendum est quomodo intelligi debeant illa verba Hieronymi."

QUAESTIO PRIMA

Circa primam partem distinctionis, in qua agitur de proprietate divini esse, duo quaeruntur: primo de ipso esse divino; secundo de mensura ejus, scilicet aeternitate.

/194a/ In primo tria quaeruntur: 1° utrum esse Deo proprie conveniat; 2° utrum suum esse sit esse cujuslibet creaturae; 3° de ordine hujus nominis, "qui est", ad alia divina nomina.

ARTICULUS PRIMUS *Utrum esse proprie dicatur de Deo*

Ad primum sic proceditur. 1. Videtur quod esse non proprie dicatur de Deo. Illud enim est proprium alicui quod sibi soli convenit. Sed esse non solum convenit Deo, immo etiam creaturis. Ergo videtur quod esse non proprie Deo conveniat.

2. Praeterea, non possumus nominare Deum, nisi secundum quod ipsum cognoscimus; unde Damascenus lib. I *Fid. orth.*, cap. XIII, col. 858, t. I: "Verbum est angelus, id est, nuntius intellectus." Sed nos non possumus cognoscere Deum in statu viae immediate sed tantum ex creaturis. Ergo nec nominare. Cum igitur "qui est" non dicat aliquem respectum ad creaturas, videtur quod non proprie nominet Deum.

3. Praeterea, sicut sapientia creata deficit a sapientia increata, ita et esse creatum ab esse increato. Sed propter hoc nomen sapientiae dicitur deficere a perfecta significatione divinae sapientiae, quia est impositum

about the unity of the essence; <in the> second, about its unchangeability, at <Chapter 22, beginning with the words> "The essence of God alone is also said <to be> unchangeable properly..."; <in the> third, about its simplicity, at <Chapter 23, beginning with the words> "And the same alone is properly and truly simple."

With regard to the first, he does two things: first he shows the truth of the divine essence; second, he eliminates a doubt, at <the words> "Here one ought diligently to consider how the words of Jerome* are to be understood."

QUESTION* I

With respect to the first part of the distinction*, in which the treatment* is concerned with the propriety* of the divine *being*, there are two topics of inquiry: first, the divine *being* itself, second its measure, namely, eternity.

/194b/ In the first <of these>, there are three points of inquiry: (1) Does *being* properly belong to God? (2) Is His *being* the *being* of any creature? (3) On the relation of the name* "He Who is"* to the other divine names.

ARTICLE* I Is *being* properly said of God?

One proceeds to the first <article> in this way: 1. It seems that *being* is not properly said of God. For that which is proper to anything is what belongs to it alone. But *being* belongs not only to God but also to creatures. Therefore, it seems that *being* does not properly belong to God.

2. Further, we cannot name God except as we know Him; hence, Damascene* in *De Fide Orthodoxa* I, chap. 13 says, "The word is an angel, i.e., a messenger of the intellect." As wayfarers we are unable to know God immediately except from creatures. Hence, neither <are we able> to name <Him>. Therefore, since "He Who is" does not predicate a relation* to creatures, it seems that it does not properly name God.

3. Further, just as created wisdom falls short of uncreated wisdom, so also does created *being* fall short of uncreated *being*. But for this reason the name "wisdom" is said to fall short of the perfect meaning

a nobis secundum apprehensionem creatae sapientiae. Ergo videtur quod eadem ratione nec hoc nomen "qui est", proprie significet divinum esse: et ita non oportet dici magis proprium nomen ejus quam alia nomina.

4. Item, Damascenus, lib. I *Fid. orth.*, cap. IX, col. 834, t. I, dicit, quod "qui est" non significat quid est Deus, sed quoddam pelagus substantiae infinitum. Sed infinitum non est comprehensible, et per consequens non nominabile sed ignotum. Ergo videtur quod "qui est" non sit divinum nomen.

Contra, Exod., III, 14, *Dixit Dominus ad Moysen*: Si quaesierint nomen meum, *sic dices filiis Israel: Qui est, misit me ad vos*. Hoc idem videtur per Damascenum, ubi supra, cap. IX, dicentem quod "qui est", maxime est proprium nomen Dei: et per Rabbi Moysen, qui dicit, hoc nomen esse nomen Dei ineffabile, quod dignissimum habebatur.

SOLUTIO.—Respondeo dicendum, quod "qui est", est /195a/ maxime proprium Dei inter alia nomina. Et ratio hujus potest esse quadruplex: prima sumitur ex littera ex verbis Hieronymi secundum perfectionem divini esse. Illud enim est perfectum cujus nihil est extra ipsum. Esse autem nostrum habet aliquid sui extra se: deest enim aliquid quod jam de ipso praeteriit, et quod futurum est. Sed in divino esse nihil praeteriit nec futurum est: et ideo totum esse suum habet perfectum, et propter hoc sibi proprie respectu aliorum convenit esse. Secunda ratio sumitur ex verbis Damasceni, lib. I *Fid. orth.*, cap. IX, qui dicit, quod "qui est" significat esse indeterminate, et non quid est: et quia in statu viae hoc tantum de ipso cognoscimus, quia est, et non quid est, nisi per negationem, et non possumus nominare nisi secundum quod cognoscimus, ideo propriissime nominatur a nobis "qui est". Tertia ratio sumitur ex verbis Dionysii, qui dicit, quod esse inter omnes alias divinae bonitatis participationes, sicut vivere et intelligere et hujusmodi, primum est, et quasi principium aliorum, praehabens in se omnia praedicta, secundum quemdam modum unita; et ita etiam Deus est principium divinum, et omnia sunt unum in ipso. Quarta ratio potest sumi ex verbis Avicennae, tract. VIII *Metaph.*, cap. I, in hunc modum, quod, cum in

of divine wisdom, since it has been imposed by us according to our <own> apprehension of created wisdom. Therefore, it seems that, for the same reason, neither does the name "He Who is" properly signify the divine *being,* and so it need not be called His proper name any more than other names.

4. Again, Damascene* says in *De Fide Orthodoxa,* I, chap. 9, that "He Who is" does not signify what God is but rather an infinite sea of substance*. But the infinite is not comprehensible and consequently is not nameable, but unknown. Hence, it seems that "He Who is" is not a divine name.

On the contrary, in *Exodus* 3, 14: *The Lord said to Moses:* If they should ask My name, *thus shalt thou speak to the sons of Israel: He Who is hath sent me to you.* The same is seen through Damascene* <*De Fide Orthodoxa,* I> chap. 9, saying that "He Who is" is the most proper Name of God, and through Rabbi Moses <Maimonides*>, who says that this name is the ineffable Name of God, which was held most worthy.

SOLUTION.—I answer that one ought to say that "He Who is" is /195b/ the most proper name of God among the other names. Four reasons* for this <claim> are possible: (I) The first is taken literally* from the words of Jerome* according to the perfection of the divine *being.* For that is perfect of which nothing is outside it. But our *being* has something of it outside itself: for there is something missing which has already passed by from it and <something> which is to come. But in the divine *being* nothing has gone past nor is anything to come; and so it has its whole *being* perfect*, and for this reason *being* belongs to it properly with respect to the rest. (ii) The second reason is taken from the words of Damascene* *De Fide Orthodoxa,* I, chap. 9, who says that "He Who is" signifies *being* indeterminately and not what He is: and since in the state of wayfaring*, we know of Him only this: that* He is (*quia est*) and not what* He is (*quid est*), except by negation; and we cannot name <anything> except according as we know <it>, and so by us He is most properly named "He Who is." (iii) The third reason is taken from the words of Dionysius,* who says that, among all the other participations of the divine goodness, such as *living**, *understanding**, and the like, *being* is the first and, as it were, the principle of the others, pre-possessing all the others in a way united within itself; and so too God is the divine principle and all things are one in Him. (iv) The fourth reason can be taken from the words of Avicenna * <*Metaphysics* VIII, chap. 1> to

omni quod est sit considerare quidditatem suam, per quam subsistit in natura determinata, et esse suum, per quod dicitur de eo quod est in actu, hoc nomen "res" imponitur rei a quidditate sua, secundum Avicennam, tract. II *Metaph.*, cap. I, hoc nomen "qui est" vel "ens" imponitur ab ipso actu essendi. Cum autem ita sit quod in qualibet re creata essentia sua differat a suo esse, res illa proprie denominatur a quidditate sua, et non ab actu eassendi, sicut homo ab humanitate. In Deo autem ipsum esse suum est sua quidditas: et ideo nomen quod sumitur ab esse, proprie nominat ipsum, et est proprium nomen ejus: sicut proprium nomen hominis quod sumitur a quidditate sua.

Ad primum ergo dicendum, quod cum dicitur aliquid proprie convenire alicui, hoc potest intelligi dupliciter: aut quod per proprietatem excludatur omne extraneum a natura subjecti, ut cum dicitur proprium hominis esse risibile, quia nulli extraneo a natura hominis convenit; et sic esse non dicitur proprium Deo, quia convenit etiam creaturis. Aut secundum quod excluditur omne extraneum a natura praedicati, ut cum dicitur, hoc proprie esse aurum, \196a\ quia non habet admixtionem alterius metalli, et hoc modo esse dicitur proprium Deo, quia non habet admixtionem divinum esse alicujus privationis vel potentialitatis, sicut esse creaturae. Et ideo pro eodem in littera sumitur proprietas et veritas: verum enim aurum dicimus esse quod est extraneo impermixtum.

Ad secundum dicendum, quod ex creaturis contingit Deum nominari tripliciter. Uno modo quando nomen ipsum actualiter connotat effectum in creatura propter relationem ad creaturam importatam in nomine, sicut Creator et Dominus. Alio modo quando ipsum nomen nominat secundum suam rationem principium alicujus actus divini in creaturis, sicut sapientia, potentia et voluntas. Alio modo quando ipsum nomen dicit aliquid repraesentatum in creaturis, sicut vivens: omnis enim vita exemplata est a vita divina. Et similiter hoc nomen "qui est" nominat Deum per esse inventum in creaturis, quod exemplariter deductum est ab ipso.

Ad tertium dicendum, quod cum esse creaturae imperfecte repraesentet divinum esse, et hoc nomen "qui est" imperfecte significat ipsum,

this effect: that, since in everything that is, it is possible to consider its quiddity*, through which it subsists in a determinate nature*, and its *being*, through which it is said of that which actually is, the name "thing*" (*res*) is imposed on a thing from its quiddity, according to Avicenna* *Metaph.* II, chap. 1*, <and> the name "He Who is" or "a being" (*ens*) is imposed* by the very act of *being*. But although it is the case that in any created thing its essence differs from its *being*, the thing is properly denominated from its quiddity and not from the act of *being*, e.g., a man* from humanity*. In God, however, His very *being* is His quiddity: and so the name that is taken from *being* properly names Him and is His proper* name, just like the proper name of man, which is taken from his quiddity.

1. So to the first <objection> one ought to say that when something is said to belong to something properly, it can be understood* in two ways: (a) either because every thing extraneous to the nature* of the subject* may be excluded by the property, as when *being* able to laugh is called a property* of man; and in this sense *being* is not called proper to God, since it belongs also to creatures; (b) or according as everything extraneous to the nature of the predicate* is excluded, as when it is said that 'this is (*esse*) properly gold,' /196b/ since it has no admixture of another metal, and in this latter sense *being* is called proper to God, since the divine *being* has no admixture of privation* or potentiality*, as does the *being* of a creature. And so in the text "property" and "truth" are taken* to stand for the same thing: for we say that true gold is what is unmixed with anything extraneous.

2. To the second <objection> one ought to say that God may be named on the basis of creatures in three ways. (1) In one way, when the name itself actually connotes* an effect* in a creature owing to a relation implied to a creature within the name, e.g., Creator, and Lord. (2) In another way, when the name itself names a principle of a divine act in creatures with respect to its own character, e.g., wisdom, power, and will. (3) In another way when the name itself utters something re-presented* in creatures, e.g., living: for all life has been modeled* by the divine life. And likewise the name "He Who is" names God through the *being* found in creatures, which has been deduced by way of example* from Him.

3. To the third <objection> one ought to say that since the *being* of a creature imperfectly* re-presents* the divine *being*, the name "He Who

quia significat per modum cujusdam concretionis et compositionis; sed adhuc imperfectius significatur per alia nomina: cum enim dico, Deum esse sapientem, tunc, cum in hoc dicto includatur esse, significatur ibi duplex imperfectio: una est ex parte ipsius esse concreti, sicut in hoc nomine "qui est;" et superadditur alia ex propria ratione divinae sapientiae. Ipsa enim sapientia creata deficit a ratione divinae sapientiae: et propter hoc major imperfectio est in aliis nominibus quam in hoc nomine "qui est;" et ideo hoc est dignius et magis Deo proprium.

Ad quartum dicendum, quod alia omnia nomina dicunt esse secundum aliam rationem determinatam; sicut sapiens dicit aliquid esse; sed hoc nomen "qui est" dicit esse absolutum et non determinatum per aliquid additum; et ideo dicit Damascenus, quod non significat quid est Deus, sed significat quoddam pelagus substantiae infinitum, quasi non determinatum. Unde quando in Deum procedimus per viam remotionis, primo negamus ab eo corporalia; et secundo etiam intellectualia, secundum quod inveniuntur in creaturis, ut bonitas et sapientia; et tunc remanet tantum in intellectu nostro, quia est, et nihil amplius: unde est sicut in quadam confusione. Ad ultimum autem etiam hoc ipsum esse, secundum quod est in creaturis, ab ipso removemus; et tunc rema /197a/ net in quadam tenebra ignorantiae, secundum quam ignorantiam, quantum ad statum viae pertinet, optime Deo conjungimur, ut dicit Dionysius et haec est quaedam caligo, in qua Deus habitare dicitur.

ARTICULUS II *Utrum Deum sit esse omnium rerum*

Ad secundum sic proceditur. 1. Videtur quod Deus sit esse omnium rerum per id quod dicit Dionysius, IV cap. *Caelest. hier.*, §1, col. 178, t. I: "Esse omnium est superesse divinitatis." Hoc etiam idem dicit, V cap. *De div. nom.*, §4, etc., col. 818, t. I: "Ipse Deus est esse existentibus."

2. Praeterea, nulla creatura est per se, sed per aliud. Esse autem non est per aliud, quia si esset per aliud esse, iterum eadem quaestio esset de illo, et sic in infinitum procederet, et ita videtur quod esse non sit quid causatum, et ita est Deus.

is" also signifies* it imperfectly, since it signifies by <indicating> concreteness* and composition*; but it is signified still more imperfectly by the other names: for when I say 'God is wise,' then, since *being* is included in this expession, two sorts of imperfection are signified there: (a) one arises from the side of the concrete *being* itself, as in the name "He Who is"; and (b) another <imperfection> is added in addition from the proper character* of wisdom. For created wisdom itself falls short of the character of divine wisdom: and for this reason there is greater imperfection in the other names than there is in the name "He Who is." And so this <name> is more fitting and more proper to God.

4. To the fourth <objection> one ought to say that all the other names say being according to another determinate aspect, as 'wise' says 'is something ' (*aliquid esse*); but the name "He Who is" says an 'is' (*esse*) absolute* and not determined* by anything additional. This is why Damascence* says that it does not signify what God is but signifies an infinite, i.e., non-determinate, sea of substance. Hence, when we proceed toward God by way of removal*, first we deny* bodily <features> of Him; and, second, <we> also <deny> intellectual <features> as they are found in creatures, e.g., goodness and wisdom; and then the only <feature> that remains in our understanding* is that it is (*quia est*) and nothing more: hence, it is, as it were, in a sort of confusion. At the last, however, we will remove even this very *being* from Him, according as it is in creatures; and then it remains /197b/ in a shadow of unknowing*, and according to this unknowing—to the extent that it pertains to the state of wayfaring*—we are best joined with God, as Dionysius* says, and this is the cloud in which God is said to dwell.

ARTICLE II: Is God the *being* of all things?

One proceeds to the second <article> in this way: 1. It seems that God is the *being* of all things because of what Dionysius says in *Caelest. hierarch.*, Chap, IV, sect. 1: "The *being* of all things is the super-*being** of divinity." He also says the same thing in the *Divine Names*, chap. V, sect. 4: "God Himself is the *being* for existent* <things>."

2. Further, no creature is through itself, but through something else. But *being* is not through something else, since, if it were through another *being*, the same question would arise about that and thus an infinite regress would arise, and so it seems that *being* is not something caused and so it is God.

3. Praeterea, ea quae sunt et nullo modo differunt, sunt idem. Sed Deus et esse rei sunt et nullo modo differunt. Ergo sunt idem. Probatio mediae. Quod sint manifestum est; quod autem non differant, videtur. Quaecumque enim differunt, aliqua differentia differunt. Sed quaecumque differunt aliqua differentia, in se habent aliquam differentiam, et ita sunt composita; sicut homo habet in se rationale. Cum igitur esse sit simplex, et similiter Deus, videtur quod non differant.

Contra, nihil est magis in re quod sit unitum sibi quam esse suum. Sed Deus non unitur rebus, quod patet etiam per Philosophum, lib. *De causis*, propos. 20: "Causa prima regit omnes res, praeterquam commisceatur cum eis." Ergo Deus non est omnium esse.

Praeterea, nihil habet esse, nisi inquantum participat divinum esse, quia ipsum est primum ens, quare causa est omnis entis. Sed omne quod est participatum in aliquo, est in eo per modum participantis: quia nihil potest recipere ultra mensuram suam. Cum igitur modus cujuslibet rei creatae sit finitus, quaelibet res creata recipit esse finitum et inferius divino esse quod est perfectissiminum. Ergo con /198a/ stat quod esse creaturae, quo est formaliter, non est divinum esse.

SOLUTIO.—Respondeo, sicut dicit Bernardus, *Serm. IV super Cant.*, Deus est esse omnium non essentiale, sed causale. Quod sic patet. Invenimus enim tres modos causae agentis. Scilicet causam aequivoce agentem, et hoc est quando effectus non convenit cum causa nec nomine nec ratione: sicut sol facit calorem qui non est calidus. Item causam univoce agentem, quando effectus convenit in nomine et ratione cum causa, sicut homo generat hominem et calor facit calorem. Neutro istorum modorum Deus agit. Non univoce, quia nihil univoce convenit cum ipso. Non aequivoce, cum effectus et causa aliquo modo conveniant in nomine et ratione, licet secundum prius et posterius; sicut Deus sua sapienta facit nos sapientes, ita tamen quod sapienta nostra semper deficit a ratione sapientiae suae, sicut accidens a ratione entis, secundum quod est in substantia. Unde est tertius modus causae agentis analogice. Unde patet quod divinum esse producit esse creaturae in similitudine sui imperfecta: et ideo esse divinum dicitur esse omnium rerum, a quo omne esse creatum effective et exemplariter manat.

3. Further, the <things> that are and in no way differ are the same*. But God and a thing's *being* exist and in no way differ. Therefore, they are the same. Proof of the minor <premise>: That they exist is obvious; but that they do not differ may be seen. For whatever things differ by a difference have the difference within themselves and so they are composite, e.g., man has rational within himself. Hence, since *being* is simple and God is likewise, it seems that they do not differ.

On the contrary, there is nothing in a thing that is more united to it than its *being*. But God is not united to things. This is clear even through the Philosopher in the *Book of Causes**, prop. 20: "The first cause rules all things without being commingled with them." Therefore, God is not the *being* of all things.

Further, nothing has *being* except inasmuch as it participates divine *being*, since it is the first being (*ens*); hence, it is the cause of every being (*entis*). But all that is participated in anything is in it through the manner* of the participant, since nothing can receive beyond its own measure*. Therefore, since the manner of any created thing is finite, any created thing receives a finite *being* inferior to the divine *being* which is the most perfect. Hence, it is /198b/ that the *being* of a creature, whereby it formally is, is not the divine *being*.

SOLUTION.—I answer, as Bernard* says in *Sermon IV on the Canticles*, God is not the essential but the causal *being* of all things. This is clear as follows: For we find three modes of agent cause, namely (1) an equivocally acting cause, and this obtains when an effect agrees neither in name nor in character* with its cause: as the sun makes heat, which is not <itself> hot. (2) Again, a univocally acting cause, when an effect agrees in name and character* with its cause, e.g., man generates man and heat makes heat. God acts in neither of these ways: not univocally, since nothing agrees with Him univocally; not equivocally, since effect and cause in a way agree in name and character, albeit with respect to prior and posterior, just as God by His wisdom makes us wise, yet such that our wisdom always falls short of the character* of His wisdom, just as an accident falls short of the character* of a being as it is in substance. (3) Hence, there is a third mode of a cause acting* analogously*. Hence, it is clear that the divine *being* produces the *being* of a creature in an imperfect likeness of Itself: and so the divine *being* is called the *being* of all things <for> all created *being* emanates effectively* and paradigmatically* from It.

Et per hoc patet solutio ad dictum Dionysii, quod ita intelligendum est, ut patet ex hoc quod dicit "superesse". Si enim Deus esset essentialiter esse creaturae, non esset superesse.

Ad secundum dicendum, quod esse creatum non est per aliquid aliud, si ly "per" dicat causam formalem intrinsecam; immo ipso formaliter est creatura; si autem dicat causam formalem extra rem, vel causam effectivam, sic est per divinum esse et non per se.

Ad tertium dicendum, quod prima non sunt diversa nisi per seipsa: sed ea quae sunt ex primis, differunt per diversitatem primorum; sicut homo et asinus differunt istis differentiis diversis, rationale et irrationale, quae non diversificantur aliis differentiis, sed seipsis: ita etiam Deus et esse creatum non differunt aliquibus differentiis utrique superadditis, sed seipsis: unde nec proprie dicuntur differre, sed diversa esse: diversum enim est absolutum, sed differens est relatum, secundum Philosophum, X *Metaph.*, text. 13. Omne enim differens, aliquo differt; sed non omne diversum, aliquo diversum est.

/199a/

ARTICULUS III *Utrum hoc nomen "qui est" sit primum inter nomina divina*

Ad tertium sic proceditur. 1. Videtur enim quod hoc nomen "qui est" non sit primum inter divina nomina. De prioribus enim prius est agendum. Sed Dionysius prius agit de bono in lib. *De div. nom.*, quam de existente. Ergo videtur bonum prius esse ente.

2. Praeterea, illud quod est communis videtur esse prius. Sed bonum est communis quam ens: quia divinum esse extendit se tantum ad entia quae etiam in esse vocat: dicitur enim bonum a boare, quod est vocare, ut Commentator dicit *Super lib.* "De div. nom.," c. IV. Ergo bonum est prius quam ens.

3. Praeterea, quaecumque sunt aequalis simplicitatis, unum non est prius altero. Sed ens, verum, bonum, et unum sunt aequalis simplicita-

1. From this, too, the solution to Dionysius's saying is clear: that it is to be understood in this way, as is clear from his saying "super-*being*". For if God were the *being* of a creature essentially, then He would not be <its> super-*being*.

2. To the second <objection> one ought to say that created *being* is not through anything else if "through" expresses the intrinsic formal cause: to be sure, by it the creature formally is. But if it expresses the formal cause outside the thing or the effective cause, in this sense it is through the divine *being* and not through itself.

3. To the third <objection> one ought to say that primes* are not diverse* except through themselves, but the things that are <derived> from the primes differ through the diversity of the primes. Just as man and ass differ by diverse differences, rational and irrational, which are diversified not by other differences but by themselves: so too God and created *being* differ not by any difference superadded to each of them, but by themselves: hence, neither are they properly said to differ but to be diverse: for the diverse is absolute, but the different* is relative, according to the Philosopher in *Metaphysics* X, text 13. For everything different differs by something, but not everything diverse differs by anything.

/199b/

ARTICLE III: Is the name "He Who is" first among the divine names?

One proceeds to the third <article> in this way. 1. For it seems that the name "He Who Is" is not first among the divine names. For one ought to treat first things first. Yet Dionysius in the *Divine Names* treats the good <chap. IV> prior to the existent <chap. V>. Therefore, the good* seems to be prior to the being.

2. Further, that which is more common seems to be prior. But the good is more common than the being, since the divine *being* extends itself only to the beings that participate* *being*, whereas the good extends itself to non-beings, which it even calls into *being*; for the good (*bonum*) is so called from *boare*, i.e., to call (*vocare*), as the Commentator* says on the book *On the Divine Names*, chap. IV. Therefore, the good is prior to the being.

3. Further, whatever things are of equal simplicity, the one is not prior to the other. But the being, the true, the good, and the one are of

tis: quod patet ex hoc quod ad invicem convertuntur. Ergo unum non est altero prius.

Contra, secundum Dionysium, *De divin. nom.*, cap. I, § 4, col. 590, t. I, divina attributa non innotescunt nobis nisi ex eorum participationibus quibus a creaturis participantur. Sed inter omnes alias participationes, esse prius est, ut dicitur V cap. *De div. nom.*, § 6, col. 819, t. I, his verbis: "Ante alias ipsius," scilicet Dei, "participationes, esse positum est." Cui etiam dictum Philosophi consonat, lib. *De causis*, propos. 4: "Prima rerum creatarum est esse." Ergo videtur quod, secundum rationem intelligendi, in Deo esse sit ante alia attributa, et "qui est" inter alia nomina.

Praeterea, illud quod est ultimum in resolutione, est primum in esse. Sed ens, ultimum est in resolutione intellectus: quia remotis omnibus aliis, ultimo remanet ens. Ergo est primum naturaliter.

SOLUTIO.—Respondeo dicendum, quod ista nomina, ens et bonum, unum et verum, simpliciter secundum rationem intelligendi praecedunt alia divina nomina: quod patet ex eorum communitate. Si autem comparemus ea ad invicem, hoc potest esse dupliciter: vel secundum suppositum; et sic convertuntur ad invicem, et sunt idem in supposito, nec unquam derelinquunt se; vel secundum intentiones eorum; /200a/ et sic simpliciter et absolute ens est prius aliis. Cujus ratio est, quia ens includitur in intellectu eorum, et non e converso. Primum enim quod cadit in imaginatione intellectus, est ens, sine quod nihil potest, apprehendi ab intellectu; sicut primum quod cadit in credulitate intellectus, sunt dignitates, et praecipue ista, contradictoria non esse simul vera: unde omnia alia includuntur quodammodo in ente unite et distincte, sicut in principio; ex quo etiam habet quamdam decentiam ut sit propriissimum divinum nomen. Alia vero quae diximus, scilicet, bonum, verum et unum, addunt, super ens, non quidem naturam aliquam, sed rationem: sed unum addit rationem indivisionis; et propter hoc est propinquissimum ad ens, quia addit tantum negationem: verum autem et bonum addunt relationem ad formam exemplarem; ex hoc enim unumquodque verum dicitur quod imitatur exemplar divinum, vel relationem ad dicitur quod imitatur exemplar divinum, vel relationem ad virtutem

equal simplicity: this is clear because they are converted* with each other. Hence, the one is not prior to the other.

On the contrary, according to Dionysius* *On the Divine Names,* chap. I, sect. 4* <the divine names> do not make known to us the divine attributes except from their participations*, by which they are participated by creatures. But *being* is prior among all the other participations, as is said in *On the Divine Names,* chap. V, sect. 6* in these words: "*Being* has been placed* before all his" i.e., God's "other participations." A saying of the Philosopher* is also in agreement with this in the *Book of Causes,** prop. 4: "The first of created things is *being.*" Hence, it seems that in God *being* is, according to the aspect of understanding, before all the other attributes, and "He Who is" among the other names.

Further, that which is last in analysis* is first in *being*. But a being is last in the mind's analysis, since, when all else has been removed, the being remains at last. Therefore, it is naturally first.

SOLUTION.—I answer that one ought to say that the names 'the being*' and 'the good,' 'the one*' and 'the true*' simply precede the other divine names according to the aspect of understanding, which is clear from their community*. But if we compare* them to each other, this can occur in two ways: either (1) with respect to the supposit,* and in this way they are converted with each other and are the same in supposit and never leave each other; or (2) with respect to their meanings* /200b/ and in this way 'being' (*ens*) is simply and absolutely prior to the others. The reason for this is that 'being' is included in the understanding* of them, but not conversely. For the first <feature> that falls within the imagination* of the intellect* is being (*ens*) without which nothing can be apprehended by the intellect; just as the axioms* are what first falls within the judgment* of the intellect, especially this one: that contradictories are not true simultaneously: hence, all the others are somehow unitedly and distinctly included within 'being' as within a principle; from this, too, <'being'> has a certain fitness for being the most proper divine name. The others which we have mentioned, viz. 'the good,' 'the true,' and 'the one'—add not a nature* but a notion* over and above 'being.' 'The one' adds the notion of undividedness*, and for this reason is closest to 'being,' since it adds only a negation*. 'The true' and 'the good,' however, add a relation*— 'the good,' a relation to an end, 'the true' a relation to an exemplar form*. For everything is called 'true,' because it imitates a divine exemplar or a relation to a knowing

cognoscitivam; dicimus enim verum aurum esse, ex eo quod habet formam auri quam demonstrat, et sic fit verum judicium de ipso. Si autem considerentur secundum rationem causalitatis, sic bonum est prius; quia bonum habet rationem causae finalis, esse autem rationem causae exemplaris et effectivae tantum in Deo: finis autem est prima causa in ratione causalitatis.

Ad primum dicendum, quod Dionysius tractat de divinis nominibus secundum quod habent rationem causalitatis, prout scilicet manifestantur in participatione creaturam; et ideo bonum ante existens determinat.

Ad secundum dicendum, quod bonum est communius non secundum ambitum praedicationis, quia sic convertitur cum ente, sed secundum rationem causalitatis; causalitas enim efficiens exemplaris extenditur tantem ad ea quae participant formam actu suae causae exemplaris; et ideo causalitas entis, secundum quod est divinum nomen, extenditur tantum ad entia, et vitae ad viventia; sed causalitas finis extenditur etiam ad ea quae nondum participant formam, quia etiam imperfecta desiderant et tendunt in finem. Vocat enim Dionysius non ens materiam propter privationem adjunctam; unde etiam dicit, IV cap. *De divin. nomin.*, § 3, col. 698, t. I, quod ipsum non existens desiderat bonum.

/201a/ Ad tertium dicendum, qoud convertuntur secundum suppositum considerata; sed tamen secundum intentionem, ens est simplicius et prius aliis, ut dictum est.

QUAESTIO II

Deinde quaeritur de mensura divini esse, quae est aeternitas; et circa hoc tria quaeruntur: 1° quid est aeternitas; 2° cui conveniat; 3° utrum de aeterno verba diversorum temporum praedicari possint.

power; for we say that gold is true because it has the form of gold which it presents and thus a true judgment* arises about it. If, however, <the transcendentals* just enumerated> are considered according to the aspect* of causality, in this way the good is prior, since the good has the aspect* of a final* cause*, whereas *being* has the aspect of exemplar* and effective* cause only in God, but the end* is the first cause in the aspect* of causality.

1. To the first <objection> one ought to say that Dionysius* is treating the divine names according as they have the aspect* of causality, viz. to the extent that they are manifested in the participation of creatures; this is why he determines the good before the existent.

2. To the second <objection> one ought to say that the good is more common not with respect to the scope of <its> predication* (since in this respect it is converted with 'being' (*ens*)), but according to the aspect of causality. For efficient exemplar causality extends only to those <items> that actually participate the form of their exemplar cause; and so the causality of a being, according as it is a divine name, extends only to beings and <that> of life <only> to living things. But the causality of the end extends even to those <items> that do not yet participate the form, since even imperfect things desire and tend to an end. For Dionysius calls matter* a non-being because of its associated privation*; hence, too, in *On the Divine Names,* chap. IV, sect. 3, he says that a non-existent itself desires the good.

/201b/ 3. To the third <objection> one ought to say that <the transcendentals> considered with respect to their supposit* are converted, but yet 'being' with respect to intention* is simpler than and prior to the others, as has been said.

QUESTION II

Then a question is asked about the measure* of the divine *being,* which is eternity*. Concerning this there are three points of inquiry: 1. What is eternity? 2. To what does <eternity> belong? 3. Can verbs of diverse tenses* be predicated of the eternal?

ARTICULUS PRIMUS *Utrum definitio aeternitatis a Boetio posita sit conveniens*

Ad primum sic proceditur. 1. Et ponitur definitio aeternitatis a Boetio, V *De consol.*, prosa ultim., col. 858, t. I: "Aeternitas est interminabilis vitae tota simul et perfecta possessio." Sed videtur quod ista definitio inconvenienter assignetur. Interminabile enim dicit negationem. Sed negatio non certificat aliquid. Ergo videtur quod in definitione aeternitatis poni non debeat.

2. Item, prima mensura respondet primo mensurato. Sed primum inter mensurata est esse. Ergo videtur quod aeternitas, quae est prima mensura, non debet definiri per vitam, sed per esse.

3. Item, simplex non habet mensuram, immo simplicissimo mensurantur omnia alia, secundum Philosophum, X *Metaphys.*, text. 3. Sed vita divina est simplicissima. Ergo non respondet aliquid sibi in ratione mensurae: sed ipsa habet rationem mensurae et ita nec aeternitas, quae rationem mensurae dicit.

4. Item, totum dicitur respectu partium. Sed de ratione durationis est quod partes ejus non sint: quia impossibile est simul esse duas durationes, nisi una includat aliam, sicut Augustinus dicit, XI *De Civitate Dei* cap. VI, col. 321, t. I. Ergo videtur duo opposita dicere, cum dicit, "tota simul."

5. Item, totum includit in se rationem perfectionis. Ergo videtur quod "perfecta" superfluit.

6. Item, aeternitas habet rationem durationis. Sed "pos /202a/ ses- ^Ssio" nihil dicit ad durationem pertinens. Ergo videtur quod non debet poni in definitione aeternitatis, ad minus in recto, et sicut genus: quia quod sic ponitur in definitione alicujus, debet dicere quid sit definitum.

SOLUTIO.—Respondeo dicendum, quod aeternitas dicitur quasi ens extra terminos. Esse autem aliquod potest dici terminatum tripliciter: vel secundum durationem totam, et hoc modo dicitur terminatum quod habet principium et finem; vel ratione partium durationis, et hoc modo dicitur terminatum illud cujus quaelibet pars accepta terminata est ad praecedens, praesens et sequens: sicut est accipere in motu; vel ratione

ARTICLE I: Is the definition of eternity posited* by Boethius fitting?

One proceeds to the first <article> in this way: 1. A definition of eternity is laid down by Boethius* *On the Consolation of Philosophy,* Book V. last prose section: "Eternity is the total* simultaneous* and perfect* possession* of interminable* life*." Yet it seems that this definition is unsuitably assigned. For 'interminable' expresses a negation. But a negation does not make anything certain. Hence, it seems that it ought not be included in the definition of eternity.

2. Again, the measure answers to the first <thing> measured. But among measured <things> the first is *being.* Therefore, it seems that eternity, which is the first measure, ought to be defined not through life, but through *being.*

3. Again, the simple does not have a measure, but rather all other things are measured by the simplest, according to the Philosopher* in *Metaphysics* Book X, text 3. But the divine life is the simplest. So nothing in the character* of a measure corresponds to It; but It itself has the character* of measure and so eternity, which expresses the character* of a measure, does not.

4. Again, the whole* is spoken of in respect to parts. But it is of the character* of duration that its parts do not exist at once; since it is impossible for two durations* to exist at once unless the one includes the other, as Augustine* says in *On the City of God,* Book XI, chap. vi. Therefore, <Boethius> seems to be saying two opposites when he says "total, simultaneous."

5. Again, the whole includes within itself the aspect* of perfection. Therefore, it seems that "perfect" is superfluous.

6. Again, eternity has the character* of a duration. But "possession" /202b/ expresses nothing pertaining to duration. Therefore, it seems as though <"possession"> ought not to be included in the definition of eternity, at least directly and as the genus*, since what is thus included in the definition of something ought to express what has been defined.

SOLUTION.—I answer that one ought to say that eternity is said as a being outside terminations. Now *being* can be terminated* (*terminatum*) in three ways: (1) according to its whole duration (and in this way that is called limited* which has a beginning and an end); or (2) by reason of the parts of the duration (and in this way that of which whatever part that is taken is terminated at the preceding, present, and following

suppositi in quo esse recipitur: esse enim recipitur in aliquo secundum modum ipsius, et ideo terminatur, sicut et quaelibet alia forma, quae de se communis est, et secundum quod recipitur in aliquo, terminatur ad illud; et hoc modo solum divinum esse non est terminatum, quia non est receptum in aliquo, quod sit diversum ab eo. Dico ergo, quod ad excludendam primam terminationem, quae est principii et finis totius durationis, ponitur, "interminabilis vitae"; et per hoc dividitur aeternum ab his quae generantur et corrumpuntur. Ad excludendum autem secundam terminationem, scilicet partium durationis, additur, "tota simul": per hoc enim excluditur successio partium, pro qua unaquaeque pars finita est et transit: et per hoc dividitur a motu et tempore, etiamsi semper fuissent et futura essent, sicut quidam posuerunt. Ad excludendum tertiam terminationem, quae est ex parte recipientis, additur, "perfecta": illud enim in quo non est esse perfectum, sed illud solum quod est suum esse: et per hoc dividitur esse aeternum ab esse rerum immobilium creatarum, quae habent esse participatum, sicut spirituales creaturae.

Ad primum ergo dicendum, quod simplicia, et praecipue divina, nullo modo melius manifestantur quam per remotionem, ut dicit Dionysius, *De divinis nomin.*, cap. VII, § 3, col. 870, t. I. Cujus ratio est, quia ipsorum esse intellectus perfecte non potest comprehendere; et ideo ex negationibus eorum quae ab ipso removentur, manuducitur intellectus ad ea aliqualiter cognoscenda. Unde et punctus negatione definitur. Et praeterea in ratione aeternitatis est quadem negatio, inquantum aeternitas est unitas, et unitas est indivisio, et hujusmodi non possunt sine negatione definiri.

Ad secundum dicendum, quod vivere hic large sumitur ad omne esse secundum etiam quod Augustinus dicit, lib. II /203a/ *Cont. Max*, cap. XII, § 2. col. 468, t. VIII, quod quaelibet mutatio creaturae, aliqua mors ejus est. Vel dicendum, quod quia in illo qui solus habet aeternitatem, esse et vivere sunt omnino idem; ideo ratione ejus, in quo est aeternitas, posuit aeternitatem mensuram vitae.

is said to be terminated, e.g., taking* in motion); or (3) by reason of the supposit* in which being is received: for being is received in something according to the <thing's> manner*, and so is terminated just as any other form that is of itself common* is also terminated at that according to which it is received in something. Only divine *being* is not terminated in this way, because It is not received in anything that is diverse from It. So I say, that "interminable life" is included to exclude the first sort of termination, i.e., of the beginning* and end* of the whole duration; and thus the eternal is divided off from the things that are generated and corrupted. To exclude the second sort of termination, that of the parts of duration, "total simultaneous" is added: for thereby a succession of parts is excluded (for which each part is rendered finite and passes by): and thus the eternal is divided off from motion* and time*, even if they had always existed and were to come, as some have claimed. To exclude the third sort of termination, i.e., on the part of the receiver, the third sort of termination, i.e., on the part of the receiver*, "perfect" is added: for that in which there is not absolute* being, but rather one terminated by a receiver, does not have perfect being; only that which is its own being <has perfect being>: and through this <feature> eternal being is divided off from the being of immobile created things, which have participated being, e.g., the spiritual* creatures*.

1. Therefore, to the first <objection> one ought to say that simple, and especially divine, things are in no way better manifested than through removal*, as Dionysius says *On the Divine Names,* chap. VII, sect. 3. The reason for this is that the intellect cannot perfectly comprehend their being; and so the intellect is guided to understand them in some way from the negations of the features that are removed from it. Here too is a point defined by negation. Moreover there is a sort of negation in the notion* of eternity, inasmuch as eternity is a unity*, and unity is undividedness, and such things cannot be defined without negation.

2. To the second <objection> one ought to say that here 'living' is taken broadly for all being, even according to what Augustine* says /203b/ in the *Contra Maximinum,* Book II, chap. 12, sect. 2: that any change of a creature is a sort of death for it. Or one ought to say that since *being* and *living* are utterly the same in Him who alone has eternity, hence he posited eternity as the measure of life by reason of that in which eternity exists.

Ad tertium dicendum, quod vivere et esse dicuntur per modum actus; et quia cuilibet actui respondet mensura sua, ideo oportet ut divino esse et vitae divinae intelligatur adjacere aeternitas, quasi mensura; quamvis realiter non sit aliud a divino esse; et quia vivere magis habet rationem actus etiam quam esse; ideo forte definit aeternitatem per vitam potius quam per esse.

Ad quartum dicendum, quod in successivis est duplex imperfectio: una ratione divisionis, alia ratione successionis, quia una pars non est cum alia parte; unde non habent esse nisi secundum aliquid sui. Ut autem excludatur omnis imperfectio a divino esse, oportet ipsum intelligere sine aliqua divisione partium perfectum, et hoc dicit nomen "tota": non enim dicit rationem partium. Item oportet ipsum intelligere sine successione, et hoc notatur per adverbium "simul".

Ad quintum dicendum, quod imperfectio esse potest considerari duplicater. Vel quantum ad durationem, et sic dicitur esse imperfectum cui deest aliquid de spatio durationis debitae; sicut dicimus vitam hominis qui moritur in pueritia, imperfectum vitam; et talis imperfectio quantum ad modum habendi, sicut omnis creatura habet imperfectum esse; et talis imperfectio tollitur per ly "perfecta", unde non superfluit.

Ad sextum dicendum, quod duratio dicit quandum distensionem ex ratione nominis: et quia in divino esse non debet intelligi aliqua talis distensio, ideo Boetius non posuit durationem, sed possessionem, metaphorice loquens ad significandum quietem divini esse; illud enim dicimus possidere quiete et plene habemus; et sic Deus possidere vitam suam dicitur, quia nulla inquietudine molestatur.

/204a/

ARTICULUS II *Utrum aeternitas tantum Deo conveniat*

Ad secundum sic proceditur. 1. Videtur quod aeternitas non tantum Deo conveniat. Aeternitas enim non est nobilior quam bonitas. Sed bonitas communicatur cum creaturis, ita quod a bono Deo creatura sit

3. To the third <objection> one ought to say that *living* and *being* are said in the manner of an act*; and since a proper measure corresponds to any act, eternity must be understood to accompany the divine *being* and the divine life as <its> measure, even though <eternity> is really nothing else but divine *being;* and since *living* has the character of act even more than *being* <does>, perhaps for that reason <Boethius> defines eternity through life rather than through *being.*

4. To the fourth <objection> one ought to say that there are two sorts of imperfection in successive <things>: one by reason of division*, the other by reason of succession*, since one part does not exist along with another part; hence, they do not have *being* except with respect to something of themselves. Now so that every imperfection may be excluded from divine *being,* it is necessary to understand It <as> perfect* without any division of parts, and the name "total" expresses this: for it does not express the notion of parts. Again, it is necessary to understand it without succession, and this is indicated by the adverb "simultaneously."

5. To the fifth <objection> one ought to say that imperfection can be considered in two ways: either* (1) with respect to duration, and in this way that is said to be imperfect to which something of the space* of the duration is missing; e.g., we call the life of a human being who dies in childhood an imperect life; such imperfection is ruled out by "total." There is also (2) an imperfection with regard to the manner of having <it>, as every creature has imperfect *being;* such imperfection is ruled out by the* <word> "perfect"; hence, it is not superfluous.

6. To the sixth <objection> one ought to say that duration expresses a certain distension* by reason of the name: and since no such distension ought to be understood in divine *being,* Boethius, speaking metaphorically, posited not duration but possession, to signify the resting of divine *being;* for we say we possess what we quietly and fully possess; and God is said to possess His life in this way, since He is not bothered by any restlessness.

/204b/

ARTICLE II: Does eternity* belong only to God?

One proceeds to the second <article> in this way: 1. It seems that eternity does belong only to God. For eternity is not more perfect than goodness. But goodness is communicated* to creatures, such that the

bona. Ergo videtur quod similiter aeternitas, ut alia ab ipso sint aeterna.

2. Praeterea, Dan., XII, 3: *Qui ad justitiam erudiunt multos, fulgebunt quasi stellae in perpetuas aeternitates.* Sed plures aeternitates non sunt unius aeterni. Ergo videtur quod sint plura aeterna, et non tantum Deus.

3. Praetera, in Psal. LXXV, 5: *Illuminans tu mirabiliter a montibus aeternis.* Sed montes sunt creaturae. Ergo etiam creaturae sunt aeternae.

4. Similiter etiam ignis inferni dicitur aeternus, Matth. XXV, 41: *Ite, maledicti, in ignem aeternum.* Ergo, etc.

5. Item, Philosophus, II *Perih.*, lect. III, et V *Metaphys.*, text. 6, dicit, quod omne necessarium est aeternum. Sed multa sunt necessaria. Ergo, etc. Huic etiam consonat quod dicit Augustinus, IV *De Trinitate*, cap. XVIII, col. 904, t. VIII, quod veritas aeterna est.

Contra, aeternum est esse interminatum, ut dictum est. Sed solus Deus est hujusmodi. Ergo, etc.

SOLUTIO.—Respondeo dicendum, quod, sicut ex praedicta definitione patet, aeternitas non potest nisi Deo convenire simpliciter et absolute secundum perfectam rationem aeternitatis. Sed secundum quod aliqua participant de interminabilitate aeternitatis, aliquo modo dicuntur aeterna participative. Quod vero nullo modo interminabilitatem participat, nullo modo aeternum dicitur, sicut temporale, quod incipit et finitur. Dico ergo, quod quibusdam communicatur interminabilitas, secundum quod excludit terminum durationis ex parte post; et hoc modo ignis inferni dicitur aeternus, quia nunquam finietur. Utrum autem aliquod aeternum possit esse, quod non habeat principium durationis, quaeretur in principio secundi. Aliquibus autem creaturis communicatur interminabilitas, secundum quod excludit terminationem quae est ex successione partium; et istae sunt spirituales creaturae, quarum esse est totum simul. Sed /205a/ interminabilitas, quae excludit omnem imperfectionem, non communicatur alicui creaturae, cum nulla creatura possit esse perfecta simplicter; sed communicatur sibi perfectio quaedam, scilicet quam nata est creatura attingere, ut sit perfecta secundum suam naturam: et sic angeli et homines beati sunt perfecti, quia totum habent id ad quod eorum natura capax est: unde angeli beati, magis sunt in

creature is good by the good God. Hence, it seems that eternity is similarly <communicated>, so that other things are eternal from Him.

2. Further, <in> *Daniel,* 12, 3: "Those who educate the many to justice" shall shine "like the stars for perpetual eternities." But many eternities do not belong to one eternal thing. Hence, it seems that there are several eternal things, and not only God.

3. Further, in *Psalm* 75, 5: "You, illuminating marvellously from the eternal mountains." But the mountains are creatures. Therefore, even creatures are eternal.

4. Similarly, even the fire of hell is called eternal. *Matthew* 25, 41: "Go ye accursed into eternal fire." Therefore, etc.

5. Again, the Philosopher* in *Perihermeneias* Book II, lect. 3* and *Metaphysics* V, text 6*, says that everything necessary* is eternal. But many things are necessary. Therefore, etc. What Augustine says in *De Trinitate* IV, chap. 18 agrees with this, viz. truth is eternal.

On the contrary, the eternal is unterminated *being,* as has been said. But only God is such. Therefore, etc.

SOLUTION.—I answer that one ought to say that, as is clear from the aforementioned definition, eternity cannot belong simply and absolutely, according to the perfect character* of eternity, to anything except God. But since some things participate in the interminability of eternity, they are called eternal in a certain way*—participatively. But what in no way participates interminability is in no way called eternal, e.g., the temporal, which starts* and is finished*. Therefore, I say that interminability is communicated to some things according as it excludes an end-point* of duration with respect to what exists afterwards; this is how the fire of hell is called eternal, since it is never brought to an end. Whether there can be anything eternal which does not have a starting-point* of duration is a question to be discussed at the beginning* of the second <book of the *Sentences*>. Interminability, however, is communicated to certain creatures according as it excludes a termination that arises from a succession of parts; these are the spiritual creatures, the *being* of which is all at once. /205b/ But the interminability which excludes every imperfection is not communicated to any creature, since no creature can be simply perfect; but a certain perfection is communicated to it, namely the one that a creature is naturally apt to attain, so as to be perfect according to its own nature: and in this way the blessed angels and humans are perfect, since they have that at which their nature is

participatione aeternitatis quam in naturalibus tantum considerati.

Ex hoc potest colligi differentia inter aeternitatem, aevum et tempus. Illud enim quod habet potentiam non recipientem actum totum simul, mensuratur tempore: hujusmodi enim habet esse terminatum: et quantum ad modum participandi, quia esse recipitur in aliqua potentia, et non est absolutum quantum ad partes durationis, quia habet prius et posterius. Illud autem quod habet potentiam differentem ab actu, sed quae totum actum simul suscipiat, mensuratur aevo: hoc enim non habet nisi unum modum terminationis, scilicet quia esse ejus est receptum in alio a se, ut dictum est. Illud vero quod non habet potentiam differentem ab esse, mensuratur aeternitate; hujusmodi enim esse est omni modo interminatum. Unde patet etiam quod aevum non est nisi quaedam aeternitas participata.

Ad primum ergo dicendum, quod quamvis divina bonitas sit communicabilis, non tamen secundum modum altissimum, prout est in Deo: unde summa bonitas non communicatur. Et quia aeternitas dicit esse secundum altissimum modum, qui est in Deo, ideo non communicatur; sed esse absolute sumptum communicatur, sicut et bonum.

Ad secundum dicendum, quod Daniel accipit ibi aeternitates participatas in beatis, quae erunt plures secundum plures beatos.

Ad tertium dicendum, quod montes aeterni possunt dici ipsi angeli, qui dicuntur aeterni participative, ut dictum est. Vel dicendum, quod potest intelligi etiam ad litteram de montibus corporalibus; et dicuntur aeterni propter longaevitatem durationis.

Ad quartum dicendum, quod ignis inferni dicitur etiam aeternus, inquantum participat aliquam conditionem aeternitatis, scilicet non habere finem.

Ad quintum dicendum, quod necessaria sunt aeterna tan /206a/ tum in mente divina, sicut etiam veritates enuntiabilium fuerunt ab aeterno in Deo, et non aliter: nisi ponerentur creaturae ab aeterno, sicut philosophi posuerunt.

capable <as> a whole: hence, the blessed angels are more in the participation* of eternity than those considered merely in their natural condition.

From this can be gathered the difference between eternity*, eviternity*, and time*. For that which has a potency* not receiving the total act simultaneously is measured by time: for such a thing has terminated *being,* both with regard to the mode of participating (since <its> *being* is received within a potency) and, with regard to the parts of duration, it is not absolute (since it has a prior and a posterior). But that which has a potency different from the act, but <a potency> that does undertake the whole act simultaneously is measured by eviternity*: for it has only one mode of termination, since its *being* has been received in something other than itself, as has been said. But that which does not have a potency different from *being* is measured by eternity*; for such *being* is unterminated in every way. Hence, it is also clear that eviternity* is nothing but a participated eternity.

1. Therefore, to the first <objection> one ought to say that although divine goodness is communicable, still <it is> not in the highest way*, as it is in God: hence, the highest goodness is not communicated. And since eternity expresses *being* in the highest way, which exists in God, it is not communicated; but *being* taken absolutely is communicated, as is the good.

2. To the second <objection> one ought to say that there Daniel is considering* eternities participated in the blessed, which will be as many as the many blessed.

3. To the third <objection> one ought to say that the angels, who are, as has been said, called eternal by way of participation, can be called "eternal mountains". Or else, one ought to say that it can even be understood literally of bodily mountains; they are also called eternal because of the length of their duration.

4. To the fourth <objection> one ought to say that the fire of hell can also be called eternal inasmuch as it participates a condition of eternity, i.e., not having an end*.

5. To the fifth <objection> one ought to say that necessary things are eternal only /206b/ in the divine mind*, just as the truths of enunciable* <propositions> have been in God from eternity, and not otherwise, unless creatures were supposed* to be from eternity, as philosophers have done.

ARTICULUS III *Utrum verba temporalia possint dici de Deo*

Ad tertium sic proceditur. 1. Videtur quod verba temporalia non possint dici de Deo. Unicuique enim respondet propria mensura. Sed tempus est propria mensura motus. Cum igitur in Deo nullus sit motus, videtur quod de Deo nullum temporale dici possit.

2. Item, quandocumque aliquid importans aliquam conditionem corporalem dicitur de Deo, metaphorice vel symbolice dicitur. Sed tempus est conditio consequens ipsa corpora, quia sequitur motum, et motus magnitudinem, secundum Philosophum, IV *Physic.*, text. 99. Ergo videtur quod quandocumque aliquid verbum temporale dicitur de Deo, sit metaphorice dictum.

3. Item, videtur quod tantum praesens de Deo debeat dici. Aeternitas enim, quae est mensura divini esse secundum rationem intelligendi, caret omni successione. Sed solum praesens non includit successionem; praeteritum enim et futurum dicuntur secundum relationem ad praesens, et non e converso; et relatio illa est in ordine successionis. Ergo solum praesens de Deo debet dici.

4. Item, videtur quod praeteritum. Divinum enim esse est perfectum. Sed inter alia tempora praeteritum magis sonat perfectionem. Ergo de Deo maxime dici debet.

5. Item, videtur quod praeteritum imperfectum. Quin Joannes in principio Evangelii sui altissime de Deo loctus est. Sed ipse ibi utitur verbis praeteriti imperfecti temporis ad designandum divinam aeternitatem, dicens: *In principio erat Verbum, et Verbum erat apud Deum, et Deus erat Verbum.* Ergo videtur quod ista verba maxime competant ad significandum divinam aeternitatem.

6. Item, videtur quod futurum. Divinum enim esse maxime distat a defectu. Cum igitur futurum remotis sit inter alia a deficiendo, videtur quod maxime competat in divinis. /207a/

SOLUTIO.—Respondeo dicendum, quod enutiatio non potest fieri de aliquo nisi secundum quod cadit in cognitionem. Omne autem cognoscens cognoscit secundum modum suum, ut dicit Boetius, lib. V *De consolat.*, pros. 2; et ideo, quia ratio nostra connaturale habet secundum

ARTICLE III: Can temporal* words* be said of God?

One proceeds to the third <article> in this way: 1. It seems that temporal words cannot be said of God. For to each thing there corresponds a proper measure. But time is the proper measure of motion. Therefore, since there is no motion in God, it seems that nothing temporal can be said of God.

2. Again, whenever anything involving a bodily condition is said of God, it is said metaphorically* or symbolically*. But time is a condition consequent upon bodies, since it follows on motion, and motion <follows on> magnitude, according to the Philosopher* in *Physics* IV, text 99*. Therefore, it seems that whenever a temporal word is said of God, it is said metaphorically.

3. Again, it seems that only the present ought to be said of God. For eternity, which is the measure of divine *being* with respect to the notion of *understanding**, is devoid of all succession. But only the present* does not include succession; for the past* and the future* are said in relation to the present and not conversely; and that relation is in the order of succession. So only the present ought to be said of God.

4. Again, it seems that the past <is predicable of God>. For divine *being* is perfect. But the past expresses perfection more than the other tenses*. So it most especially ought to be said of God.

5. Again, it seems that the past imperfect <tense is predicable of God>, since at the beginning of his Gospel, John spoke in a most elevated way about God. But there he uses verbs of the past imperfect tense* to designate the divine eternity, saying: "In the beginning was the Word, and the Word was with God, and the Word was God." Hence, it seems that these words are most fitting to signify the divine eternity.

6. Again, it seems that the future <tense is predicable of God>. For divine *being* is most distant from defect. Therefore, since the future is more remote than the rest from being defective, it seems that it is most appropriate in divine things. /207b/

SOLUTION.—I answer that one ought to say that an enunciation* cannot be made except with regard to what falls into cognition*. Now every knower* knows in his own way, as Boethius* says in *De consolatione* Book V, prose 2*; and so, since in the state of wayfaring* our reason has <as> a connatural <feature> to consider* <things> along with

statum viae accipere cum tempore, propter hoc quod ejus cognitio oritur a sensibilibus, quae in tempore sunt, ideo non potest formare enuntiationes nisi per verba temporalia: unde cogitur de Deo enuntians, verbis temporalibus uti, quamvis intelligat eum supra tempus esse: nihilominus tamen istae locutiones non sunt falsae. Divinum enim esse, ut dicit Dionysius, *De divinis nominibus* c. V, § 4, etc., col. 818, t. I, praeaccipit sicut causa in se omne quantum ad id quod est perfectionis in omnibus; et ideo enuntiamus de ipso verba omnium temporum, propter id quod ipse nulli tempori deest, et quidquid est perfectionis in omnibus temporibus, ipse habet.

Ad primum ergo dicendum, quod quando verba temporalia dicuntur de Deo, intellectus noster non attribuit divino esse illud quod est imperfectionis in singulis temporibus, sed quod est perfectionis in omnibus; aeternitas enim includit in se omnem perfectionem modo simplici, quae est in temporalibus divisum, cum tempus imitetur perfectionem aeternitatis, quantum potest.

Ad secundum dicendum, quod aliqua dictio potest importare conditionem corporalem dupliciter. Vel quantum ad rem significatam principaliter in nomine; et tale quid non dicitur de Deo nisi symbolice, sicut leo, et agnus, et ira, et hujusmodi. Vel quantum modum significandi, et non quantum ad rem significatam; et ista proprie dicuntur de Deo, quamvis non perfecte ipsum repreasentent: alias omnia nomina dicta de Deo essent symbolica, quia modus significandi ipsorum est secundum quod de creaturis dicuntur; et de talibus haec sunt verba, "fuit et erit" quae significant essentiam per modum actus et consignificant tempus.

Ad tertium dicendum, quod quantum ad id quod praesens non implicat successionem, nec habet aliquid de non esse inclusum, inter alia proprius Deo competit; nihilominus tamen verba aliorum temporum dicuntur de Deo secundum id quod perfectionis est in ipsis, et non ratione successionis vel alicujus defectus.

Ad quartum dicendum, quod nomine perfectionis praeteritum de Deo dicitur, et quia non est novum, secundum /208a/ quod ipse praeteritis non defuit. Nihilominus tamen intelligendum est, quod aliquando per praesens magis designatur perfectio quam per praeteritum: quae-

time, because its cognition originates from sensible things which exist in time, it cannot form enunciations except through temporal words; hence, while framing an enunciation about God, it is compelled to use temporal words, although it understands Him to be above time: but, nevertheless, these utterances are not false. For, as Dionysius* says in *On the Divine Names* chap. V, sect. 4*, divine *being* as a cause preaccepts within Itself everything by way of perfection in all things; and so we enunciate verbs of all tenses of It, because It is lacking to no time, and It has whatever there is of perfection at all times.

1. To the first <objection>, therefore, one ought to say that when temporal words are said of God, our intellect does not attribute to divine *being* that which is of imperfection at single times, but that which is of perfection at all <times>; for eternity includes within itself all perfection in a simple way, < a perfection> which is something divided in temporal things, although time imitates the perfection of eternity as much as possible.

2. To the second <objection> one ought to say that an expression can involve a bodily condition in two ways: either (1) with respect to the thing principally signified in the name, and such a thing is said of God only symbolically, e.g., lion, lamb, wrath, and the like; or else (2) with respect to their mode* of signifying* and not with respect to the thing signified*, and these things are properly said of God, even though they do not represent Him perfectly: otherwise all names said of God would be symbolic, since their mode of signifying is according as they are said of creatures. Among such things are the verbs "was" and "will be," which signify* an essence in the manner of act, and co-signify* a time.

3. To the third <objection> one ought to say that inasmuch as that which is present does not imply succession and does not have anything of non-*being* included, it belongs more properly to God than <do the> other <tenses>; nevertheless, however, verbs of other tenses are said of God according to that bit of perfection that is in them, and not by reason of succession or any defect.

4. To the fourth <objection> one ought to say that the past is said of God as a name of perfection, not because it is something new, because /208b/ He was not lacking to past things. But, nevertheless, it is to be understood that perfection is sometimes designated more by the present <tense> than by the past: for there are some things whose *being* consists

dam enim sunt quorum esse est in fieri, et horum perfectio non est nisi quando venitur ad terminum, et horum perfectio non est nisi quando venitur ad terminum, et horum perfectio magis significatur per praeteritum, sicut sunt motus, et hujusmodi successiva. Quaedam autem sunt quorum esse consistit in permanendo; et horum perfectio designatur magis per praesens quam per praeteritum: quia in hoc quod sunt, habent perfectionem; et praeteritum dicitur secundum recessum ab esse. Unde etiam in divinis ea quae dicuntur per modum rei permanentis verius signantur per praesens, ut, Deus est bonus, et hujusmodi; quae autem signantur per modum actus, verius signantur per praeteritum, sicut infra, dist. IX, dicit Gregorius quod magis proprie dicimus Filium natum, quam nasci.

Ad quintum dicendum, quod quoad aliquid magis proprie dicitur de ipso Deo praeteritum imperfectum quam praeteritum perfectum, eo scilicet quod terminationem non includit, sicut verbum praeteriti perfecti; unde in illis quae significantur per modum actus, verius dicitur praeteritum perfectum, quia horum perfectio non potest significari nisi ex termino; quae autem significantur non per modum operationis, verius significantur per praeteritum imperfectum, quia horum perfectio non dependet ex termino.

Ad sextum dicendum, quod futurum maxime removetur a divina praedicatione, propter hoc quod nondum est, nisi in potentia. Nihilominus tamen secundum id quod est perfectionis in ipso, scilicet quod longius distat a deficiendo, de Deo dicitur, abjecta imperfectione.

EXPOSITIO PRIMAE PARTIS TEXTUS

"Nunc de veritate, sive proprietate, sive incommutabilitate atque simplicitate divinae naturae, sive substantiae, sive essentiae agendum est." Quaeritur cum multa sint attributa essentialia, quare tantum de his tribus facit mentionem?—Et dicendum, quod Magister intendit tantum ea tangere quae pertinent ad perfectionem divini esse, inquantum est esse perfectum. Perfectio autem esse potest attendi tripliciter: vel secundum quod excluditur privatio vel non esse; et ista perfectio

in becoming, and, of these, the perfect does not exist except when it is made to come to term; the perfection of these things is signified to a greater degree by the past <tense>, e.g., motions and successive <things> of that sort. There are other things whose *being* consists in lasting*; and their perfection is designated more by the present than by the past, since they have perfection in that they are, whereas the past is said with respect to a receding* from *being*. Hence, too, in divine things, those that are spoken of in the fashion* of a permanent thing are more truly marked by the present <tense>, e.g., "God is good" and the like; whereas those that are signified in the fashion of an act are more truly marked by the past (as <is discussed> below <in> Distinction 9*), as Gregory* says that we more properly say that the Son has been born than that He is born.

5. To the fifth <objection> one ought to say that something is more properly said of God Himself <in> the past imperfect than the past perfect <tense> inasmuch as <the former> does not include an end-point* as a verb of the past perfect does. Hence, in those <cases> which are signified by way of act, the past perfect* is said more truly, since their perfection can be signified only from <their> end-point*; whereas those that are signified not by way of operation are more truly marked by the past imperfect*, since their perfection does not depend on <their> end-point*.

6. To the sixth <objection> one ought to say that the future is <the tense> most removed from divine predication, because it does not yet exist, except in potency*. But, nevertheless, according to that which is of perfection in it, viz. that it is further from being defective, it is said of God, once the imperfection is eliminated.

EXPOSITION* OF THE FIRST PART* OF THE TEXT*

"One ought now to deal with the truth* or propriety* or incommutability* and simplicity* of the divine nature or substance* or essence*." The question is asked: since there are many essential attributes, why mention only these three?—One ought to say that the Master* intends to touch only those <topics> that pertain to the perfection of the divine *being* inasmuch as it is perfect *being*. Perfection* <of> *being* can be regarded in three ways: either (1) according as privation or non-*being* is

tangitur per veritatem vel proprietatem, quae pro eodem sumuntur, ut dictum est. Vel secundum quod excluditur potentialitas; et quantum ad hoc ponitur immutabilitas. Vel quantum ad integritatem ipsius esse; et quantum ad hoc ponitur simplicitas: quia quidquid est in simplici, est ipsum suum esse. /209a/

"Natura vel substantia sive essentia." Sciendum, quod ista tria sumuntur hic pro eodem. Non enim sumitur hic natura secundum quod nominat principium alicujus actus, sed prout dicit formam consequentem totum, sicut humanitas est natura hominis. Similiter substantia non sumitur hic pro individuo subsistente in genere substantiae, sed secundum quod nominat esse praedicati primi, prout dividitur contra accidens; et hoc idem est quod essentia non existens in aliquo sicut in subjecto.

"Sicut enim ab eo quod est sapere, dicta est sapientia ... ita ab eo quod est esse, dicta est essentia." Videtur e contrario debere dici, quod sapere procedit a sapientia.—Dicendum quod non loquitur secundum ordinem rei, sed secundum ordinem cognitionis nostrae, quae in habitus ex actibus venit.

"Et quis magis est quam ille qui dixit famulo suo: 'Ego sum qui sum'?" Videtur inconvenienter loqui: quia esse non suscipit magis et minus.—Dicendum, quod magis et minus potest dici aliquid dupliciter: vel quantum ad ipsam naturam participatam, quae secundum se intenditur et remittitur secundum accessum ad terminum vel recessum, et hoc non est nisi in accidentibus; vel quantum ad modum participandi; et sic etiam in essentialibus dicitur magis et minus secundum diversum modum participandi, sicut angelus dicitur magis intellectualis quam homo.

"Deus autem tantum est, qui non novit fuisse vel futurum esse", notitia quasi experimentali, ut scilicet successiones temporum in suo esse experiatur.

"Cujus essentiae comparatum nostrum esse non est." Videtur esse falsum: quia esse nostrum nihil est nisi per comparationem ad ipsum Deum: quia, secundum Gregorium, lib. XVI *Moralium*, cap. XXXVII, col. 1143, t. I, omnia in nihilum deciderent, nisi ea manus omnipotentis contineret.—Dicendum, quod esse nostrum potest ad Deum comparari

excluded, and this perfection is touched on through truth or propriety*, which are taken* for the same <thing>, as has been said; or (2) according as potentiality* is excluded, and in this respect immutability is posited; or (3) with respect to the integrity* of *being* itself, and in this regard simplicity is posited, since whatever is within the simple is its very *being*. /209b/

"Nature or substance or essence." One ought to know that these three <names> are here taken for the same thing. For here 'nature'* is not taken inasmuch as it names the principle of a certain act but as it expresses a form* consequent on the whole, as humanity is the nature of man. Similarly here 'substance'* is taken not as an individual subsisting* in the category of substance, but according as it names the *being* of the first predicate as it is distinguished against accident. And this is the same thing as 'essence' not existing in anything as its subject.

"For just as wisdom is so called from being wise (*sapere*) ... so is essence so called from *being* (*esse*)." It seems on the contrary that it ought to be said that being wise proceeds from wisdom.—It ought to be said <in response> that he is speaking <here> not according to the order* of reality* but according to the order of our cognition, which develops into habits on the basis of <our> acts.

"And who is greater than He Who said to His servant: 'I am Who AM?' " It seems that he spoke unfittingly since *being* is not susceptible of more and less.—It ought to be said that something can be said to be more and less in two ways: either (1) with respect to the nature participated, which in itself suffers intension and remission according to its movement toward or away from a term, and this exists only in accidents; or else (2) with respect to the manner of participating, and in this way 'more and less' are said even in essentials according to <their> diverse way<s> of participating, as an angel is said to be more intellectual than a human being.

"God, however, Who did not know *was* or *about to be* merely is," with a sort of experiential knowledge, so that He experiences the successions of times within His own *being*.

"Our *being* compared with His essence is not." <This> seems to be false, since our *being* is nothing except through a comparison to God Himself, since, as Gregory* says in the *Moralia*, Book XVI, chap. 37, all things would collapse into nothing unless the hand of the Almighty should contain them.—One ought to say that our *being* can be compared

dupliciter: vel sicut ad principium a quo est; et sic esse nostrum est solum per hoc quod ad Deum comparatur; vel secundum comparationem proportionis vel aequiparantiae, et sic esse nostrum comparatum ad divinum quasi nihil est, quia in infinitum ab eo distat.

"Esse non est accidens Deo." Videtur quod nec alicui creaturae, cum nihil sit essentialius rei quam suum esse.—Ad quod dicendum, quod accidens dicitur hic quod non est de intellectu alicujus, sicut rationale dicitur animali accidere; et ita cuilibet quidditati creatae accidit esse, quia non est de intellectu quidditatis; potest enim intelligi humanitas, et tamen dubitari, utrum homo habeat esse.

"Sed subsistens veritas." Excludit Hilarius triplicem imperfectionem a divino esse. Esse enim creaturae non est aliquid /210a/ per se subsistens, immo est actus subsistentis; sed in Deo suum esse est ipse Deus subsistens: et ideo dicit, quod est subsistens veritas. Item esse creaturae est acquisitum ab alio, et habet, quantum in se est, potentialitatem et mutabilitatem; sed esse divinum est causa omnis esse, immutabiliter permanens; et ideo dicit quod est manens causa. Item esse creaturae differt a quidditate sua, unde per esse suum homo non ponitur in genere humano, sed per quidditatem suam; sed esse divinum est sua quidditas, et ideo per esse suum ponitur Deus in genere divino; et ideo per esse suum ponitur Deus in genere divino; et ideo dicitur, quod est naturalis generis proprietas.

QUAESTIO III

"Dei etiam solius essentia incommutabilis dicitur proprie." Hic prosequitur de secundo attributo, scilicet immutabilitate, ostendens solum Deum incommutabilem esse, alias autem omnes creaturas aliquo modo mutabiles; et circa hoc tria quaeruntur: 1° utrum Deus sit omnino immutabilis 2° utrum omnis creatura sit mutabilis; 3° de modis mutationum, quos Augustinus assignat in *Littera*.

to God in two ways: either (1) as to the principle by Whom it is, and in this sense our *being* is only because it is compared to God; or (2) according to a comparison of proportion or equivalence*, and in this way our *being* is as nothing compared to the divine <*being*>, since it is infinitely distant from It.

"*Being* is not an accident to God." It seems that neither is <*being* an accident> to any creature, since nothing is more essential to a thing than its own *being*.—To this <objection> one ought to say that here whatever is involved in the understanding of a thing is said to be an accident, e.g., rational is said to be accidental to animal, and in this fashion *being* is accidental to any created quiddity, since it is not <part> of the concept of the quiddity itself; for humanity can be understood and it can still be doubted whether a human has *being*.

"But subsistent Truth": Hilary* rules out three sorts of imperfection from divine *being*. For (1) a creature's *being* is not anything /210b/ subsisting through itself, but is rather the act of the subsisting <thing>; but in God, His *being* is the subsisting God Himself; and so he says that He is "subsistent Truth." (2) Again, a creature's *being* has been acquired from another, and, to the extent that it is in itself, has potentiality and mutability; but divine *being* is the immutably permanent cause of every being; and so he says that it is a "lasting cause." (3) Again, a creature's *being* differs from its quiddity; hence, a human is put within the human genus not by its *being* but by its quiddity, whereas divine *being* is its own quiddity, and so God is put within the divine genus by His *being*, and in this sense it is said that it is a "natural property of the genus."

QUESTION III

"Also the essence of God alone is properly said <to be> unchangeable." Here he is in pursuit of the second attribute, viz. immutability, showing that God alone is unchangeable, whereas all other creatures are somehow changeable. There are three points of inquiry on this topic: 1. Is God utterly immutable? 2. Is every creature mutable? 3. On the modes of the changes that Augustine assigns in the text.

ARTICULUS PRIMUS *Utrum Deus aliquo modo sit mutabilis*

Ad primum sic proceditur. 1. Videtur quod Deus sit aliquo modo mutabilis. Sap., VII, 24: *Omnibus mobilibus mobilior est sapientia.* Sed sapientia divina, de qua loquitur, est ipse Deus. Ergo, etc.

2. Praeterea, quidquid movet seipsum, movetur a seipso. Sed, sicut dicit Augustinus, *Sup. Genes. ad litt.*, lib. VIII, cap. XX. col. 388, t. III: "spiritus creator movet se nec per tempus nec per locum." Ergo videtur quod moveatur.

3. Item, omne quod est per alterum, reducitur ad illud quod est per se. Sed invenimus multa quae moventur per alios motores. Ergo oportet esse aliquid quod moveatur a seipso. Sed omnis creatura mota movetur ab alio, quia a Deo. Ergo Deus est motus a se.

4. Praeterea, omne quod exit de otio in actum aliquo modo movetur, secundum Philosophum, III *Phys.*, text. 16, quia /211a/ omnis operatio quae est ab operante non moto est semper. Sed Deus quandoque creat in actu, vel infundit gratiam, cum prius hoc non fecerit. Ergo videtur quod ad minus sit in eo mutatio de habitu in actum.

Contra Malach., III, 6: *Ego Deus et non mutor*; et Jacob., I, 17: *Apud quem non est transmutatio, nec vicissitudinis obumbratio.*

Praeterea, sicut probat Philosophus, VIII *Physic.*, text. 34, omne quod movetur, ab alio movetur. Si igitur illud a quo movetur mobile ipsum, etiam movetur, oportet quod ab aliquo motore moveatur. Sed impossibile est ire in infinitum. Ergo oportet devenire ad primum motorem, qui movet et nullo modo movetur; et hic est Deus. Ergo omnino est immutabilis.

SOLUTIO.—Respondeo dicendum, quod omnis motus vel mutatio, quocumque modo dicatur, consequitur aliquam possibilitatem, cum motus sit actus existentis in potentia. Cum igitur Deus sit actus purus, nihil habens de potentia admixtum non potest in eo esse aliqua mutatio.

Ad primum ergo dicendum, quod divina sapientia non dicitur mobilis quia in se moveatur, sed inquantum procedit in effectus; et ista

ARTICLE I: Is God in any way mutable?

One proceeds in this way to the first <article>. 1. It seems that God is somehow mutable. *Wisdom* 7, 24: "Wisdom is more mobile than all mobile things." But the divine Wisdom, of which it is speaking, is God Himself. Therefore, etc.

2. Further, whatever moves itself is moved by itself. But, as Augustine* says in the *Phrase-by-phrase* Commentary on Genesis,* Book VIII, chap. 20, "The Creator Spirit moves itself neither through time nor through place." Therefore, it seems that He is moved.

3. Again, everything that is through another is reduced to that which is through itself. But we find many things that are being moved through other movers. Hence, there must be something that is being moved by itself. But every moved creature is moved by another, since <it is moved> by God. So God is moved by Himself.

4. Further, everything that departs from rest into act is somehow being moved, according to the Philosopher* in *Physics,* Book III, text 16,* since /211b/ every operation that arises from a non-moved operator exists perpetually. But, God sometimes actually creates or infuses grace, since previously He did not do it. Hence, it seems that there is in Him at least a change from habit into act.

On the contrary, *Malachi* 3, 6: "I <am> God and I am not changed"; and *James* 1, 17: "With Whom there is no transmutation nor even a shadow of change."

Further, as the Philosopher* proves in *Physics* VIII, text 34,* everything that is being moved, is being moved by something else. Therefore, if that by which a mobile thing is being moved is itself also being moved, it would have to be moved by a mover. But it is impossible to go on to infinity. Hence, one must arrive at a first mover that moves and is in no way being moved, and this is God. Therefore, He is utterly immutable.

SOLUTION.—I answer that one ought to say that every motion or mutation, howsoever it be said follows upon some possibility, since motion is an act of an existent in potency. Hence, since God is pure act, having nothing of potency* admixed, there can not be any mutation in Him.

1. Hence, to the first <objection> one ought to say that divine wisdom is not called mobile because it is moved in itself, but inasmuch as

processio non est proprie motus, sed quamdam similitudinem motus habet. In motu enim locali processivo, illud quod est in uno loco fit postmodum in alio, et deinde in alio, et sic deinceps quousque compleatur motus. Similiter autem divina sapientia, quae est exemplar rerum, facit similitudinem suam in creatura secundum ordinem: quia prius efficiuntur in participatione divinae similitudinis creaturae superiores, et posterius inferiores. Unde in hoc habet similitudinem motus: quia ipsa divina sapientia secundum similitudinem suam efficitur in creatura. In duobus autem deficit a ratione motus: primo quia non est idem numero quod est in hoc et in illo; sed similitudo ejus; secundo, quia non est ibi ordo temporis, secundum quod procedit in diversas creaturas, sed tantum ordo naturae: quia prius naturaliter sunt in participatione divinae bonitatis creaturae nobiliores, et si non tempore; et sic etiam intelligitur quod Dionysius dicit in principio *Cael. hier.*, col. 119, t. 1: "Sed et patre luminum moto", etc., et quod frequenter dicit, divinam bonitatem vel sapientiam procedere in creaturas. /212a/

Ad secundum dicendum, quod Augustinus accipit large moveri, secundum quo<d> ipsum intelligere est moveri quoddam et velle, quae proprie non sunt motus, sed comparatione. In hoc enim verificatur dictum Platonis in Parmenide, qui dicit: "Deus movet se", sicut dicit Commentator, XII *Metaph.*, cap. II, qui dicit quod Deus intelligit se et vult se: sicut etiam dicimus, quod finis movet efficientem. Vel dicendum, quod movet se in creaturam productione, ut dictum est.

Ad tertium dicendum, quod impossibile est aliquid movere seipsum nisi secundum diversas partes, ita quod una pars sit movens et alia mota; sicut etiam in animali est anima movens et corpus motum. Cujus ratio est, quia nihil movet nisi secundum quod est in actu, nec movetur nisi secundum quod est in potentia, et haec duo non possunt simul eidem inesse respectu ejusdem. Et quia Deus est simplex, non potest esse quod seipsum moveat, proprie loquendo. Quod ergo objicitur quod omne mobile per aliud reducitur ad mobile per se, verum est de

it proceeds to effects; this process is not properly motion, but it has a certain likeness to motion. For in processive* local motion, that which is in one place is afterwards made to be in another, and then in another, and so on till the motion is completed. Similarly, divine wisdom, which is the exemplar of things, makes its likeness in a creature in an orderly way: since first the superior and later the inferior creatures are effected in participation of the divine likeness. Hence, <divine wisdom> has a similarity to motion in this respect: that it is effected in a creature according to a likeness of itself; it falls short of the character of motion, however, in two respects: first (1) it is not numerically the same thing that exists in this <instance> as in that, but <only> a likeness of It; second (2), since it is not an order of time with respect to which <divine wisdom> proceeds into diverse creatures, but only the order of nature: since nobler creatures are naturally prior in <their> participation of divine goodness even if not in time; and this is also how what Dionysius* says at the beginning of the *Celestial Hierarchy** is to be understood: "But also when the Father of lights has been moved, etc.," and what he says frequently, <namely> that the divine goodness or wisdom proceeds into creatures. /212b/

2. To the second <objection> one ought to say that Augustine* is taking <the term> 'to be moved' broadly, inasmuch as* *understanding* is itself a sort of *'being-moved'**, and so is willing, which are not motions properly, but <only> by <way of> comparison. For in this <sense> Plato's* remark in the *Parmenides**—viz. "God 'moves' Himself"—is justified*, as the Commentator* says on *Metaphysics* Book XII, chap. 2*, who says that God understands Himself and wills Himself, as we also say that the end 'moves' the efficient <cause>. Or else one ought to say that He 'moves' Himself in the production of creatures, as has been said.

3. To the third <objection> one ought to say that it is impossible for anything to move itself except with respect to diverse parts, such that the one part is moving and the other moved, just as in an animal the soul is moving and the body moved. The reason for this is that nothing moves except to the extent that it is in act, nor is anything being moved except to the extent that it is in potency, and these two cannot be in the same thing in the same respect at the same time. Moreover, since God is simple, it is not possible for Him to move Himself, properly speaking. Hence, the objection that everything mobile through another is reduced

reductione quae est ad primum in genere illo. Unde secundum philosophos, VIII *Phy<sic.>*, text. 34, omnia mobilia reducuntur ad primum mobile, quod dicebant motum ex se, quia est compositum ex motore et moto. Sed hoc ulterius oportet reducere in primum simplex, quod est omnino immobile.

Ad quartum dicendum, quod in omnibus in quibus operatio differt a substantia, oportet esse aliquem modum motus ex hoc quod exit de novo in operationem; quia acquiritur in ipso operatio, quae prius non erat. In Deo autem operatio sua est sua substantia: unde sicut substantia est aeterna, ita et operatio. Sed non sequitur operationem operatum ab aeterno, sed secundum ordinem sapientiae, quae est principium operati.

ARTICULUS II *Utrum omnis creatura sit mutabilis*

Ad secundum sic proceditur. 1. Videtur quod non omnis creatura sit mutabilis. Omnis enim mutatio, ut dicitur in V /213a/ *Phys.*, text. 7, est generatio vel corruptio vel motus. Sed quaedam sunt in quibus nullum horum est, sicut angeli, et hujusmodi, quae sunt separata a materia et motu, secundum philosophos, ut patet XII *Metaph.*, text. 30. Ergo non omnis creatura mutabilis est.

2. Praeterea, quidquid est mutabile pertinet ad considerationem naturalis, cujus est considerare motum. Sed substantiae separatae a materia non considerantur a naturali. Ergo non sunt mutabiles.

3. Praeterea, quidquid mutatur, subjicitur mutationi. Sed formae simplices non possunt esse subjectum, ut dicit Boetius, *De Trinit.*, cap. II, col. 1250, t. II. Ergo non possunt mutari.

4. Praeterea, sicut in *Littera* dicitur, omnis creatura movetur per tempus vel per locum. Sed quaedam sunt creaturae quorum non est locus et tempus sicut universale, quod, secundum Philosophum, I *Post.*, text. 7, est ubique et semper; et sicut materia prima, de qua dicit

to <something> mobile through itself is true with respect to the reduction that is to a prime <instance> in that genus. Hence, according to the philosophers <referred to in> *Physics* Book VIII, text 34*, all movable things are reduced to a first mobile <object> which they used to call something "moved out of itself*," since it was composed of mover and moved. But one must reduce this still further to a simple first which is utterly immovable.

4. To the fourth <objection> one ought to say that in all things in which operation differs from substance, there must be a sort of motion from that which originally goes off into operation, since an operation that previously did not exist is being acquired in it. In God, however, His operation is His substance: hence, just as <His> substance is eternal, so too <is His> operation. But it does not follow that <His> operation was performed from eternity, but only following the order of <His> wisdom, which is the starting-point* of the <act> performed.

ARTICLE II: Is every creature mutable?

One proceeds in this way to the second <article>. 1. It seems that not every creature is mutable. For, as is said in *Physics,* Book V, text 7*, every mutation /213b/ is either a generation or a corruption or a motion. But there are certain things in which there is none of these, e.g., angels and the like, which are separate from matter and motion according to the philosophers, as is clear in *Metaphysics* Book XII, text 30. Hence, not every creature is mutable.

2. Further, whatever is mutable pertains to the consideration of the natural <philosopher> whose <task> is to consider motion. But substances separate from matter are not considered by the natural <philosopher>. So they are not mutable.

3. Further, whatever is mutated is subjected to mutation. But simple forms cannot be <anything> subjected, as Boethius* says in *De Trinitate,* chap. 2*. Therefore, <simple forms> cannot be mutated.

4. Further, as is said in the text*, every creature is moved either through time or through place. But there are some creatures of which there is no time and place, e.g., a universal, which is, according to the Philosopher* in the *Posterior Analytics,* Book I, text 7*, always and everywhere; and again, e.g., prime matter, of which Augustine* in *Confessions*

Augustinus, XII *Confess.*, cap. XIX, col. 836, t. I, quod successiones temporum non habet. Ergo non omnis creatura mutatur.

Contra, Ps. CI, 28: *Mutabis eos, et mutabuntur.*

Praeterea, Damascenus, lib. I *Fidei orth.*, cap. III, col. 795 t. I, dicit: "Omne quod est ex nihilo, vertibile est in nihil; quod enim a mutatione incepit, subjacere mutationi necesse est." Sed omnis creatura est hujusmodi. Ergo, etc.

SOLUTIO.—Respondeo dicendum, quod, sicut dictum est, motus, quocumque modo dicatur, sequitur potentiam. Cum igitur omnis creatura habeat aliquid de potentia, quia solus Deus est purus actus, oportet omnes creaturas mutabiles esse, et solum Deum immutabilem. Est autem considerare duplicem possibilitatem: unam secundum id quod creatura habet; alteram secundum id quod nata est habere. Prima consequitur creaturam secundum quod habet esse ab alio; omne enim quod esse suum ab alio habet, non est per se necesse esse, ut probat Avicenna, tract. VIII *Metaphys.*, cap. [L]IV, unde, quantum est in se, est possibile, et ista possibilitas dicit dependentiam ad id a quo est. Haec autem possibilitas est duplex. Quaedam secundum dependentiam totius esse ad id a quo est res, secundum totum esse suum, et illud est Deus; et hanc dependentiam sive possibilitatem consequitur mutabilitas quaedam, /214a/ quae est vertibilitas in nihil, secundum Damascenum, ubi supra. Tamen haec non proprie est mutabilitas, nec creatura secundum hoc proprie dicitur mutabilis; et ideo Augustinus de hoc non facit mentionem in *Littera*. Et hujus ratio est duplex. Quia in omni mutabili est invenire aliquid quod substernitur ei quod per mutationem amovetur, et de hoc dicitur quod potest mutari. Sed si accipiamus totum esse creaturae quod dependet a Deo, non inveniemus aliquid substratum de quo possit dici quod potest mutari. Alia ratio est, quia nihil dicitur possibile cujus contrarium est necessarium, vel quod non potest esse, nisi impossibili posito. Esse autem creaturae omnino deficere non potest, nisi retrahatur inde fluxus divinae bonitatis in creaturis, et hoc est impossibile ex immutabilitate divinae voluntatis, et contrarium necessarium; et ideo ex hoc creatura non potest dici simpliciter corruptibilis vel

Book XII, chap. 19* says that it does not have successions of time. Hence, not every creature is mutated.

On the contrary, *Psalm* 101, 28: "Thou shalt change them and they shall be changed."

Further, Damascene* in *De Fide Orthodoxa* Book I, chap. 3* says: "All that is from nothing can be turned* back into nothing; for whatever began from a mutation is necessarily subject to mutation." But every creature is of this sort. Therefore, etc.

SOLUTION.—I answer that one ought to say that, as has been said, howsoever motion be spoken of, it follows potency. Hence, since every creature has something of potency (since God alone is pure act), all creatures must be mutable and God alone immutable. But there are two sorts of possibility to consider: the one, according to what a creature does have; the other, according to what it is naturally apt to have. (1) The first follows the creature according as it has *being* from another; for everything that has its *being* from another is not through itself necessary *being*, as Avicenna* proves in *Metaphysics* Treatise VIII, chap. 4*; hence, to the extent that it is in itself, it is possible, and that possibility expresses dependency upon that by which it is. This possibility, moreover, is of two sorts: <there is> a certain <sort of possibility> with respect to the dependency of <its> whole *being* on that by which the thing is with respect to its whole *being*, and that is God; a certain mutability follows on this dependency or possibility /214b/ <a dependency> which is vertibility* into nothing, according to Damascene*. Nevertheless this is not properly mutability, nor is a creature properly said to be mutable in this respect; and so Augustine makes no mention of it in the text. There are two reasons for this: (a) Since in everything mutable it is <possible> to find something that is laid* under what is moved off through mutation, and being able to be changed is said of this. But if we accept <the fact> that the whole *being* of a creature depends on God we shall not find any substrate* of which it can be said that it can be changed. (b) The other reason is that nothing is said to be possible whose contrary is necessary or which is not able to be unless something impossible is affirmed. But the *being* of a creature is completely unable to fail unless the influence of the divine goodness upon creatures be withdrawn from them, and this is impossible on the basis of the immutability of the divine will, and its contrary <is> necessary; and so on this basis a creature can be said to be simply corruptible or mutable, except subject to the condition

mutabilis sed sub conditione si sibi relinquatur; et hoc est quod dicit Gregorius, lib. XVI *Moralium*, cap. XXXVII, col. 1143, t. 1: "In nihilum omnia deciderent, nisi ea manus omnipotentis contineret." Est etiam quaedam dependentia sive possibilitas rei secundum partem sui esse, scilicet formam praesupposita materia, vel eo quod est loco materiae; et hanc possibilitas rei secundum partem sui esse, scilicet formam praesupposita materia, vel eo quod est loco materiae; et hanc possibilitatem sequitur mutatio variabilitatis, ex eo quod id quod habet ab alio, potest amittere, quantum est in se, nisi forte impediatur ex immutabilitate causae, ut dictum est; et hoc modo sancti in gloria sunt immutabiles in esse gloriae propter immutabilitatem divinae voluntatis. Secunda possibilitas consequitur creaturam secundum quod non est perfecta simpliciter; secundum hoc enim semper possibilis est ad receptionem, accipiendo large mutationem, secundum quod omne recipere dictur pati quoddam et moveri, sicut dicit Philosophus in lib. III *De anima*, text. 12: "Intelligere quoddam pati est."

Ad primum ergo dicendum, quod philosophi consideraverunt tantum illam mutationem quae est secundum variationem formae substantialis vel accidentalis cujus causa non est immutabilis; et hanc diviserunt per generationem, et corruptionem, et motum. Talem autem mutationem non est possibile in angelis esse quantum ad id quod in natura eorum est. /215a/

Et per hoc patet solutio ad secundum, quia naturalis non considerat nisi dictam mutationem.

Ad tertium dicendum, quod Magister et Augustinus loquuntur hic de creaturis quae habent esse perfectum; formae autem non habent esse perfectum, cum non subsistant in se, sed in alio. Vel dicendum, quod dupliciter dicitur aliquid mutabile; vel quia subjicitur mutationi, et hoc modo id tantum quod est in potentia, mutatur; aut sicut id quod removetur vel abjicitur mutatione; et sic formae, quae sunt actus, mutabiles sunt. Non hoc tamen videtur esse de intentione Augustini.

Ad quartum dicendum similiter, quod materia prima et universale non habent in se esse completum; sed esse eorum est in particularibus

'if it be left to itself'; and this is what Gregory* says in *Moralia* Book XVI, chap. 37*: "All things would collapse into nothing if the hand of the Almighty did not hold them together." (2) There is also another sort of dependency or possibility of a thing with respect to a part of its own *being,* i.e., <its> form, once matter or its equivalent has been posited: the mutation of variability follows the latter possibility, because <a thing> can lose what it has from another to the extent that it is in itself, unless, as has been said, it perchance be impeded by the immutability of <its> cause; and this is how the saints in glory are immutable in the *being* of glory owing to the immutability of the divine will. <This> second <sort of> possibility follows on a creature inasmuch as it is not simply perfect; for in this way it is always possible with respect to reception*. Hence, in this respect, too, every creature is said to be mutable—taking mutation broadly—since every receiving is a sort of *being affected** and *being moved**, as the Philosopher* says in *De anima,* Book III, text 12*: "Understanding is a way of *being-affected* *."

1. Hence, to the first <objection> one ought to say that the philosophers have considered only the <sort of> mutation that exists with respect to a variation of a substantial or accidental form whose cause is not immutable; and they divided this <mutation> into generation, corruption, and motion. But it is not possible for such mutation to exist in angels with respect to what is in their nature.

/215b/ 2. The solution to the second <objection> is also clear for this reason: since the natural <philosopher> considers only the aforementioned sort of mutation.

3. To the third <objection> one ought to say that the Master* and Augustine* are here speaking about creatures that have perfect *being;* but the forms do not have perfect *being,* since they do not subsist in themselves but in another. Or else one ought to say that something is called mutable in two ways: either (1) because it is subjected to mutation, and in this sense only that which is in potency is mutated; or else (2) as that which is removed or cast off by a mutation, and the latter sense forms that are acts are mutable. But this does not seem to be what Augustine meant.

4. To the fourth <objection> it ought likewise to be said that prime matter and the universal do not have complete *being* in themselves, but

compositis: et ideo esse non mutant per se, sed tantum per accidens, sicut est de formis.

ARTICULUS III *Utrum modi mutationis creaturarum convenienter assignentur ab Augustino*

Ad tertium sic proceditur. 1. Videtur quod Augustinus inconvenienter assignet modus mutationis creaturam. Secundum illud enim est mutatio in quo invenitur motus, sicut secundum quantitatem vel qualitatem. Sed in quando non est motus, ut dicit Philosophus, V *Phys.*, text. 9. Ergo videtur quod nihil dicat creaturas moveri per tempora.

2. Praeterea, in nulla divisione debet unum membrum contineri sub alio. Sed omnis motus qui est per locum, est etiam per tempus. Ergo videtur inconvenienter dividere mutationem in mutationem loci et temporis.

3. Praeterea, motus, secundum Philosophum, ut supra, est in tribus generibus, scilicet quantitate, qualitate et ubi: et adhuc est in substantia generatio et corruptio simpliciter, et in omnibus generibus generatio et corruptio secundum quid: qui omnes inveniuntur in creatura corporali. Ergo videtur quod diminute assignet mutationem creaturam corporalium per ubi, sive per locum tantum.

4. Praeterea, tempus est mensura primi mobilis. Ergo quod non habet ordinem ad motum primi mobilis, non habet relationem ad tempus. Sed affectiones animarum non ordinantur /216a/ ad motum caeli nec subjacent sibi. Ergo inconvenienter dicit, quod moveri per tempus est per affectiones mutari.

SOLUTIO.—Respondeo dicendum, quod in motu proprie accepto est duo reperire, scilicet continuitatem et successionem: et secundum quod habet continuitatem, sic proprie mensuratur per locum, quia ex continuitate magnitudinis est continuitas motus, ut dicitur IV *Phys.*, text. 99, et V, text. 39; secundum autem quod habet successionem, sic proprie mensuratur per tempus; unde tempus dicitur numerus motus secundum prius et posterius. Quia autem inveniuntur aliqui motus habentes continuitatem et successionem, aliqui autem habentes successionem et non

their *being* exists in particular composite <things>; and so they do not change <their> *being* through themselves but only by accident, as is the case with forms.

ARTICLE III: Are the modes of mutation of creatures suitably assigned by Augustine?

One proceeds to the third <article> in this way. 1. It seems that Augustine* assigned the modes of mutation in creatures unsuitably. For mutation exists according to that in which there is found motion, e.g., in quantity or quality. But motion does not exist in <the category* of> 'when,' as the Philosopher* says in *Physics* Book V, text 9*. Hence, it seems that nothing says that creatures are being moved through times.

2. Further, one member in a division ought never to be contained under another. But every motion that is through place is also through time. Hence, it seems unsuitable to divide mutation into mutation of place and <that> of time.

3. Further, according to the Philosopher* (as above)* motion exists in three categories—quantity, quality, and where: and moreover in substance there is generation and corruption simply, and in all categories <there is> generation and corruption relatively speaking. Therefore, it seems that he defectively assigns the mutation of bodily creatures only in terms of where or place.

4. Further, time is the measure of the prime mobile. Hence, what does not have a relation to the motion of the prime mobile does not have a relation to time. But the affections of souls are not related /216b/ to the motion of the heavens and are not subject to it. Hence, he speaks unsuitably <in saying> that being moved through time is to be mutated through affections.

SOLUTION.—I answer that one ought to say that in motion taken properly it is <possible> to find two <features>, namely continuity and succession: (1) with respect to <the fact> that it has continuity, <motion> is properly measured by place, since the continuity of motion arises from continuity of magnitude, as is said in *Physics* Book IV, text 99 and V, text 39*; (2) with respect to <the fact> that it has succession, however, <motion> is properly measured through time; hence, time is called 'the number of motion with respect to the before and after.' But since some motions are found having continuity and succession, and

continuitatem, sicut motus affectionum et etiam cogitationum, quando scilicet anima transit de una cogitatione in aliam, inter enim illas duas intentiones cogitatas non est aliqua continuitas, ideo divisit mutationem creeaturae per locum et tempus.

Ad primum ergo dicendum, quod in genere "quando" non est motus, sicut in terminante motum; nullus enim motus terminatur ad "quando" sicut ad "ubi": est tamen motus in "quando" sicut in mensurante.

Ad secundum dicendum, quod divisio intelligenda est cum praecisione, ut sic scilicet intelligatur, quod quaedam mutatio est per locum et tempus; quaedam autem per tempus tantum; quod patet ex his quae dicta sunt.

Ad tertium dicendum, quod quamvis in corporalibus sint plures motus, omnes tamen ordinantur ad motum localem caeli, qui est causa omnis motus corporalis; et ideo per motum localem tanguntur omnes. Vel potest dici, quod alii motus a motu locali tanguntur per mutationem quae est per tempus: quia, sicut Commentator probat in VIII *Phys.*, text. 53, nullus alius motus est simpliciter continus nisi motus localis; et ipse Augustinus dicit in *Littera,* quod Deus creaturam corporalem movet et per tempus et per locum.

Ad quartum dicendum, quod tempus dupliciter dicitur: uno modo numerus prioris et posterioris inventorum in motu caeli; et istud tempus continuitatem habet a motu, et motus a magnitudine, et hoc tempore mensurantur omnia quae habent ordinem ad motum caeli, sive per se sicut motus corporales, sive per accidens, sicut aliquae operationes animae, secundum quod habent aliquam relationem ad corpus. Et hoc modo tantum accipitur a philosophis. Alio modo, ut IV *Phys.*, text. 101 et 102, dicitur tempus magis communiter /217a/ numerus ejus quod habet quocumque modo prius et posterius; et sic dicimus esse tempus mensurans simplices conceptiones intellectus, quae sunt sibi succedentes: et istud tempus non oportet quod habeat continuitatem, cum illud secundum quod attenditur motus, non sit continuum. Et sic accipitur hic tempus, et frequenter a theologis.

others having succession but not continuity, e.g., the motions of the emotions and even of thoughts when the soul moves from one thought to another (for there is no continuity between those two intentions* that have been thought); so he divided the mutation of the creature into place and time.

1. Therefore, to the first <objection> one ought to say that in the category of 'when' there is no motion in the sense of something terminating a motion (for no motion is terminated at a 'when' as it is at a 'where'): but there is motion in 'when' in the sense of something measuring <a motion>.

2. To the second <objection> one ought to say that the division is to be understood with precision, i.e., so as to be understood such that one sort of mutation through place and time, and another through time only, which is clear from what has been said.

3. To the third <objection> one ought to say that, although there are many motions in bodily things, nevertheless, they are related to the local motion of the sky, which is the cause of all bodily motion; and so they are all touched through local motion. Or it can be said that other motions than local motion are touched upon through the motion that is through time: since, as the Commentator* proves on *Physics* VIII text 53*, no motion is simply continuous other than local motion; and in the text* Augustine* himself says that God moves the bodily creature both through time and through place.

4. To the fourth <objection> one ought to say that time is spoken of in two ways: (1) in one way, <as> the number of the prior and posterior in things found in the motion of the sky; that time has continuity from motion, and motion <has it> from magnitude, and by this time all things that have a relation to the sky's motion are measured, whether through themselves (e.g., bodily motions) or through accident (e.g., some operations of the soul, according as they have some relation to body), and <time> is taken only in this way by the philosophers. (2) In the other way, as in <the Philosopher*> *Physics* Book IV, texts 101 and 102, time is spoken of more generally /217b/ <as> the number of that which in any way has a before and after; and in this way we say there is a time measuring the simple conceptions of the intellect which are succeeding each other: and that time need not have continuity, since that according to which motion is involved is not continuous. And this is how time is taken here and frequently by theologians.

DIVISIO SECUNDAE PARTIS TEXTUS

"Eademque sola proprie ac vere simplex est." Haec est tertia pars distinctionis, in qua Magister determinat de divina simplicitate, et dividitur in partes duas: in prima proponit quod intendit; in secunda probat propositum, ibi: "Ut autem scias quod simplex sit illa substantia, te docet Augustinus;" quae dividitur in duas: in prima ostendit creaturae multiplicitatem; in secunda divinam simplicitatem, ibi: "Deus vero, etsi multiplex dicatur, vere tamen et summe simplex est." Prima in duas: in prima excludit simplicitatem a creatura corporali; in secunda a spirituali, ibi: "Creatura quoque spiritualis, ut est anima, in comparatione quidem corporis est simplex; sine comparatione vero corporis est mutiplex."

"Deus vero, etsi multiplex dicatur, vere tamen et summe simplex est." Hic ostendit divinam simplicitatem, et dividitur in partes duas: in prima ostendit simplicitatem; in secunda excludit omnem compositionem ab ipso, ibi: "Quod autem in natura divina nulla sit accidentium diversitas. . ., ostendit Augustinus." Prima in duas: in prima ostendit veritatem; in secunda excludit dubitationem, ibi: "Hic diligenter attendendum est."

"Quod autem in natura divina nulla sit accidentium diversitas, nullaque penitus mutabilitas, sed perfecta simplicitas, ostendit Augustinus." Hic excludit a Deo omnem compositionem vel multiplicitatem; et circa hoc duo facit: primo ostendit specialiter quod in Deo non est compositio accidentis ad subjectum; secundo ostendit universaliter quod in ipso nulla est compositio, ibi: "Hujus autem essentiae simplicitas ac sinceritas tanta est quod non est in ea aliquid quod non sit ipsa." Circa

DIVISION* OF THE SECOND PART* OF THE TEXT

"And the same alone is properly and truly simple." This <Chapters 23–28> is the third part of the distinction, in which the Master* determines* about the divine simplicity, and <Chapter 23> is divided into two parts: in the first he proposes what he intends <to do>; in the second, at <the words> "Augustine teaches you that you may know that that substance is simple," he proves what he proposed, which <part> is divided into two <divisions>.

In the first <division, beginning with Chapter 24, n. 1> he shows the multiplicity of the creature; in the second, at <Chapter 24, n. 3, beginning with the words> "But even though God is spoken of in many ways, nevertheless, He is truly and most highly simple," the divine simplicity.

The first <division is in turn divided> into two <sections>: In the first <Chapter 24, n. 1> he excludes simplicity from the bodily creature; in the second < he excludes it> from the spiritual <creature>, at <Chapter 24, n. 2, beginning with the words> "The spiritual creature, too, e.g., the soul, is simple in comparison with the body, but is multiple apart from comparison with the body."

"But even though God is spoken of in many ways, nevertheless, He is truly and most highly simple." Here <Chapter 24, n. 3>, he shows the divine simplicity, and <this again> is divided into two parts: in the first he shows the simplicity; in the second <Chapter 26> he excludes all composition from Him, at <the words> "Augustine explains ... that there is, however, no diversity of accidents in the divine nature." The first <part is divided> into two: in the first <Chapter 24, n. 3> he shows the truth; in the second, at <Chapter 25, beginning with the words> "Here one ought diligently to pay attention," he excludes a <point of> doubt.

"Augustine explains that there is, however, no diversity of accidents, and absolutely no mutability, in the divine nature, but perfect simplicity." Here <Chapter 26> he excludes all composition or multiplicity from God; and he does two things in this regard: first he specifically shows that there is no composition of accident to subject in God; second, he shows universally that there is no composition in Him, at <Chapter 28, beginning with the words> "The simplicity and purity of this essence is so great that there is not a thing which is not itself in It."

primum duo facit: primo excludit a Deo accidentium praedicationem; secundo concludit, quod nec etiam substantia de eo proprie praedicatur, ibi: "Unde nec proprie dicitur substantia."
/218a/

QUAESTIO IV

Ad intellectum hujus partis duo quaeruntur: primo de divina simplicitate; secundo de simplicitate creaturae.

Circa primum tria quaeruntur: 1° si in Deo sit omnimoda simplicitas; 2° an contineatur in praedicamento substantiae ; 3° si alia praedicamenta de ipso dicantur.

ARTICULUS PRIMUS *Utrum Deus sit omnino simplex*

Ad primum sic proceditur. 1. Videtur quod Deus non sit simplex omnino. Ens enim cui non fit additio, est ens commune praedicatum de omnibus de quo nihil potest vere negari. Sed Deus non est hujusmodi. Ergo ad esse suum fit aliqua additio. Non est ergo simplex.

2. Praeterea, Boetius, lib. *De hebdom.*, col. 1311, t. II: "Omne quod est, esse participat ut sit; alia autem participat, ut aliquid sit." Sed Deus verissime est ens et est aliquid, quia bonus et sapiens et hujusmodi. Ergo Deus habet esse suum quo est, et super hoc habet aliquid aliud quo aliquid est. Ergo non est simplex.

3. Item, de quocumque praedicatur aliquid quod non est de substantia sua, illud non est simplex. Sed quidquid praedicatur de aliquo postquam non praedicabatur, illud non est de substantia sua, cum nulli rei substantia sua de novo adveniat. Cum igitur de Deo praedicetur aliquid postquam non praedicabatur, ut esse dominum et creatorem quae dicuntur de ipso ex tempore, videtur quod ipse non sit simplex.

4. Praeterea, ubicumque sunt plures res in uno, ibi oportet esse aliquem modum compositionis. Sed in divina natura sunt tres personae

With respect to the first he does two things: first <Chapter 26> he excludes predication of accidents from God; second, he concludes that not even substance is properly predicated of Him, at <Chapter 27, beginning with the words> "Hence, He is not properly called substance, either."
/218b/

QUESTION IV

To understand this part two questions are asked: first, about the divine simplicity; second, about the creature's simplicity.

As to the first, there are three points of inquiry: (1) if simplicity be in God in every way; (2) whether He be contained in the category of substance; (3) if other categories be said of Him.

ARTICLE I: Is God entirely simple?

One proceeds to the first <article> in this way: 1. It seems that God is not entirely simple. For the being (*ens*) to which no addition is made is the common being (*ens commune*) predicated of all things <and> of which nothing can be truly negated. But God is not of this sort. Therefore, an addition can be made to His *being* (*esse*). Therefore, He is not simple.

2. Further, Boethius* in the *De Hebdomadibus** says: "Everything that is participates *being* so as to be; but it participates* other <characteristics> so as to be something." But God most truly is a being and is something (*aliquid*), since <He is> good and wise and such. Therefore, God has His *being*, by which He is, and over and above this He has something else by which He is something. Therefore, He is not simple.

3. Again, anything of which something is predicated that is not of its substance is not simple. But whatever is being predicated of something after it was not being predicated <of it> is not of its substance, since no thing has its own substance popping suddenly* into it. Hence, since something is predicated of God after it was not <so> predicated (e.g., *being* Lord and Creator, which are said of Him on the basis of time), it seems that He is not simple.

4. Further, wherever many things exist in one, there must be a sort of composition there. But in the divine nature there are three really dis-

realiter distinctae, convenientes in una essentia. Ergo videtur ibi esse aliquis modus compositionis.

Contra, omne compositum est posterius suis componentibus: quia simplicius est prius in se quam addatur sibi aliquid ad compositionem tertii. Sed primo simpliciter nihil est prius. Cum igitur Deus sit primum principium, non est compositus.

Praeterea, illud quod est primum dans omnibus esse, habet esse non dependens ab alio: quod enim habet esse dependens /219a/ ab alio, habet esse ab alio, et nullum tale est primum dans esse. Sed Deus est primum dans omnibus esse. Ergo suum esse non dependet ab alio. Sed cujuslibet compositi esse dependet ex componentibus, quibus remotis, et esse compositi tollitur et secundum rem et secundum intellectum. Ergo Deus non est compositus.

Item, illud quod est primum principium essendi, nobilissimo modo habet esse, cum semper sit aliquid nobilius in causa quam in causato. Sed nobilissimus modus habendi esse, est quo totum aliquid est suum esse. Ergo Deus est suum esse. Sed nullum compositum totum est suum esse, quia esse ipsius sequitur componentia, quae non sunt ipsum esse. Ergo Deus non est compositus. Et hoc simpliciter concedendum est.

Ad primum ergo dicendum, quod aliquid esse sine additione dicitur dupliciter. Aut de cujus ratione est ut nihil sibi addatur: et sic dicitur de Deo: hoc enim oportet perfectum esse in se ex quo additionem non recipit; nec potest esse commune, quia omne commune salvatur in proprio, ubi sibi fit additio. Aut ita quod non sit de ratione ejus quod fiat sibi additio, neque quod non fiat, et hoc modo ens commune est sine additione. In intellectu enim entis non includitur ista conditio, sine additione; alias nunquam posset sibi fieri additio, quia esset contra rationem ejus; et ideo commune est, quia in sui ratione non dicit aliquam additionem, sed potest sibi fieri additio ut determinetur ad proprium; sicut

tinct Persons agreeing in one essence. Therefore, a certain manner of composition seems to be there.

On the contrary, every composite is posterior to its components: since the simpler exists in itself before anything is added to it for the composition of a third. But nothing is prior to the first. Therefore, since God is the first principle, He is not composite.

Further, that which is first, giving *being* to all <things>, has *being* not dependent upon anything else: for what has *being* dependent /219b/ upon something else has *being* from another, and nothing of that sort is a first, giving *being*. But God is the first, giving *being* to all <things>. Therefore, His *being* does not depend on another. But the *being* of any composite depends on <its> components, <and> these having been removed, the *being* of the composite is removed as well—both with respect to the thing and with respect to understanding. Hence, God has not been composed.

Again, that which is the first principle of *being* has *being* in the most perfect way, since something always exists more perfectly in the cause than in the caused. But the most perfect way of having *being* is that by which some whole is its own *being*. Hence, God is His own being. But no composite whole is its own *being*, since its *being* follows <its> components, which are not *being* itself. Hence, God is not composite. This is to be granted without qualification.

1. To the first <objection>, therefore, one ought to say that '*being* something without addition' is said in two ways: Either (1) that whose very meaning is <such> that nothing may be added to it, and this is how <something added> is said of God: for this must be perfect in itself from which <fact> it does not receive an addition; but it cannot be <something> common, since everything common is preserved in the proper, where addition is made to it. Or (2) <something is said to be without addition> in such a way that it is not of its very meaning that addition should be made to it, nor that <addition> should not be made <to it>, and this is how a common being (*ens commune*) is without addition. For the condition <of being> 'without addition' is not included in what is understood of a being; otherwise addition could never be made to it, since <addition> would be contrary to its very meaning; and so <addition> is <something> common, since it does not express any addition within its very meaning but an addition can be made to it such that it be determined to the proper <instance>; 'common animal' is said to

etiam animal commune dicitur esse sine ratione, quia de intellectu ejus non est habere rationem, neque non habere; asinus autem dicitur sine ratione esse, quia in intellectu ejus includitur negatio rationis, et per hoc determinatur secundum differentiam propriam. Ita etiam divinum esse est determinatum in se et ab omnibus aliis divisum, per hoc quod sibi nulla additio fieri potest. Unde patet quod negationes dictae de Deo non designant in ipso aliquam compositionem.

Ad secundum dicendum quod in rebus creatis res determinatur ut sit aliquid, tripliciter: aut per additionem alicujus differentiae, quae potentialiter in genere erat; aut ex eo quod natura communis recipitur in aliquo, et fit hoc aliquid; aut ex eo quod additur aliquid accidens, per quod dicitur esse vel sciens vel albus. Nullus istorum modorum potest esse in Deo, quia ipse non est commune aliquid, cum de intellectu suo sit quod non addatur sibi aliquid; nec etiam ejus natura est recepta in aliquo, cum sit actus purus; nec etiam recipit /220a/ aliquid extra essentiam suam, eo quod essentia sua continet omnem perfectionem. Remanet autem quod sit aliquid determinatum per conditionem negandi ab ipso omnem additionem, et per hoc removetur ab eo omne illud quod possibile est additionem recipere. Unde per suum esse absolutum non tantum est, sed aliquid est. Nec differt in eo quod est et aliquid esse, nisi per modum significandi, vel ratione, ut supra dictum est de attributis. Dictum autem Boetii intelligitur de participantibus esse, et non de eo qui essentialiter est suum esse. Ex quo patet quod attributa nulla compositionem in ipso faciunt. Sapientia enim secundum suam rationem non facit compositionem, sed secundum suum esse, prout in subjecto realiter differens est ab ipso; qualiter in Deo non est, ut dictum est.

Ad tertium dicendum, quod hujusmodi relationes quae dicuntur de Deo ex tempore, non ponunt aliquid in ipso realiter sed tantum in creatura. Contingit enim, ut dicit Philosophus, V *Metaph.*, text. 20, aliquid dici relative, non quod ipsum referatur, sed quia aliquid refertur ad ipsum; sicut est in omnibus quorum unum dependet ab altero, et non e contrario; sicut scibile non est relativum, nisi quia scientia refertur

'be without reason' in this way, too, since neither having nor not having reason is <involved> with what is understood by it; 'ass,' however, is said to 'be without reason' because a negation of reason is included in what is understood of it, and thus it is determined according to a proper difference. So too divine *being* is determined within Itself and divided from all other <things>, because no addition can be made to It. Hence, it is clear that the negations said of God do not designate any composition in Him.

2. To the second <objection> one ought to say that in created things a thing is determined to be something (*aliquid*) in three ways: either (1) by the addition of some difference which was potentially in the genus, or (2) because a common nature is received in something and becomes this something, or (3) because some accident is added, through which it is said to be knowing or white. None of these ways can be in God, since He is not something common, since (1) <the fact> that something is not added to Him is <a mark> of what is understood of Him; nor again (2) is His nature received in anything, since He is pure act; nor again (3) does He receive /220b/ anything outside His own essence, because His essence contains every perfection. It remains that there is something determined through the condition of negating every addition from Him, and thus everything that is able to receive addition is removed from Him. Hence, through His own absolute *being* He not only is, but <also> is something (*aliquid*). Nor is there any difference between that which is and *being* something, except in terms of the mode of signifying or by the meaning*, as was said above* about the attributes. Boethius' saying is understood of <things> participating *being* and not of Him who essentially is His own *being*. Hence, it is clear that the attributes make no composition in Him. For wisdom makes a composition not with respect to its meaning but with respect to its *being*, as in a subject <wisdom> is really different from it, but this is not how it is in God, as has been said.*

3. To the third <objection> one ought to say that such relations as are said of God on the basis of time do not really posit anything in Him but only in the creature. For, as the Philosopher* says in *Metaphysics* V, text 20*, something may be spoken of relatively not because it is itself related but because something <else> is related to it; e.g., in all <things> one of which depends upon another but not contrariwise: as the knowable <thing> is not relative except because knowledge is related to it;

ad ipsum; scibile enim non dependet a scientia, sed e converso. Sed quia intellectus noster non potest accipere relationem in uno relativorum, quin intelligatur in illo ad quod refertur, ideo ponit relationem quamdam circa ipsum scibile, et significat ipsum relative. Unde illa relatio quae significatur in scibili, non est realiter in ipso, sed secundum rationem tantum; in scientia autem relatio importata per hoc nomen Deus, vel Creator, cum de Deo dicatur, non ponit aliquid in Deo nisi secundum intellectum, sed tantum in creatura. Ex quo patet quod diversitas relationum ipsius Dei ad creaturas non ponit compositionem in ipso.

Ad quartum dicendum, quod, sicut supra dictum est, proprietas personalis comparata ad essentiam, non differt re ab ipsa, et ideo non facit compositionem cum ea; sed comparata ad suum correlativum, facit distinctionem realem; sed ex illa parte non est aliqua unio, et ideo nec compositio. Unde reliquitur ibi tres esse res et tamen nullam compositionem. Ex hoc patet nomina personalia nullam in Deo compositionem significare.

/221a/

ARTICULUS II *Utrum Deus sit in praedicamento substantiae*

Ad secundum sic proceditur. 1. Videtur quod Deus sit in praedicamento substantiae. Omne enim quod est, vel est substantia vel accidens. Sed Deus non est accidens, ergo est substantia. Cum igitur substantia praedicetur de ipso sicut praedicatum substantiale, et non conversim, quia non omnis substantia est Deus, videtur quod de ipso praedicetur sicut genus, et ita Deus est in genere substantiae.

2. Praeterea, substantia est quod non est in subjecto, sed est ens per se. Cum igitur Deo hoc maxime conveniat, videtur quod ipse sit in genere substantiae.

3. Praeterea, secundum Philosophum, X *Metaph.*, text. 3, ac deinceps, unumquodque mensuratur minimo sui generis, et dicit ibi Commentator quod illud ad quod mensurantur omnes substantiae est primus motor, qui, secundum ipsum, est Deus. Ergo Deus est in genere substantiae.

for the knowable <thing> does not depend upon knowledge, but the other way around. But since our intellect cannot grasp a relation in one of the relatives unless that to which it is related be understood in it, for this reason it posits a relation with respect to the knowable <thing> itself and signifies it relatively. Hence, the relation that is signified in the known <thing> is not in it really, but only notionally; in knowledge, however, <such a relation is found> really. So too when a relation implied by the name "God" or "Creator" is said of God, it does not posit something in God except according to understanding, but only in the creature. From this it is clear that the diversity of God's relations to creatures does not posit any composition in Him.

4. To the fourth <objection> one ought to say that, as was said above*, a personal property compared to the essence does not differ from it by a thing*, and so does not make a composition with it; but <a personal property> compared to its correlative does make a real distinction; but from that side, there is not <any> union, and so neither <is there any> composition. Hence, it remains that three things are there and yet no composition. From this it is clear that the personal names signify no composition in God.

/221b/

ARTICLE II Is God in the category of substance?

One proceeds to the second <article> in this way: 1. It seems that God is in the category of substance. For everything that exists is either a substance or an accident. But God is not an accident. So He is a substance. Hence, since substance is predicated of Him as a substantial predicate and not conversely (since not every substance is God), it seems that <substance> is predicated of Him categorically* and so God is in the category of substance.

2. Further, substance is that which is not in a subject but is a being through itself. Hence, since this <sort of being> especially belongs to God, it seems that He is in the category of substance.

3. Further, according to the Philosopher* in *Metaphysics* Book X, text 3 and following*, each and every thing is measured by the least <element> of its kind, and the Commentator* says there that that toward which all substances are measured is the first mover, who, according to him, is God. Hence, God is in the category of substance.

Contra, quidquid est in genere, aut est sicut generalissimum, aut est sicut contentum sub ipso. Sed Deus non est in genere substantiae sicut generalissimum, quia praedicaretur de omnibus substantiis; nec etiam sicut contentum sub genere, quia adderet aliquid supra genus, et ita non esset divina essentia simplicissima. Ergo Deus non est in genere substantiae.

Praeterea, quidquid est in genere, habet esse suum determinatum ad illud genus. Sed esse divinum nullo modo determinatum est ad aliquid genus; quinimo comprehendit in se nobilitates omnium generum, ut dicit Philosophus et Commentator in V *Metaph.*, text. 21. Ergo Deus non est in genere substantiae. Quod simpliciter concedendum est.

Hujus autem ratio quadruplex assignatur: prima ponitur in *littera* ex parte nominis sumpta. Nomen enim substantiae imponitur a substando; Deus autem nulli substat. Secunda sumitur ex ratione ejus quod est in genere. Omne enim hujusmodi addit aliquid supra genus, et ideo illud quod est summe /221a/ simplex, non potest esse in genere. Tertia ratio subtilior est Avicennae, tract. V *Metaph.*, cap. IV, et tract. IX, cap. I. Omne quod est in genere, habet quidditatem differentem ab esse, sicut homo; humanitati enim ex hoc quod est humanitas, non debetur esse in actu; potest enim cogitari humanitas et tamen ignorari an aliquis homo sit. Et ratio hujus est, quia commune, quod praedicatur de his quae sunt in genere, praedicat quidditatem, cum genus et species praedicentur in eo quod quid est. Illi autem quidditati non debetur esse nisi per hoc quod suscepta est in hoc vel in illo. Et ideo quidditas generis vel speciei non communicatur secundum unum esse omnibus, sed solum secundum unam rationem communem. Unde constat quod esse suum non est quidditas sua. In Deo autem esse suum est quidditas sua: aliter enim accideret quidditati, et ita esset acquisitum sibi ab alio, et non haberet esse per essentiam suam. Et ideo Deo non potest esse in aliquo genere. Quarta causa est ex perfectione divini esse, quae colligit omnes nobilitates generum. Unde ad nullum genus determinatur, ut objectum est.

On the contrary, whatever is in a genus is either there as most general or is there as contained under it. But God is not in the genus of substance as most general, since <in that case> He would be predicated of all substances; nor again <is He> as contained under a genus, since He would be adding something over and above the genus, and so the divine essence would not be most simple. Therefore, God is not in the genus of substance.

Further, whatever is in a genus has its being determined to that genus. But divine being is in no way determined to some genus; no, it rather comprehends within itself the perfections of all genera, as the Philosopher* and the Commentator* say at *Metaphysics* Book V, text 21*. Therefore, God is not in the genus of substance. This is to be granted without qualification.

<Solution.> Four reasons* are assigned for this <position>. The first is posited in the text, based on etymology. For the name of substance is established from standing (*stando*) under (*sub*); but God substands nothing. The second <reason> is drawn from the meaning of that which is in a genus. For everything of this sort adds something over and above the genus, and so that which is to the highest degree /221b/ simple cannot be in a genus. The third, subtler reason is that of Avicenna* <in his> *Metaphysics,* Treatise V, chap. 4 and Treatise IX, chap. 1*: Everything that is in a genus has a quiddity different from *being,* e.g., man; for *being* in act is not owed to humanity precisely as humanity; for humanity can be thought of and it is still possible for it to be unknown whether some man is. The reason for this is that the common <feature> that is predicated of the <things> that are in the genus predicates the quiddity, since genus and species are predicated quidditatively (*in eo quod quid est*). But *being* is not owed to that quiddity except by the <fact> that <the quiddity> has been received in this or that <instance>. And so the quiddity of a genus or species is communicated to all <things> not with respect to one *being* but only with respect to one common notion. Hence, it arises that its *being* is not its quiddity. In God, however, His *being* is His quiddity: for otherwise <His *being*> would be accidental to the quiddity, and so It would be acquired by it from another and it would not have *being* through its own essence. And so it is not possible for God to be in a genus. The fourth cause is from the perfection of divine *being,* which gathers together all the perfections of all kinds. Hence, it is not, as was objected, determined to any kind.

Ad primum ergo dicendum, quod Deus simpliciter non est accidens, nec tamen omnino proprie potest dici substantia tum quia nomen substantiae dicitur a substando, tum quia substantia quidditatem nominat, quae est aliud ab esse ejus. Unde illa est divisio entis creati. Si tamen non fieret in hoc vis, largo modo potest dici substantia, quae tamen intelligitur supra omnem substantiam creatam, quantum ad id quod est perfectionis in substantia, ut non esse in alio et hujusmodi, et tunc est idem in praedicato et in subjecto, sicut in omnibus quae de Deo praedicantur; et ideo non sequitur quod omne quod est substantia, sit Deus; quia nihil aliud ab ipso recipit praedicationem substantiae sic acceptae, secundum quod dicitur de ipso; et propter diversum modum praedicandi non dicitur substantia de Deo et creaturis univoce, sed analogice. Et haec potest esse alia ratio quare Deus non est in aliquo genere, quia scilicet nihil de ipso et de aliis univoce praedicatur.

Ad secundum dicendum, quod ista definitio, secundum Avicennam, tract. II *Metaph.*, cap. I, et tract. III, cap. VIII, non potest esse substantiae: substantia est quae non est in subjecto. Ens enim non est genus. Haec autem negatio "non in subjecto" nihil ponit; unde hoc quod dico, ens non est in subjecto, non dicit aliquod genus: quia in quolibet genere oportet signi /223a/ ficare quidditatem aliquam, ut dictum est, de cujus intellectu non est esse. Ens autem non dicit quidditatem, sed solum actum essendi, cum sit principium ipsum; et ideo non sequitur: est non in subjecto, ergo est in genere substantiae; sed oportet addi: est habens quidditatem quam consequitur esse non in subjecto; ergo est in genere substantiae. Sed hoc dictum Deo convenit, ut dictum est.

Ad tertium dicendum, quod mensura proprie dicitur in quantitatibus: dicitur enim mensura illud per quod innotescit quantitas rei, et hoc est minimum in genere quantitatis vel simpliciter, ut in numeris, quae mensurantur unitate, quae est minimum simpliciter; aut minimum secundum positionem nostram, sicut in continuis, in quibus non est

1. Therefore, to the first <objection> one ought to say that God is simply not an accident, nor yet can He at all properly be called a substance, both because the name 'substance' is said from 'sub-standing' and because substance names a quiddity which is other than its *being*. Hence, that is a division of a created being. If, however, <such a> connotation* were not to come about in this, He can, broadly speaking, be called substance, which, nevertheless, is understood <to be> above every created substance with respect to that which belongs to perfection in a substance, as not *being* in another and so on, and in that case it is the same in the predicate as in the subject, as in all <features> that are predicated of God; and so it does not follow that everything which is substance is God; since nothing else besides Him receives a predication of substance taken as it is said of Him; and so, because of the diverse mode of predication substance is said of God and creatures not univocally* but analogously. And this might be another reason why God is not in a genus: namely, that nothing is predicated univocally of Him and other things.

2. To the second <objection> one ought to say that this definition—according to Avicenna* <in his> *Metaphysics,* Treatise II, chap. 1 and Treatise III, chap. 8*—cannot belong to substance: "substance is that which is not in a subject." For a being (*ens*) is not a genus. But the negation "not in a subject" does not posit anything; hence, my saying "not in a subject" does not express any genus, since in any genus one must signify /223b/ some quiddity, as has been said, <and> *being* is not involved in the understanding of it. A being, however, states not a quiddity but only the act of *being,* since it is the principle itself; and so <to say> "it is not in a subject; therefore, it is in the genus of substance" does not follow, but "it is <something> having a quiddity upon which *being* not in a subject follows" must be added; therefore, it is in the genus of substance. But this saying* does not apply to God, as has been said.

3. To the third <objection> one ought to say that measure is properly said in <the case of> quantities: for that through which the quantity of a thing becomes known is the measure, and this is a minimum in the category of quantity—either without qualification, as in numbers, which are measured by unity, which is the minimum without qualification; or a minimum with respect to our stand-point, as in continuous <quantities>, in which there is no minimum without qualification; hence, we

minimum simpliciter; unde ponimus palmum loco minimi ad mensurandum pannos, vel stadium ad mensurandum viam. Exinde transumptum est nomen mensurae ad omnia genera, ut illud quod est primum in quolibet genere et simplicissimum et perfectissimum dicatur mensura omnium quae sunt in genere illo eo quod unumquodque cognoscitur habere de veritate generis plus et minus, secundum quod magis accedit ad ipsum vel recedit, ut album in genere colorum. Ita etiam in genere substantiae, illud quod habet esse perfectissimum et simplicissimum dicitur mensura omnium substantiarum, sicut Deus. Unde non oportet quod sit in genere substantiae sicut contentum, sed solum sicut principium, habens in se omnem perfectionem generis sicut unitas in numeris, sed tamen diversimode quia unitate non mensurantur nisi numeri; sed Deus est mensura non tantum subtantialium perfectionum, sed omnium quae sunt in omnibus generibus, sicut sapientiae, virtutis et hujusmodi. Et ideo quamvis unitas contineatur in uno genere determinato sicut principium, non tamen Deus.

ARTICULUS III *Utrum alia praedicamenta de Deo dicantur*

Ad tertium sic proceditur. 1. Videtur etiam quod alia praedicamenta de Deo dicatur. De quocumque enim praedicatur species, et genus. Sed scientia, quae est species qualitatis, /224a/ invenitur in Deo, et magnitudo, quae est species quantitatis. Ergo et quantitas et qualitas.

2. Praeterea, Philosophus, in IV *Metaph.*, text. 4 et seq., dicit: "Unum in substantia facit idem, in quantitate aequale, in qualitate simile." Sed in Deo dicitur vere aequalitas et similitudo. Ergo oportet de eo dici aliquid per modum qualitatis et quantitatis, sicut scientiam vel magnitudinem.

3. Praeterea, natura generis propriissime reperitur in eo in quo primo est. Sed Deus est primum agens. Ergo in eo actio praecipue invenitur.

4. Praeterea, quanto aliquid est debilioris esse, tanto magis repugnat summae perfectioni. Sed inter omnia alia entia relatio habet debilissimum esse, ut dicit Commentator, XI *Metaph.*, text. 11; unde etiam fundatur super alia omnia entia, sicut supra quantitatem aequalitas, et sic

posit the span* instead of the minimum to measure pieces of cloth or the stadium to measure a road. From here the name of measure was taken over to all the categories (*genera*), so that that which is first, most simple, and most perfect in any category is said <to be> the measure of all <things> that are in it, because each and every thing is known to have more or less of the truth of a genus the more it approaches to or recedes from it, e.g., white in the genus of colors. So too in the genus of substance, that which has the most perfect and most simple *being* is the measure of all substances, i.e., God. Hence, <the most perfect and simple *being*> need not be in the genus of substance as <something> contained <in it>, but only as the principle, having within itself all the perfection of a genus, like unity in <the case of> numbers, but yet diversely*, since only numbers are measured by <quantitative> unity; but God is the measure not only of substantial perfections but <also> of all those that are in all the categories (*generibus*), e.g., wisdom, virtue, and the like. And so, although unity is contained within one determinate genus as <its> principle, God is not.

ARTICLE III: Are the other categories said of God?

One proceeds to the third <article> in this way: 1. It seems that the other categories are said of God, too. For species and genus are predicated of each and every <thing>. But knowledge, which is a species of quality /224b/ is found in God, as is magnitude, which is a species of quantity. Hence, both quantity and quality <are predicable of God>.

2. Further, the Philosopher* says in *Metaphysics* Book IV, text 4 and following*, "The one in substance makes the same; <the one> in quantity, the equal; <the one> in quality, the similar." But equality and similarity are truly said <to be> in God. Hence, something must be said of Him by way of quality and quantity, e.g., knowledge or magnitude.

3. Further, the nature of a genus is most properly found in that in which it primarily is. But God is the prime agent. So action is chiefly found in Him.

4. Further, by as much as something is of weaker *being*, by so much is it the more repugnant to the highest perfection. But relation has the weakest *being* among all beings, as the Commentator* says in *Metaphysics*, Book XI, text 11*; hence, too <relation> is based on all the other beings, e.g., equality <is based> on quantity, and so on for the others.

de aliis. Cum igitur in divinis inveniatur relatio, multo fortius alia praedicamenta.

Contra, Augustinus, V *De Trin.*, cap. VIII, col. 916, t. VIII "Omne quod de Deo dicitur, aut secundum substantiam aut secundum relationem dicitur"; et ita alia praedicamenta non erunt in divinis. Hoc etiam habetur ex auctoritate Augustini in *Littera*.

SOLUTIO.—Respondeo dicendum, quod quidquid inventum in creaturis, de Deo praedicatur, praedicatur eminenter, ut dicit Dionysius, VII *De divinis nominibus*, § 3, col. 870, t. I, sicut etiam est in omnibus aliis causis et causatis. Unde oportet omnem imperfectionem removeri ab eo quod divinam praedicationem venit. Sed in unoquoque novem praedicamentorum duo invenio: scilicet rationem accidentis et rationem propriam illius generis, sicut quantitatis vel qualitatis. Ratio autem accidentis imperfectionem continet: quia esse accidentis est inesse et dependere, et compositionem facere cum subjecto per consequens. Unde secundum rationem accidentis nihil potest de Deo praedicari. Si autem consideremus propriam rationem cujuslibet generis, quodlibet aliorum generum, praeter "ad aliquid," importat imperfectionem; quantitas enim habet propriam rationem in comparatione ad subjectum; est enim quantitas mensura substantiae, qualitas dispositio substantiae, et sic patet in omnibus aliis. Unde eadem ratione removentur a divina praedicatione secundum rationem generis, sicut removebantur per rationem accidentis. Si autem consideremus species ipsarum, tunc aliqua secundum differentias completivas important aliquid perfectionis, ut scientia, virtus et hujusmodi. Et ideo ista praedicantur de Deo secundum propriam rationem speciei et non secundum rationem generis. "Ad /225a/ aliquid" autem, etiam secundum rationem generis, non importat aliquam dependentiam ad subjectum; immo refertur ad aliquid extra: et ideo etiam secundum rationem generis in divinis invenitur. Et propter hoc tantum remanent duo modi praedicandi in divinis, scilicet secundum substantiam et secundum relationem; non enim speciei contentae in genere debetur aliquis modus praedicandi, sed ipsi generi.

Therefore, since relation is found in divine <affairs>, much more are the other categories.

On the contrary, Augustine* in *De Trinitate* Book V, chap. 8* <says>, "Everything that is said about God is said either according to substance, or according to relation"; and so the other categories will not exist in divine <things>. The same <position> is also held on the authority* of Augustine in the text*.

SOLUTION.—I answer that one ought to say that whatever is predicated of God that is found in creatures is, as Dionysius* says in the *On the Divine Names* chap. VII, sect. 3*, predicated eminently, as also is <the case> in all other causes and caused <things>. Hence, every imperfection must be removed from that which comes into divine predication. But I find two <features> in each of the nine <accidental> categories*, namely the aspect* of accident and the proper aspect* of the category*, e.g., quantity or quality. (1) The aspect* of accident contains imperfection, since the being of an accident* is a *being-in** (*inesse*) and a depending-upon and consequently a making-a-composition-with-a-subject. Hence, nothing can be predicated of God according to the aspect of an accident. (2) If, however, we consider the proper aspect of any category*, any of the other categories aside from relation* implies imperfection; for quantity has a proper aspect in comparison to a subject; for quantity is the measure of a substance; quality, the disposition of a substance; and the same is clear in all the other <categories>. Hence, they are removed from divine predication according to the aspect of the category for the same reason as they are removed through the aspect of accident. If, however, we consider their species, then some <things>, like knowledge, virtue, etc. imply something of perfection with respect to their completing differences*. And so they are predicated of God according to the proper aspect of <their> species and not according to the aspect of <their> genus. Relation, /225b/ however, does not, even according to the aspect of <its> genus, imply any dependence upon a subject, but is rather related to something outside: and so even with respect to the aspect of the genus <relation> is found in divine <things>. For this reason also there remain only two modes of predicating in divine <things>, namely with respect to substance and with respect to relation; for a certain mode of predicating is owed not to the species contained in the genus but to the genus itself.

Ad primum ergo dicendum, quod, sicut dictum est, scientia non praedicatur de Deo secundum rationem generis, sed secundum propriam differentiam, quae complet rationem ipsius. Unde non praedicatur univoce de Deo et de aliis; sed secundum prius et posterius.

Ad secundum dicendum, quod in divinis quaedam dicuntur habere modum quantitatis vel qualitatis; non quia secundum talem modum praedicentur de Deo, sed secundum modum quo inveniuntur in creaturis, nomina quae a nobis imposita sunt, modum habent qualitatis et quantitatis: sicut etiam Damascenus dicit, lib. I *Fidei orth.*, cap. XII, col. 834, t. I, quod quaedam de Deo sicut assequentia substantiam cum tamen, prout in ipso est, nihil sit assequens.

Ad tertium dicendum, quod actio, secundum quod est praedicamentum, dicut aliquid fluens ab agente, et cum motu; sed in Deo non est aliquid medium secundum rem inter ipsum et opus suum, et ideo non dicitur agens actione quae est praedicamentum, sed actio sua est substantia. De hoc tamen plenius dicetur in principio secundi.

Ad quartum dicendum, quod debilitas esse relationis consideratur secundum inhaerentiam sui ad subjectum: quia non ponit aliquid absolutum in subjecto, sed tantum per respectum ad aliud. Unde ex hoc habet magis quod veniat in divinam praedicationem: quia quanto minus addit, tanto minus repugnat simplicitati.

QUAESTIO V

Deinde quaeritur de simplicitate ex parte creaturae; et circa hoc tria quaeruntur: 1° utrum aliqua creatura sit simplex; 2° utrum anima sit simplex, quia hoc habet specialem difficultatem; 3° utrum sit tota in qualibet parte corporis.

1. Therefore, to the first <objection> one ought to say that, as has been said before, knowledge is predicated of God not with respect to the aspect of the genus, but according to the proper difference which completes its aspect. Hence, <knowledge> is predicated of God and other things not univocally but with respect to the prior and posterior.

2. To the second <objection> one ought to say that in divine <things> some <features> are said to have the mode of quantity or quality not because <those features> are predicated of God in this manner but according to the manner in which they are found in creatures, i.e., as the names that have been established by us have the mode of quality and quantity, as Damascene* also says in *De Fide Orthodoxa* Book I, chap. 12*, that some <things> are said of God as following* <His> substance, even though there is nothing following* precisely as it is in Him.

3. To the third <objection> one ought to say that the action*, as a category, expresses something flowing* from the agent* involving motion; but in God there is nothing really* intermediate between Him and His work*, and so He is not called an agent with the action that is a category, but His action is <His> substance. More will be said of this, however, at the beginning of <Book> II <distinction 1, article 2>.

4. To the fourth <objection> one ought to say that the weakness of the *being* of relation* is considered* with respect* to its inherence* upon a subject*: since <its *being*> does not posit* anything absolute* within a subject but only by a looking-back* at <something> else. Hence, <the *being* of relation> has greater <suitability> for coming into divine predication <precisely> because to the extent that it adds* less, by so much is it less repugnant to <His> simplicity.

QUESTION V

Then <the question> is asked about simplicity* from the side of the creature*, and there are three points of inquiry about this: (1) Is any creature simple? (2) Is the soul* simple?—since this involves a special difficulty; (3) Is <the soul as> a whole in each part* of the body*?

/226a/

ARTICULUS PRIMUS *Utrum aliqua creatura sit simplex*

Ad primum sic proceditur. 1. Videtur quod aliqua creatura simplex sit. Forma enim est compositioni contingens, simplici et invariabili essentia consistens. Sed forma est creatura. Ergo, etc.

2. Praeterea, resolutio intellectus non stat quousque invenit compositionem, sive sint separabilia secundum rem, sive non; multa enim separantur intellectu quae non separantur actu, secundum Boetium, lib. *De hebdom.*, col. 1311, t. II. Illud ergo in quo ultima stat resolutio intellectus est omnino simplex. Sed ens commune est hujusmodi. Ergo, etc.

3. Praeterea, si omnis creatura est composita, constat quod non est composita nisi ex creaturis. Ergo et componentia sua erunt composita. Igitur vel itur in infinitum, quod natura et intellectus non patitur; vel erit devenire ad prima componentia simplicia, quae tamen creaturae sunt. Ergo, etc.

4. Si dicatur, quod ista componentia non possunt esse simplicia, quia habent habitudinem concretam, quod sint ab alio: Contra: illud quod est extrinsecum rei non facit compositionem cum re ipsa. Sed agens est extrinsecum a re. Ergo per hoc quod res est ab aliquo agente, non inducitur in ipsam aliqua compositio.

Contra, Boetius, 1 *De Trinitate*. cap. II, col. 1250, t. II: "In omni eo quod est citra primum, differt et quod est et quo est." Sed omnis creatura est citra primum. Ergo est composita ex esse et quodest.

Praeterea, omnis creatura habet esse finitum. Sed esse non receptum in aliquo, non est finitum, immo absolutum. Ergo omnis creatura habet esse receptum in aliquo; et ita oportet quod habeat duo ad minus, scilicet esse, et id quod esse recipit.

SOLUTIO.—Respondeo dicendum, quod omne quod procedit a Deo in diversitate essentiae, deficit a simplicitate ejus. Ex hoc autem quod deficit a simplicitate, non oportet quod incidat in compositionem; sicut ex quod deficit a summa bonitate, non oportet quod incidat in ipsum aliqua malitia. Dico ergo quod creatura est duplex. Quaedam enim

/122b/

ARTICLE I Is any creature simple?

One proceeds to the first <article> in this way: 1. It seems that some creature is simple. For form* is contingent* upon composition* and consistent* with a simple and invariable creature. But a form is a creature. Therefore, etc.

2. Further, the analysis* of the intellect* does not halt* as long as it discovers* a composition, whether or not <the things> are really* separable*; for, according to Boethius* *De Hebdomadibus**, many <features> are separated* by the intellect that are not separated in act. Hence, that within which the ultimate analysis of the intellect halts is utterly* simple. But common* being* is of this sort. Therefore, etc.

3. Further, if every creature is composite*, then it is composed of nothing but creatures. Hence, its components* will also be composed. Therefore, there will either be an infinite regress (which nature and intellect do not allow*) or there will be an arrival at prime simple components which are nevertheless creatures. Hence, etc.

4. If it be said that those components cannot be simple since they have a concrete* relation*, because they exist from <something> else, <to the> contrary <one might object>: That which is extrinsic to a thing* does not make a composition with the thing itself. But the agent is extrinsic to the thing. Hence, a composition is not induced into <the thing> itself <just> because the thing exists from an agent.

On the contrary, Boethius* <says> in *De Trinitate* Book I, chap. 2*, "In all that is this side of the First, <that>-which-is* and <that>-by-which-it-is* differ." But every creature is this side of the First. Hence, it is composed of *being* and <that> which is.

Further, every creature has finite* *being*. But *being* not received in something is not rendered finite* but rather is absolute. Hence, every creature has *being* received in something; and so <every creature> must have at least two <constitutents>, namely *being* and that which receives* *being*.

SOLUTION.—I answer that one ought to say that everything that proceeds from God in a diversity of essence* falls short of His simplicity. But from the fact that it falls short of simplicity, it need not be the case that it falls into composition; just as from the fact that <something> falls short of the highest goodness, it need not be the case that any badness* occur in it. Therefore, I say that there are two sorts of creature.

est quae habet esse completum in se, sicut homo et hujusmodi, et talis creatura ita deficit a simplicitate divina quod incidit in compositionem. Cum enim in solo Deo esse suum sit sua quidditas, /227a/ oportet quod in qualibet creatura, vel in corporali vel in spirituali, inveniatur quidditas vel natura sua, et esse suum, quod est sibi acquisitum a Deo, cujus essentia est suum esse; et ita componitur ex esse, vel quo est, et quod est. Est etiam quaedam creatura quae non habet esse in se, sed tantum in alio, sicut materia prima, sicut forma quaelibet, sicut universale; non enim est esse alicujus, nisi particularis subsistentis in natura, et talis creatura non deficit a simplicitate, ita quod sit composita. Si enim dicatur, quod componitur ex ipsa sua natura et habitudinibus quibus refertur ed Deum vel ad illud cum quo componitur, item quaeritur de illis habitudinibus utrum sint res, vel non: et si non sunt res, non faciunt compositionem; si autem sunt res, ipsae non referuntur habitudinibus aliis, sed seipsis: quia illud quod per se est relatio, non refertur per aliam relationem. Unde oportebit devenire ad aliquid quod non est compositum, sed tamen defecit a simplicitate primi: et defectus iste perpenditur ex duobus: vel quia est divisibile in potentia vel per accidens, sicut materia prima, et forma, et universale; vel quia est componibile alteri, quod divina simplicitas non patitur.

Et per hoc patet solutio ad ea quae objecta sunt. Primae enim rationes procedebant de illis creaturis quae non habent esse completum, quae non componuntur ex aliis sicut ex partibus; et aliae duae procedebant de creaturis quae habent esse completum.

ARTICULUS II *Utrum anima sit simplex*

Ad secundum sic proceditur. 1. Videtur quod anima sit simplex. Sicut enim dicit Philosophus, II *De anima*, text. 2, anima est forma corporis. Sed *ibidem* dicit, quod forma neque est materia neque compositum. Ergo anima non est composita.

(1) For there is a <creature> that has *being* complete in itself, e.g., a human* being and the like, and such a creature falls short of the divine simplicity in such a way as to fall into composition. For since in God alone His *being* is His quiddity*, /227b/ in any creature, corporeal or spiritual, there must be found its quiddity or nature as well as its *being*, which is acquired* for it by God, Whose essence is His *being;* and so <any such creature> is composed of *being* or that by which it is and that which is. (2) There is also a creature which does not have *being* in itself, but only in another, like prime matter*, like any form, like a universal*; for it is not the *being* of something except of a particular* subsisting* within a nature, and such a creature does not fall short of simplicity in such a way as to be composite. For if it be said that <such a creature> is composed out of its own nature and the relationships* by which it is related to God or to that with which it is composed, the same question arises about those relationships: are they things or not? And if they are not things, they do not make a composition; but if they are things, they themselves are not related by means of other relationships but by themselves: since that which is a relation in its own right* is not related through another relation. Hence, one will have to arrive at something which is not composite, but yet which falls short of the simplicity of the First: and that short-fall* depends on two <things>: <it arises> either because <the something in question> is divisible in potency* or by accident, like prime matter, and form, and the universal; or because it is able-to-be-composed* with another, which <latter> the divine simplicity does not undergo*.

And for this reason the solution* to the objections* is clear. For the first arguments proceed regarding those creatures that do not have complete *being,* <those> that are not composed of other <components> as out of parts; and the other two proceed regarding creatures that do have complete *being.*

ARTICLE II Is the soul* simple?

One proceeds to the second <article> in this way: 1. It seems that the soul is simple*. For, as the Philosopher* says in *De anima,* Book II, text 2*, the soul is the form of the body*. But he says in the same place that form is neither matter nor composite. Therefore, the soul is not composite.

2. Praeterea, omne quod est compositum, habet esse ex suis componentibus. Si igitur anima sit composita, tunc ipsa in se habet aliquod esse, et illud esse nunquam removetur ab ea. Sed ex conjunctione animae ad corpus relinquitur quoddam esse quod est esse hominis. Ergo in homine est esse duplex, scilicet esse animae, et esse conjuncti: quod non potest esse, cum unius rei sit unicum esse.

/228a/ 3. Praeterea, omnis compositio quae advenit rei post suum esse completum, est sibi accidentalis. Si igitur anima est composita ex suis principiis, habens in se esse perfectum, compositio ipsius ad corpus erit sibi accidentalis. Sed compositio accidentalis terminatur ad unum per accidens. Ergo ex anima et corpore non efficitur nisi unum per accidens; et ita homo non est ens per se, sed per accidens.

4. Contra, Boetius, 1 *De Trinit.*, cap. II, col. 1250, t. II: Nulla forma simplex potest esse subjectum. Sed anima est subjectum et potentiarum, et habituum, et specierum intelligibilium. Ergo non est forma simplex.

5. Praeterea, forma simplex non habet esse per se, ut dictum est. Sed illud quod non habet esse nisi per hoc quod est in altero, non potest remanere post illud, nec etiam potest esse motor, quamvis possit esse principium motus, quia movens est ens perfectum in se; unde forma ignis non est motor, ut dicitur VIII *Physic.*, text. 40. Anima autem manet post corpus, et est motor corporis. Ergo non est forma simplex.

6. Praeterea, nulla forma simplex habet in se unde individuetur, cum omnis forma sit de se communis. Si igitur anima est forma simplex, non habebit in se unde individuetur; sed tantum individuabitur per corpus. Remoto autem eo quod est causa individuationis, tollitur individuatio. Ergo, remoto corpore, non remanebunt animae diversae secundum individua; et ita non remanebit nisi una anima quae erit natura animae.

SOLUTIO.—Respondeo dicendum, quod hic est duplex opinio. *Quidam* enim dicunt, quod anima, est composita ex materia et forma; quorum etiam sunt *quidam* dicentes, eamdem esse materiam animae et aliorum corporalium et spiritualium. Sed hoc non videtur esse verum,

2. Further, everything that is composite has *being* from its components. Therefore, if the soul is composite, then it has *being* within itself, and that *being* is never removed from it. But a *being* that is the *being* of the human* being remains on the basis of the soul's conjunction* to the body. Therefore, there are two sorts of *being* in a human* being—namely, the soul's *being* and the *being* of the conjunct*, which cannot be, since there is a unique* *being* of one thing.

/228b/ 3. Further, every composition that comes to a thing after its completed* *being* is accidental to it. Therefore, if the soul is composed out of its own principles*—having a perfected* *being* in itself, its compositon with the body will be accidental to it. But an accidental composition is terminated at <something> one* by accident*. Hence, only <something> one by accident is effected out of a soul and a body; and thus a human* is not a being in its own right but by accident.

4. On the other hand, Boethius* *De Trinitate* I, chap. 2*, <says that> no simple form can be a subject*. But the soul is a subject both of powers* and habits* as well as of intelligible species*. Therefore, the soul is not a simple form.

5. Further, a simple form does not have being in its own right, as has been said. But that which does not have *being* except by being in another cannot remain after that <other is gone>, nor can it even be a mover*, although it can be a principle of motion*, since a mover is a being perfect in itself; hence, the form of fire is not a mover*, as is said <by the Philosopher*> in *Physics* Book VIII, text 40*. But the soul remains after the body, and it is the mover of the body. Hence, <the soul> is not a simple form.

6. Further, no simple form has within itself the wherewithal to be individuated*, since every form is of itself* common*. If, then, the soul is a simple form, it will not have within itself the wherewithal to be individuated; but it will be individuated only through a body. But when that which is the cause of individuation* has been removed*, individuation is cancelled. Hence, once the body is removed, individually* diverse souls will not remain; and so there will remain only one soul, which will be the very nature of soul.

SOLUTION.—I answer that one ought to say that there are two sorts of opinion* here. For (1) some** say that the soul is composed of matter and form; of these, again, there are some** saying that the matter of the soul and of other bodily* and spiritual things is the same. But this

quia nulla forma efficitur intelligibilis, nisi per hoc quod separatur a materia et ab appendentiis materiae. Hoc autem non est inquantum est materia corporalis perfecta corporeitate, cum ipsa forma corporeitatis sit intelligibilis per separationem a materia. Unde illae substantiae quae sunt intelligibiles per naturam, non videntur esse materiales: alias species rerum in ipsis non essent secundum esse intelligibile. Unde Avicenna, tract. III, cap. VIII, dicit, quod aliquod dicitur esse intellectivum, quia est immune a materia. Et propterea materia prima, prout consideratur nuda ab omni forma, non habet aliquam diversitatem, sed efficitur diversa per aliqua accidentia ante adventum formae substantialis cum esse accidentale non praecedat substantiale. Uni autem perfectibili debetur una perfectio. /229a/ Ergo oportet quod prima forma substantialis perficiat totam materiam. Sed prima forma quae recipitur in materia, est corporeitas, a qua nunquam denudatur, ut dicit Comment. in I *Physic.*, text. com. 63. Ergo forma corporeitatis est in tota materia, et ita materia non erit nisi in corporibus. Si enim diceres, quod quidditas substantiae esset prima forma recepta in materia, adhuc redibit in idem; quia ex quidditate substantiae materia non habet divisionem. sed ex corporeitate, quam consequuntur dimensiones quantitatis in actu; et postea per divisionem materiae, secundum quod disponitur diversis sitibus, acquiruntur in ipsa diversae formae. Ordo enim nobilitatis in corporibus videtur esse secundum ordinem situs ipsorum, sicut ignis aerem; et ideo non videtur quod anima habeat materiam, nisi materia aequivoce sumatur.

Alii dicunt, quod anima est composita ex "quo est" et "quod est." Differt autem "quod est" a materia; quia "quod est," dicit ipsum suppositum habens esse; materia autem non habet esse, sed compositum ex materia et forma; unde materia non est "quod est," sed compositum. Unde in omnibus illis in quibus est compositio ex materia et forma, est etiam compositio ex "quo est" et "quod est." In compositis autem ex materia et forma "quo est" potest dici tripliciter. Potest enim dici "quo est" ipsa forma partis, quae dat esse materiae. Potest etiam dici "quo

<position> does not seem to be true, since no form is rendered intelligible except through being separated from matter and from the appurtenances* of matter. But this is not <the case> inasmuch as corporeal* matter has been perfected by corporeity*, since the very form of corporeity is intelligible through separation* from matter. Hence, those substances that are intelligible by nature do not seem to be material: otherwise the species of things in them would not be intelligible with respect to <their> *being*. Hence, in <*Metaphysics*> Treatise III, chap. 8*, Avicenna* says that something is said to be intellective, since it is immune from matter. And for this reason, to the extent that prime matter is considered denuded* of every form, it does not have any diversity, but it is rendered diverse through certain accidents prior to the arrival of the substantial form, although accidental *being* does not precede substantial <*being*>. One perfection, however, is owing to one perfectible <thing>. /229b/ Hence, the first substantial form* must perfect the whole matter. But the first form that is received in matter is corporeity, from which <matter> is never denuded*, as the Commentator* says in I *Phys.* text. com. 63*. Hence, the form of corporeity is in the whole of matter, and in this sense matter will not exist except in bodies. For if you were to say that the quiddity of a substance were the first form received in matter, the same point would come up still again; since matter has division not from the quiddity of a substance, but from the corporeity upon which the dimensions of quantity follow in act; and afterwards through the division of matter, according as it is disposed with diverse positions*, diverse forms are acquired within it. For the order* of perfection in bodies is seen to exist according to the order of their position, e.g., <the natural place of> fire is above <that of> air; and so it does not seem that the soul has matter unless "matter" be taken equivocally.

(2) Others say that the soul is composed of "that by which it is" and "that which is." "That which is" differs, however, from matter, since "that which is" denotes the supposit itself having *being;* it is not matter that has *being* but rather the composite of matter and form; hence, not matter but rather the composite is "that which is." Hence, in all those <things> in which there is a composition of matter and form there is also a composition of "that by which it is" and "that which is." But in composites of matter and form "that by which it is" can be said in three ways: For (2.1) the very form* of the part which gives being to matter

est" ipse actus essendi, scilicet esse, sicut quo curritur, est actus curren-di. Potest etiam dici "quo est" ipsa natura quae relinquitur ex conjun-ctione formae cum materia, ut humanitas; praecipue secundum ponen-tes quod forma, quae est totum, quae dicitur quidditas, non est forma partis, de quibus est Avicenna, tract. V, cap. III. Cum autem de ratione quidditatis, vel essentiae, non sit quod sit composita vel compositum; consequens poterit inveniri et intelligi aliqua quidditas simplex, non consequens compositionem formae et materiae. Si autem inveniamus aliquam quidditatem quae non sit composita ex materia et forma, illa quidditas aut est esse suum, aut non. Si illa quidditas sit esse suum, sic erit essentia ipsius Dei, quae est suum esse, et erit omnino simplex. Si vero non sit ipsum esse, oportet quod habeat esse acquisitum ab alio, sicut est omnis quidditas creata. Et quia haec quidditas posita est non subsistere in materia, non acquiretur sibi esse in altero, sicut quidditati-bus compositis, immo acquiretur sibi esse in se; et ita ipsa quidditas erit hoc "quod est," et ipsum esse suum erit "quo est." Et quia omne quod non habet aliquid a se, est possibile respectu illius; hujusmodi quidditas cum habeat esse ab alio, erit possibilis respectu /230a/ illius esse, et respectu ejus a quo esse habet, in quo nulla cadit potentia; et ita in tali quidditate invenietur potentia et actus, secundum quod ipsa quidditas est possibliis, et esse suum est actus ejus. Et hoc modo intelligo in angelis compositionem potentiae et actus, et de "quo est" et "quod est," et similiter in anima. Unde angelus vel anima potest dici quidditas vel natura vel forma simplex, inquantum eorum quidditas non componitur ex diversis; sed tamen advenit ibi compositio horum duorum, scilicet quidditatis et esse.

Ad primum ergo dicendum, quod anima non est composita ex ali-quibus quae sint partes quidditatis ipsius, sicut nec quaelibet alia forma; sed quia anima est forma absoluta, non dependens a materia, quod con-venit sibi propter assimilationem et propinquitatem ad Deum, ipsa

can be called "that by which it is." (2.2) The very act* of *being,* viz. *being,* just as that by which running is done is the act of running, can also be called "that by which it is." (2.3) The nature itself that is left from the conjunction of form with matter, e.g., humanity, can also be called "that by which it is"—especially according to those who assert that the form* which is a whole, which is called the quiddity, is not the form of the part, about <both of> which <topics> there is Avicenna* <*Metaphysics*>, Treatise V, chap. 3*. Now since it is not of the character* of a quiddity or essence that it should be composed or composite, it will be possible for a simple quiddity to be found and to be understood <as a> consequent, <but> not consequent on a composition of matter and form. If, however, we do find a quiddity which is not composed of matter and form, that quiddity is either its own *being* or <it is> not. If that quiddity is its own *being,* it will thus be the essence of God Himself, which is His *being,* and it will be utterly simple. But if <that quiddity> is not *being* itself, it must have *being* acquired from another, as is every created quiddity. And since this quiddity has been supposed* not to subsist* in matter, *being* within another would not be acquired by it, in the fashion of composite quiddities, but rather *being* in itself would be acquired by it; and thus the quiddity itself will be the "that which is" and its *being* will itself be "that by which it is." And since everything that does not have something from itself is possible with respect to that <something> (since a quiddity of this sort has *being* from another*), it will be possible with respect /230b/ to that *being* and with respect to that by which <such a quiddity> has *being,* in which there befalls no potency; and thus in such a quiddity there will be found potency and act, since the quiddity itself is possible and its *being* is its act. And this is how I understand the composition of potency and act and of "that by which it is" and "that which is" in angels and likewise in the soul. Hence, an angel or a soul can be called a simple quiddity, nature, or form, inasmuch as their quiddity is not composed out of diverse <things>, but a composition of these two—namely quiddity and *being*—does occur* there.

1. Therefore, to the first <objection> one ought to say that the soul is not composed out of certain <things> that are parts of its quiddity, any more than any other form is; but since the soul is an absolute form, <i.e.,> not dependent upon matter, <a characteristic> which belongs to it because of <its> likeness and nearness to God, <the soul> has *being* in

habet esse per se quod non habent aliae formae corporales. Unde in anima invenitur compositio "esse" et "quod est," et non in aliis formis: quia ipsum esse non est formarum corporalium absolute, sicut eorum quae sunt, sed compositi.

Ad secundum dicendum, quod anima sine dubio habet in se esse perfectum, quamvis hoc esse non resultet ex partibus componentibus quidditatem ipsius, nec per conjunctionem corporis efficitur aliquod aliud esse; immo hoc ipsum esse quod est animae per se, fit esse conjuncti: esse enim conjuncti non est nisi esse ipsius formae. Sed verum est quod aliae formae materiales, propter earum imperfectionem, non subsistunt per illud esse, sed sunt tantum principia essendi.

Et per hoc etiam patet solutio ad tertium: quia compositio quae advenit animae post esse completum, secundum modum intelligendi, non facit aliud esse, quia sine dubio illud esse esset accidentale, et ideo non sequitur quod homo sit ens per accidens.

Ad quartum dicendum, quod si Boetius loquitur de subjecto respectu quorumcumque accidentium, dictum suum est verum de forma quae est ita simplex quod etiam est suum esse, sicut est Deus: et talis simplicitas nec in anima nec in angelo est. Si autem loquitur de subjecto respectu accidentium quae habent esse firmum in natura, et quae sunt accidentia individui; tunc est verum dictum suum etiam de forma simplici, cujus quidditas non componitur ex partibus. Sunt enim quaedam accidentia quae non habent esse vere, sed tantum sunt /231a/ intentiones rerum naturalium; et hujusmodi sunt species rerum, quae sunt in anima; item accidentium habentium esse naturae quaedam consequuntur naturam individui, scilicet materiam, per quam natura individuatur, sicut album et nigrum in homine; unde etiam non consequuntur totam speciem: et talibus accidentibus non potest subjici anima. Quaedam autem habent esse naturae, sed consequuntur ex principiis speciei, sicut sunt proprietates consequentes speciem et talibus accidentibus potest forma simplex subjici; quae tamen non est suum esse ratione possibilitatis quae est in quidditate ejus, ut dictum est, et talia accidentia sunt potentiae animae; sic enim et punctus et unitas habent suas proprietates.

its own right <a characteristic> which other corporeal forms do not have. Hence, a composition of *being* and of "that which is" is found in the soul and not in other forms: since *being* itself does not belong to corporeal forms absolutely, <i.e.,> in the fashion of <things> that exist, but rather to the composite.

2. To the second <objection> one ought to say that the soul doubtless has perfect *being* within itself, although this *being* does not result from parts* composing its quiddity, nor is any other *being* effected there through conjunction <with> a body; no, rather this very *being* which belongs to the soul in its own right becomes the *being* of the conjunct: for the *being* of the conjunct is nothing but the *being* of the form itself. But it is true that other material forms, owing to their imperfection, do not subsist through that *being* but are only principles of *being*.

3. And for this reason the solution to the third <objection> is also clear: since the composition which comes to the soul after the complete *being* does not make any other *being* according to the mode of understanding, since that *being* would doubtless be accidental, and so it does not follow that a human being is a being by accident.

4. To the fourth <objection> one ought to say that if Boethius* is speaking about a subject with respect to any accidents whatsoever, his saying is true of the form that is so simple that it is even its own *being*, as is God: and such simplicity is neither in a soul nor in an angel. If, however, he is speaking about a subject with respect to accidents which have *being* fixed* in nature, and which are accidents of an individual—then his saying is true even of the simple form whose quiddity is not composed of parts. For there are certain accidents that do not truly have *being* but are merely /231b/ intentions* of natural things; and the species of things that are in the soul are <notions> of this sort; again, of the accidents having a *being* of nature, some follow along with the nature of the individual, namely the matter through which the nature is individuated, e.g., the white and the black in a human being; hence, too, they do not follow the whole species, and the soul cannot be subjected to such accidents. Others have a *being* of nature, but follow from the principles of the species, as are the properties following on the species; and a simple form can be subjected to such accidents (provided that it is not its own *being*) by reason of the possibility that is in its quiddity, as has been said, and such accidents are powers of the soul; for a point and unity have their properties in this way, too.

Ad quintum dicendum, quod omnis forma est aliqua similitudo primi principii, qui est actus purus: unde quanto forma magis accedit ad similitudinem ipsius, plures participat de perfectionibus ejus. Inter formas autem corporum magis appropinquat ad similitudinem Dei, anima rationalis; et ideo participat de nobilitatibus Dei, scilicet quod intelligit, et quod potest movere, et quod habet esse per se; et anima sensibilis minus, et vegetabilis adhuc minus, et sic deinceps. Dico igitur, quod animae non convenit movere, vel habere esse absolutum, inquantum est forma; sed inquantum est similitudo Dei.

Ad sextum dicendum, quod secundum praedicta, in anima non est aliquod quo ipsa individuetur, et hoc intellexerunt qui negaverunt eam esse hoc aliquid, et non quod non habeat per se absolutum esse. Et dico quod non individuatur nisi ex corpore. Unde impossibilis est error ponentium animas prius creatas, et postea incorporatas: quia non efficiuntur plures nisi secundum quod infunduntur pluribus corporibus. Sed quamvis individuatio animarum dependeat a corpore quantum ad sui principium, non tamen quantum ad sui finem, ita scilicet quod cessantibus corporibus, esset individuatio animarum. Cujus ratio est, quod cum omnis perfectio infundatur materiae secundum capacitatem suam, natura animae ita infundetur diversis corporibus, non secundum eamdem nobilitatem et puritatem: unde in unoquoque corpore habebit esse terminatum secundum mensuram corporis. Hoc autem esse terminatum, quamvis acquiratur animae in corpore, non tamen ex corpore, nec per dependentiam ad corpus. Unde, remotis corporibus, adhuc remanebit unicuique animae esse suum terminatum, secundum affectiones vel dispositiones quae /232a/ consecutae sunt ipsam, prout fuit perfectio talis corporis. Et haec est solutio Avicennae, *De anima*, part. L<sic>, cap. III, et potest manifestari per exemplum sensible. Si enim aliquid unum non retinens figuram distinguatur per diversa vasa, sicut aqua; quando vasa removebuntur, non remanebunt proprie figurae distinctae; sed remanebit una tantum aqua. Ita est de formis materialibus quae non retinent esse per se. Si autem sit aliquid retinens figuram quod distinguatur

5. To the fifth <objection> one ought to say that every form is a likeness of the first Principle, Who is pure act: hence, the more a form approached to a likeness of Him the more of His perfections it participates. Now, among the forms of bodies, the rational soul more approaches to a likeness of God <than do the others>; and so it participates in God's perfections*, e.g., that it understands, that it can move, and that it has being in its own right; and the sensible soul <participates His perfections> less, and the vegetable soul still less, and so on. I say, therefore, that moving or having being absolutely belongs to soul not inasmuch as it is form, but rather inasmuch as it is a likeness of God.

6. To the sixth <objection> one ought to say that according to what has previously been said, there is not anything within the soul by which<the soul> is *. And those* who denied that <the soul> is a this* something and <did> not <deny> that it does not have absolute *being* in its own right understood this. I say that <the soul> is not individuated except from the body. Hence, the error of those* who assert* that souls were created first and later embodied is impossible: since <souls> are not rendered plural except as they are infused in many bodies. But although the individuation of souls depends upon the body from the standpoint of their starting-point, nevertheless, <this is> not <true> from that of their end, so that there would be an individuation of souls <even> after the cessation of <their> bodies. The reason for this is that since every perfection is infused in matter according to its capacity, the nature of soul is infused in diverse bodies in the same way, not according to the same perfection and purity: hence, in each body <a soul> will have a determinate *being* according to the measure of the body. Now although this determinate *being* is acquired for the soul in a body, nevertheless, <this is> not <acquired> from the body nor through a dependency upon a body. Hence, when bodies are removed, there will still remain for each soul its own determinate *being,* according to the affections or dispositions /232b/ that follow on <that soul> inasmuch as it was the perfection of such and such a body. This is Avicenna's solution <in his> *De anima,** part <V*>, chap. 3*, and it can be clarified by means of a sensible example. For if something* one not retaining <any> shape, e.g., water, is distinguished through various* containers, <then> when the vessels are removed, properly distinct figures will not remain, but there will remain only one water. So it is with material forms that do not retain *being* in their own right. If, however, there be

secundum diversas figuras per diversa instrumenta, etiam remotis illis, remanebit distinctio figuram, ut patet in cera; et ita est de anima, quae retinet esse suum post corporis destructionem, quod etiam manet in ipsa esse individuatum et distinctum.

ARTICULUS III *Utrum anima sit tota in toto, et tota in qualibet parte*

Ad tertium sic proceaitur. 1. Videtur quod anima non sit tota in qualibet parte corporis. Cum enim anima sit forma simplex, totalitas ejus attenditur secundum potentias. Sed non in qualibet parte corpori, sunt omnes ejus potentiae. Ergo non est tota in qualibet parte corporis.

2. Praeterea, animal est quod est compositum ex anima et corpore. Si igitur anima esset in qualibet parte corporis tota, quaelibet pars corporis esset animal sicut quaelibet pars ignis est ignis. Ergo, etc.

3. Praeterea, constat quod anima influit vitam corpori. Si igitur anima esset tota in qualibet parte corporis, quaelibet pars corporis immediate acciperet vitam ab anima; et ita vita unius partis non dependeret ab alia: quod videtur falsum, quia vita totius corporis dependet ex corde. Ergo, etc.

4. Praeterea, corpus habet diversas parte distinctas. Si igitur anima esset in qualibet parte corporis tota, totum esset in pluribus locis simul. Hoc autem non videtur convenire nisi Deo. Ergo, etc.

Contra, forma substantialis adest cuilibet parti materiae: non enim perficit tantum totum, sed singulas partes. Sed anima est forma substantialis corporis animati. Ergo est in qualibet parte ejus tota.

Praeterea, videmus quod anima aequaliter sentit laesionem in qualibet parte corporis. Hoc autem non esset, nisi anima /233a/ adesset cuilibet parti. Ergo anima est tota in qualibet parte corporis.

SOLUTIO. —Respondeo dicendum, quod quidam posuerunt animam dupliciter posse considerari: aut secundum suam essentiam, aut secundum quod est quoddam totum potentiale. Si primo modo, sic dice-

something retaining <its> shape, <something> that is distinguished according to various shapes by means of various tools*, <then> even when those <tools> have been removed, the distinction of shapes will remain, as is clear in the case of wax; so too is it with the soul, which retains its *being* after the destruction of the body, <a *being*> which also remains in <the soul as> individuated and distinct *being*.

ARTICLE III Is the soul a whole within the whole, and a whole in any part?

One proceeds in this way to the third <article>. 1. It seems that the soul is not a whole in any part of the body whatever. For since the soul is a simple form, its totality is attended to with respect to <its> powers. But all its powers are not in just any part of the body. Hence, <the soul> is not a whole in just any part of the body.

2. Further, an animal is <something> which is composed of soul and body. Therefore, if the soul were a whole in any part of the body, each part of the body would be an animal just as any part of fire is fire.

3. Further, it is the case that the soul pours life into the body. If, therefore, the soul were a whole in any part of the body, any part of the body would accept life immediately from the soul; and so the life of the one part would not depend on the other: which seems to be false, since the life of the whole body depends on the heart. Therefore, etc.

4. Further, the body has diverse distinct parts. Therefore, if the soul were a whole within any part of the body, <something> whole would be in many places at the same time. But this does not seem to be fitting <for anything> except for God. Therefore, etc.

On the contrary, the substantial form is present to any part of matter: for it perfects not only the whole but <also> each of the parts. But the soul is the substantial form of the animated body. Hence, <the soul> is a whole in each part of <the body>.

Further, we see that the soul senses injury equally fast in any part of the body. But this would not be the case unless the soul /233b/ were present to each part. Therefore, the soul is a whole in each part of the body.

SOLUTION.—I answer that one ought to say that some* have asserted* that the soul can be considered in two ways: (1) either with respect to its essence, or (2) inasmuch as it is a potential whole. (1) If <it be considered> in the first way, in this sense they* used to say that <the

bant, ipsam non esse in toto corpore, sed in aliqua parte ejus, scilicet corde, et per cor vivificare totum corpus per spiritus vitales procedentes a corde. Si secundo modo, sic anima consideratur ut quaedam potentia integrata ex omnibus particularibus potentiis, et sic tota anima est in toto corpore, et non tota in qualibet parte corporis: immo sicut dicit Philosophus, II *De anima*, text. 9, partes animae se habent ad partes corporis, sicut tota anima ad corpus totam; unde si pupilla esset animal, visus esset anima ejus. Hujus autem positionis causa, fuit duplex falsa imaginatio: una est, quia imaginati sunt animam esse in corpore sicut in loco, ac si tantum esset motor, et non forma, sicut est nauta in navi; alia est, quia imaginati sunt simplicitatem animae esse ad modum puncti, ut sit aliquid indivisibile habens situm indivisibilem. Et utrumque horum stultum est. Et ideo dicendum cum Augustino, VI *De Trinit.*, cap. VI, col. 928, t. VIII, quod anima secundum essentiam suam considerata, tota est in qualibet parte corporis. Non tamen tota, si accipiatur secundum totalitem potentiarum, sic enim est tota in toto animali. Et ratio hujus est, quia nulli substantiae simplici debetur locus, nisi secundum relationem quam habet ad corpus. Anima autem comparatur ad corpus ut ejus forma a qua totum corpus et quaelibet pars ejus habet esse, sicut a forma substantiali. Sed tamen potentias ejus, non omnes partes corporis participant; immo sunt aliquae potentiae quibus non est possibile perfici aliquid corporeum, sicut potentiae intellectivae; aliae autem sunt quae possunt esse perfectiones corporum, non tamen eas omnes influit anima in qualibet parte corporis, cum non quaelibet pars corporis sit ejusdem harmoniae et commixtionis; et nihil recipitur in aliquo nisi secundum proportionem recipientis; et ideo non eamdem perfectionem recipit ab anima auris et oculus, cum tamen quaelibet pars recipiat esse. Unde si consideretur anima prout est forma et essentia, est in qualibet corporis tota; si /234a/ autem prout est motor secundum potentias suas, sic est tota in toto, et in diversis partibus secundum diversas potentias.

soul> is not in the whole body, but in a certain part of it, namely the heart, and that through the heart it vivifies the whole body by means of the vital spirits* proceeding from the heart. (2) If <it be considered> in the second way, in this sense the soul is considered as a certain power integrated out of all <its> particular powers, and in this sense the whole soul is in the whole body and not a whole in just any part of the body; indeed, as the Philosopher* says in *De anima* II, text 9*, the parts of the soul are related to parts of the body as the whole soul <is related> to the whole body; hence, if the pupil <of the eye> were an animal, sight would be its soul. The cause for this position, however, was a false imagining* of two sorts: (2.1) the one is that they imagined that the soul is in the body as in a place, as though it were merely a mover and not a form, the way a sailor is in a ship; (2.2) the other is that they imagined that the simplicity of the soul is the same way as that of a point, so that it is an indivisible something having an indivisible position. And each of these is stupid. And so one ought to say, with Augustine* *De Trinitate* <Book> VI, chap. 6*, that the soul, considered with respect to its essence, is a whole in each part of the body, but not a whole if <soul> be taken as the totality of powers; for in <the latter> sense <the soul> is a whole in the whole animal body. The reason for this is that since a place* is not required for any simple substance except according to the relation it has to the body. Moreover, the soul is related to the body as its form, by which the whole body and each part of it has *being* as by a substantial form. But yet not all the parts of the body participate <the soul's> powers: indeed there are some powers by which it is not possible for anything bodily to be perfected, e.g., the intellective powers; there are others that can be perfections of bodies, but the soul does not infuse all these <powers> in every part of the body, since not every part of the body is of the same harmony* or constitution*; and nothing is received in something except according to the proportion* of the receiver; and so the ear and the eye do not receive the same perfection from the soul, though, nevertheless, each part receives *being*. Hence, if the soul is considered as form and essence, the whole <soul> is in each part; if, /234b/ however, <the soul is considered> inasmuch as it is a mover according to its own powers, in this sense it is a whole <soul> in the whole <body> and <it is> in the diverse parts with respect to diverse powers.

Ad primum ergo dicendum, quod cum dicimus totam animam esse in qualibet parte corporis, intelligimus per totum perfectionem naturae suae, et non aliquam totalitatem partium; totum enim et perfectum est idem, ut dicit Philosophus in III *Physic.*, text. 61.

Ad secundum dicendum, quod perfectibile debet esse proportionatum suae perfectioni. Anima autem quamvis sit forma simplex, est tamen multiplex in virtute, secundum quod ex ejus essentia oriuntur diversae potentiae; et ideo oportet corpus proportionatum sibi habere partes distinctas ad recipiendum diversas potentias; unde etiam anima dicitur esse actus corporis organici. Et quia non quaelibet pars animalis habet talem distinctionem, non potest dici animal. Sed animae minus nobiles quae habent parvam diversitatem in potentiis, perficiunt etiam corpus quod est quasi uniforme in toto et partibus; et ideo ad divisionem partium efficiuntur diversae animae actu in partibus, sicut etiam in animalibus annulosis et plantis. Non tamen ante divisionem in hujusmodi animalibus quaelibet pars dicitur animal, nisi in potentia; sicut nullius continui pars est nisi in potentia: unde nec pars ignis est aliquid actu, nisi post divisionem.

Ad tertium dicendum, quod vivere in animali dicitur dupliciter: uno modo vivere est ipsum esse viventis, sicut dicit Philosophus, II *De anima*, text. 37<:> "Vivere viventibus est esse;" et hoc modo anima immediate facit vivere quamlibet partem corporis, inquantum est ejus forma; alio modo dicitur vivere pro operatione animae quam facit in corde prout est motor; et talis est vita quae defertur per spiritus vitales; et talem vitam influit primo in cor, et postea in omnes alias partes. Et inde est quod laeso corde perit operatio animae in omnibus partibus corporis, et per consequens esse ipsarum partium, quod conservatur per operationem animae.

Ad quartum dicendum, quod anima non est in corpore vel in partibus corporis, sicut in loco, sed sicut forma in materia, et ideo non sequitur quod sit in pluribus locis.

1. Therefore, to the first <objection> one ought to say that when we say that the whole soul is in each part of the body, we understand by "the whole" the perfection of its nature and not any totality of parts; for, as the Philosopher* says in *Physics* <Book> III, text. 61*, "the whole and the perfect is the same."

2. To the second <objection> one ought to say that the perfectible ought to be proportioned to its own perfection. Now although the soul is a simple form, it is, nevertheless, manifold in power, since diverse powers arise from its essence; and so a body proportionate* to it must have distinct parts to receive the diverse powers; this is also why the soul is said to be the act of an organic* body. And since not just any part of an animal has such a distinction, it cannot be called an animal. But less perfect souls that have little diversity in <their> parts perfect even a body which is almost* uniform in the whole and the parts; and so at the division of parts diverse souls are actually effected in the parts, as also in ringed* animals and plants. Nevertheless in such animals <it is> not <the case that> any part is called an animal prior to division, except potentially*; just as no part of anything continuous exists except potentially; hence, neither is a part of fire actually* anything except after division.

3. To the third <objection> one ought to say that in an animal, *living* is said in two ways: (1) in one way, *living* is the *being* itself of a living <thing>, as the Philosopher* says in *De anima* <Book> II, text 37*: "For living <things> *living* is *being*"; and in this way the soul immediately makes each part of the body to live*, inasmuch as <the soul> is the form of <the body>; (2) in the other way, *living* is said <to stand> for the soul's operation that it produces in the heart inasmuch as it is a mover, and such is the life* that is conveyed by means of the vital spirits; and <the soul> first infuses such a life into the heart and then into all the other parts of the body, and consequently <infuses> the *being* of the parts themselves, which is conserved through the soul's operation.

4. To the fourth <objection> one ought to say that the soul is not in a body or the parts of a body as in a place but as form in matter, and so it does not follow that it is in many places.

EXPOSITIO SECUNDAE PARTIS TEXTUS

"Aliud timor, aliud laetitia, aliud tristitia" <Mandonnet, p. 190, line 26>. Videtur per hoc designari compositio animae, cum ista, secundum Philo /235a/ sophum, lib. I *De anima*, text. 12, sint passiones conjuncti. Et dicendum, quod amor, et timor, et hujusmodi omnia dicuntur dupliciter: vel secundum corporalem passionem; et sic sunt passiones conjuncti, nec remanent in anima separata; vel secundum quod consistunt in apprehensione et affectione intellectiva; et sic accidunt ipsi animae secundum se, et sunt in ipsa post separationem a corpore. Unde etiam Philosophus, VII *Ethic.*, cap. XVII, et XII *Metaph.*, text. 39, ponit delectationem etiam in natura divina.

"Sine indigentia Creatorem" <Mandonnet, p. 191, line 24>. Hoc ideo dicit, quia omnia alia agentia ab ipso agunt propter finem alium a se, et ideo acquisitione illius finis indigent; ipse autem Deus propter seipsum omnia facit, ut dicitur Proverb., XVI, 4: Universa propter seipsum operatus est Dominus, et ideo agit sine indigentia.

"Sine habitu omnia continentem" <Mandonnet, p. 191, line 25>. Hoc ideo dicit, quia habitus est eorum quae circa corpus adjacent, in quibus quodammodo ipsum corpus est, sicut in vestimento. Cum autem continere dicatur alio modo in corporalibus quam in spiritualibus, quia in corporalibus, quod inest, continetur ab eo in quo est, sicut aqua a vase; in spiritualibus autem quod inest, continet illud in quo est, sicut anima corpus, Deus qui est in rebus sicut continens ipsas, non dicitur in eis esse sicut habens habitum in habitu, ut includatur ab eis: est enim intra omnia non inclusus. Et ideo quamvis sit in omnibus sicut continens, non tamen omnia se habent ad ipsum per modum habitus.

"Non enim ex compositis Deus, qui vita est, subsistit" <Mandonnet, p. 192, line 15>. Ad intellectum hujus litterae sciendum est, quod quando aliquid substantialiter componitur ex partibus, perfectio est ipsius compositi, et non alicujus partium: sicut forma non habet esse, nec materia, sed totum compositum. In Deo autem invenitur perfectio

EXPOSITION OF THE SECOND PART OF THE TEXT

"Fear is one thing; joy another; sadness still another" <Mandonnet, p. 190, line 26>. A composition of the soul seems to be designated by this <phrase>, since, according to the Philo /235b/ sopher*, lib. I *De anima,* text. 12, these are passions of the composite. Further, one must say that love, fear, and all such things are said in two ways: either with respect to a bodily passion, and in this way they are passions belonging to the composite and do not remain in the separated soul; or according as they consist in an intellective apprehension or affection; and in this way they belong to the soul itself in its own right and are in it after separation from the body. This is also why the Philosopher*, VII *Ethic.*, chap. XVII, et XII *Metăph.*, text. 39, asserts* <there is> delight even in the divine nature.

"<We understand God to be> Creator without neediness" <Mandonnet, p. 191, line 24>. <Augustine> says this because all other things acting by Him act for an end other than themselves, and so they need to acquire that end; God Himself, however, does all things for His own sake, as is said in Proverbs XVI, 4: *The Lord has made all things for Himself,* and so He acts without needing to.

"<We understand God to be> containing all things without being held (*habitu*)" <Mandonnet, p. 191, line 25>. He says this since a habit is among the things that are next to the body in which the body itself is somehow <contained>, e.g., clothing. In bodily things, however, containments is spoken of otherwise than in spiritual ones, since that which is in bodily things is contained by that in which it is, like watter by a vase, whereas that which is in spiritual things contains that in which it is, as the soul contains the body. Thus God, Who is in things as containing them, is not said to be in them as something having to be held in a habit, so as to be enclosed by them: for He is within all things but not as having been enclosed. So although He is in them all as containing them, nevertheless they are not related to Him as something held <by them>.

"God, Who is life, does not subsist out of composites" <Mandonnet, p. 192, line 15>. To understand this text one must know that when anything is substantially composed out of parts, the perfection belongs to the composite itself and not to any of its parts; thus the form does not have *being* nor does the matter, but the whole composite does. Perfec-

et quantum ad esse, et quantum ad bene esse. Quantum ad esse, quia vita est: unde si vita divina esset alicujus ut compositi, oporteret quod ea ex quibus illud componeretur, non essent viventia. Et quia vita non habet aliquid admixtum quod non sit vita, sicut nec esse, ut dicit Boetius, lib. *De hebdom.*, col. 1311, t. II, ideo non potest esse ut Deus, qui non tantum vivit per vitam, sed ipsemet est vita, sit ex aliquibus compositis ad invicem ad constitutionem alicujus tertii. Quantum ad bene esse consideratur divina perfectio quantum ad tria. Primo, quantum ad potestatem, et secundum hoc ipse Deus dicitur virtus et non tantum habens virtutem. Unde non potest esse quod componatur ex aliquibus, quia in componentibus non esset virtus illa, et ita componeretur ex infirmis, id est carentibus virtute quae est totius. Virtus autem non habet aliquid admixtum, sicut nec esse; sed habens /236a/ virtutem potest habere infirmitatem admixtam. Secundo, quantum ad pulchritudinem, et sic Deus dicitur lux. Si autem ista lux sequeretur compositionem aliquam, componentia non essent lucentia; sicut videmus, quia ex congregatione diaphani efficitur corpus lucidum, ut chrystallus, cum tamen partes dispersae non haberent prius luciditatem. Nihil autem obscurum in Deo potest esse, qui est lux, sicut nec non esse in esse. Tertio, quantum ad naturae subtilitatem, dicitur enim spiritus essentialiter. Unde formalitas sua, sive quidditas, non est ex aliquibus disparibus, id est dissimiliter se habentibus ad formalitatem; sicut humanitas ex anima et corpore, per quam homo formaliter est.

"Vivens per totum" <Mandonnet, p. 190, line 26>, quia nihil est in eo nisi vita.

tion is found in God, however, both with respect to *being* and with respect to well *being*. <Perfection is found in God> with respect to *being*, since He is life: hence, if the divine life were to belong to something as composed, then the items out of which that <composite> was composed would have to be non-living. Since, moreover, life does not have anything that is not life mixed into it, any more than *being* does, as Boethius* says in *De hebdom.*, it cannot be the case that God, Who does not just live through life but is life itself, should be out of any items composed with each other to constitute some third thing. The divine perfection is considered with respect to well *being* in regard to three things. In the first place, with regard to power, God is said to be active-power* and not merely to have it. Hence it cannot be the case that He should be composed of things, since that active-power would not be in the components, and so He would be composed from weak items, i.e., those lacking the active-power that belongs to the whole. But neither the active-power nor *being* can have anything admixed with it; but something having /236b/ the active-power can have weakness mixed in. In the second place, in regard to beauty*, God is said to be light*. If, however, that light were a consequence of some composition, the components <themselves> would not be bright*; just as we see because a body, e.g., a chrystal, is rendered bright from a gathering together of the transparent* <medium> though, its dispersed parts did not previously possess brightness*. But in God, Who is light, there can be nothing obscure any more that there can be non-*being* in *being*. In the third place, <divine perfection with respect to well *being* is found> in regard to subtlety* of nature; for He is called a spirit* essentially. Hence His formality* or quiddity is not out of unequals, i.e., items dissimilarly related to the formality; e.g., out of soul and body, humanity, through which man formally is.

"<Hilary* understands God to be a nature> living as a whole" <Mandonnet, p. 192, line 23>, since in Him there is nothing but life.

Annotated Select Bibliography

1.0 BIBLIOGRAPHICAL TOOLS

1.1 Works of Orientation

DeGeorge, Richard. *The Philosopher's Guide to Sources, Research Tools, Professional Life, and Related Fields.* Lawrence: The Regents Press of Kansas, 1980. See especially Chapter 4 on medieval and renaissance philosophy. Publications are sorted by increasing specificity (4.1 General: Histories, Bibliographies, Dictionaries, Journals; 4.2 General Collections; 4.3 Individual philosophers, alphabetically arranged).

Ingardia, Richard. *Thomas Aquinas: International Bibliography, 1977–1990.* Bowling Green, OH: Philosophy Documentation Center, 1993. Publications are sorted into Primary Sources, Secondary Sources, and "Congresses, Special Collections, Unpublished Papers, and Disserations" and arranged within these headings by language (I. English, II. French, III. German, IV. Italian, V. Latin, VI. Spanish, VII. Miscellaneous), with six indexes.

Macierowski, E. M. "Medieval Philosophy Studies." *The New Catholic Encyclopedia.* New York: McGraw-Hill, 1967. *Supplement* (1978–1988) vol. 18. Publications are sorted by Aquinas's recommended pedagogical order (1. Logic, 2. Mathematics, 3. Natural philosophy, 4. Moral philosophy, 5. Metaphysics).

Miethe, Terry L. and Vernon J. Bourke. *Thomistic Bibliography 1940–1978.* Westport, CT & London: Greenwood Press, 1980.

Wallace, William A. *The Elements of Philosophy: A Compendium for Philosophers and Theologians.* New York: Alba House, 1977. A 338–page survey keyed to the volume, page, and quadrant of the articles on philosophical topics, both systematic and historical, in the *New*

Catholic Encyclopedia (New York: McGraw-Hill, 1967), up to and including the 1974 Supplement volume.

1.2 Major Bibliographical Series. (The following items are the most important resources providing the essential data for students to complete interlibrary loan requests.)

Le Bulletin de philosophie médiévale. Annual published by the Société Internationale pour l'Étude de la Philosophie Médiévale. Louvain (Belgium), 1954– .

Bulletin thomiste. Le Saulchoir, 1924–1965. 12 vols., continued by the *Rassegna di letteratura tomistica.*

The Philosopher's Index. Bowling Green, OH: Philosophy Documentation Center, 1978– .

Rassegna di Letteratura Tomistica, nuova serie del Bulletin thomiste. Rome: Pontificia Università s. Tommaso d'Aquino, 1969– .

Repertoire bibliographique de la philosophie. Louvain (Belgium), 1949– . The directions for using this series are given in English and the other chief European languages at the beginning of each issue.

2.0 HISTORICAL, GEOGRAPHICAL AND PHILOLOGICAL BACKGROUND

2.1 Chronology

Bernath, Klaus, ed. *Thomas von Aquin.* Bd. I: *Chronologie und Werkanalyse.* Wege der Forschung 188. Darmstadt: Wissenschaftliche Buchgesellschaft, 1978.

Cappelli, A. *Cronologia, cronografia e calendario perpetuo dal principio dell' È ra Cristiana ai giorni nostri.* 2a ed. Milano: Ulricho Hoepli, 1930; rpt. 1960.

"I Sommi Pontefici Romani" in *Annuario Pontificio,* pp. 7*–23*. Città del Vaticano: Libreria Editrice Vaticana, 1994.

McGuire, M. R. P. "Popes, List of" in *The New Catholic Encyclopedia,* vol. 11. New York: McGraw-Hill, 1967.

2.2 Historical Geography

2.21 Ancient Background

Cary, M. *The Geographic Background of Greek & Roman History*. Westport, CT: Greenwood Press, 1981 rpt.; orig. Oxford 1949. It contains 33 maps with shaded elevations, the chief land-routes, Latin place-names. Bibliography pp. [314]–18.

Hammond, Nicholas G. L., ed. *Atlas of the Greek and Roman World in Antiquity*. Park Ridge, NJ: Noyes Press, 1981.

2.22 Medieval

Grosser historischer Weltaltlas, zweite, verbesserte Auflage. München: Bayerischer Schulbuch-Verlag, I. Teil: Vorgeschichte und Altertum, 1954; II. Teil: Mittelalter; III. Teil: Neuzeit, 1957.

Muir's Atlas of Ancient, Mediaeval and Modern History, comprising Muir's Atlas of Ancient and Classical History and Muir's Historical Atlas—Mediaeval and Modern, ed. George Goodall. London: The London Geographical Institute (George Philip & Son), 1947.

Walz, Angelus. *Saint Thomas Aquinas: A Biographical Study,* trans. Sebastian Bullough. Westminster, MD: Newman, 1951. "A Sketch Map of the Coastal District round Rome & Naples" (inside front cover).

2.23 Physical Geography and Routes

Great Britain. Naval Intelligence Division. Geographical Handbook Series.

France (B. R. 503)	vol. 1, Physical Geography, 1942.
Germany (B. R. 529)	vol. 1, Physical Geography, 1944.
Italy (B. R. 517)	vol. 1 <Introduction & Physical Geography>, 1944.

Note especially the carto-bibliographies.

For a more comprehensive treatment of these extremely valuable Books of Reference, see

Macierowski, E. M. "British Naval Geography in World War I: Holdings in the Library of Congress," Special Libraries Association, Geography and Map Division *Bulletin,* No. 147 (March 1987) 9–17.

———. "British Naval Geography in World War II: Holdings in the Library of Congress." SLA, G&M Div. *Bulletin,* No. 140 (June 1985), 15–21.

Road Atlas & City Guide of Europe. Edinburgh: Bartholomew; Chicago: Rand McNally, 1991.

United States Government. Defense Mapping Agency. *Pub. 131. Sailing Directions (Enroute) for the Western Mediterranean.* Fourth Edition. 1986. DMA Stock No. SDPUB131.

2.3 Historical Surveys

2.31 Historical Method

Garraghan, Gilbert J., S. J. *A Guide to Historical Method.* New York: Fordham University Press, 1946.

Samaran, Charles (ed.). *L'Histoire et ses méthodes.* Encyclopédie de la Pléiade. Paris: Librairie Gallimard, 1961.

2.32 Recent Introductory Surveys of the Middle Ages

Lynch, Joseph H. *The Medieval Church: A Brief History.* London: Longman Group, 1992.

Nicholas, David. *The Evolution of the Medieval World: Society, Government and Thought in Europe, 312–1500.* Longman Group, 1992. Social history, non-clerical.

Tierney, Brian and Sydney Painter. *Western Europe in the Middle Ages, 300–1475,* 5th ed. New York: McGraw-Hill, 1992. Bibliographies in English at the end of each chapter.

2.4 Technical Vocabulary

2.41 Latin

Busa, R., ed. *Index Thomisticus.* Sect. I, 10 vols.; Sect. II (1), 23 vols.; Sect. II (2), 8 vols.; Sect. III, 6 vols. Stuttgart-Bad Cannstatt: Frommann-Holzboog, 1975.

———. "Introduzione alla bibliografia, agli indici e lessici tomistici." *Seminarium* (Città del Vaticano, 1977), pp. 922–58.

Defarrari, Roy J. et al., *A Lexicon of St. Thomas Aquinas,* based on the *Summa Theologica* and selected passages of his other works. 5 vols. Washington, DC: Catholic University of America Press, 1948–1953.

Giacon, Carlo. "Sussidi lessicali e bibliografia per lo studio di San Tommaso." *Seminarium* (Città del Vaticano, 1977), pp. 918–93.

Petrus de Bergamo. *Tabula Aurea.* Contained in v. 25 of the Parma ed. (see below, 3.112) and in vols. 33–34 of the Vivès ed. (see below, 3.113).

Rosset, Vincent. *L'Index Thomisticus: Mode d'emploi,* ed. J. P. Torelli. Fribourg (Suisse): Université de Fribourg, 1989.

Schütz, Ludwig. *Thomas-Lexikon.* 2. Aufl. Paderborn: Schöningh, 1895; rpt. Stuttgart-Bad Cannstatt: Frommann-Holzboog, 1983.

2.42 Greek

Ast, Friedrich. *Lexikon Platonicum sive vocum Platonicarum index.* 3 vols. Bonn: Habelt, 1956; orig. 1835–1838.

Brandwood, Leonard. *A Word Index to Plato.* Leeds: W. S. Maney & Sons, 1976.

Bonitz, Hermann. *Index Aristotelicus.* Berlin: de Gruyter, 1961; orig. vol. 5 of Immanuel Bekker's edition of *Aristotelis opera.* Berlin: Prussian Academy, 1831–1870.

2.43 Arabic

Goichon, A.-M. *Lexique de la langue philosophique d'Ibn Sina (Avicenne).* Paris: Desclée de Brouwer, 1938.

———. *Vocabulaires comparés d'Aristote et d'Ibn Sina.* Paris: Desclée de Brouwer, 1939.

2.5 Composition and Transmission of Manuscripts and the Work of the Leonine Commission

Bataillon, Louis-Jacques. "Problèmes posés par l'édition critique des textes latins médiévaux." *Revue philosophique de Louvain,* 75 (1977) 234–50.

———. "L'Édition léonine des oeuvres de Saint Thomas et les études médiévales." *Atti dell'VIII Congresso Tomistico Internazionale I,* pp.

452–64. Città del Vaticano: Pontificia Accademia di San Tommaso e di Religione Cattolica, 1981.

Booth, Edward. "The Three *Pecia* Systems of St. Thomas Aquinas' Commentary in *I Sententiarum.*" *La Production du livre universitaire au Moyen Âge: Exemplares et Specia,* pp. 225–51. Ed. Louis J. Bataillon, Bertrand G. Guyot, and Richard H. Rouse. Actes du Symposium tenu au Collegio San Bonaventura de Grottaferrata en mai 1983. Paris: Éditions du Centre National de la Recherche Scientifique, 1988. Describes some of the technical detective work being done in the Leonine Commission to unravel how St. Thomas's book was copied and distributed in the Middle Ages: preliminary work paving the way toward the Latin critical edition.

Cappelli, Adriano. *Dizionario di abbreviature latine ed italiane usate nelle carte e codici specialmente del medio-evo riprodotte con oltre 14000 segni incisi, con l'aggiunta di uno studio sulla brachigrafia medioevale, un prontuario di Sigle Epigrafiche, l'antica numerazione romana ed arabica ed i segni indicanti monete, pesi, misure, etc.* 6th ed., Milan: Editore Ulrico Hoepli, 1967. An important and useful manual for decoding the abbreviations and condensed forms of writing used in medieval manuscripts and early printed books; intelligent use of it requires a good reading knowledge of Latin.

Contenson, Pierre Marie, de. "L'Édition critique des oeuvres de Saint Thomas d'Aquin: principes, méthodes, problèmes et perspectives." *Hilfswissenschaften und Quellenkunde,* pp. 55–74. Eds. Ludwig Hödl and Dieter Wuttke. Boppard: H. B. Verlag, 1978.

———. "Documents sur les origines et les premières années de la Commission Léonine," vol. 1, pp. 331–88 in in Maurer (ed.) *St. Thomas Aquinas 1274–1974: Commemorative Studies,* 2 vols. Toronto: Pontifical Institute of Mediaeval Studies, 1974.

Reilly, James P. "The Leonine Enterprise: An Exercise in Historical Discovery." *Proceedings of the Patristic, Medieval and Renaissance Conference,* 7 (1982) 1–12.

3.0 AQUINAS—SELECT INTRODUCTIONS TO HIS LIFE, TIMES, THOUGHT AND WORKS

3.1 Aquinas's Works and Translations of Them into English

3.11 Latin Editions

3.111 Thomas Aquinas. *Opera omnia.* Editio Leonina. Rome: Typographia Polyglotta, 1882– .

This series of critical editions is still incomplete as of 1997. In addition, most libraries (particularly those using computers) no longer provide analytical cataloguing. Accordingly, it is hard for librarians to keep track of their holdings and almost impossible for students to find what they are looking for without a check-list. Here is a conspectus (updates are included as a fly-leaf of the most recently published volumes) of the contents of the whole Leonine edition which is projected as a set of 50 parts (*tomi*), some of which are subdivided into volumes (*volumina*):

Tomus	**Title**	**Date or status of publication**
1	In Aristotelis liberos Peri hermeneias et Posteriorum analyticorum	1882
1*, 1	Expositio libri Peryermeneias, Editio altera retractata	1989
1*, 2	Expositio libri Posteriorum, Editio altera retractata	1989
2	In Aristotelis libros Physicorum	1884
3	In Arist. libros De caelo, De generatione ... et Meteorologicorum	1886
4–12	Summa theologiae cum Supplemento et commentariis Caietani	1888–1906
13–15	Summa contra Gentiles cum commentariis Ferrariensis	1918–1930
16	Indices in tomos IV–XV	1948
17–20	Super IV Sententiarum	(Books III, II, and I in

		preparation; IV not yet undertaken.)
21	Quaestiones disputatae de potentia	in preparation
22	Quaestiones disputatae de veritate (3 volumes)	1970–1976
23	Quaestiones diputatae de malo	1982
24	Quaestiones disputatae de immortalitate anime, de spiritualibus creaturis, etc.	in preparation
25	Quaestiones quodlibetales	in preparation
26	Expositio super Iob ad litteram	1965
27	Super Psalmos	in preparation
28	Expositio super Isaiam ad litteram	1974
29	Super Ieremiam et Threnos	in preparation
30	Super Matthaeum	———
31	Super Ioannem	in preparation
32–35	Super Epistolas Pauli Apostoli	in preparation
36–39	Glossa continua super Evangelia (Catena aurea)	———
40	Contra errores Graecorum, De rationibus fidei, De forma absolutionis, De substantiis separatis, Super Decretales	1967–1968
41	Contra impugnantes . . . , De perfectione . . . , Contra doctrinam retrahentium . . .	1970
42	Compendium theologiae, De articulis fidei, De 108 art., De 43 art., De 36 art., De 6 art., Ad ducissam Brabantiae, De emptione, Ad Bernardum abbatem, De regno—De secreto	1979
43	De principiis naturae, De aeternitate mundi, De motu cordis, De mixtione elementorum, De operationibus occultis naturae, De iudiciis astrorum, De sortibus, De unitate intellectus, De ente et essentia—De fallaciis, De propositionibus modalibus	1976
44	De decem praeceptis, Super Credo, Super Pater, Super Ave Maria, Sermones, Principia	in preparation
45, 1	Sentencia libri De anima	1984
45, 2	Sentencia libri De Sensu (De memoria)	1985

46	Sententia libri Metaphysicae	in press
47	Sententia libri Ethicorum (2 volumes)	1969
48	Sententia libri Politicorum, Tabula libri Ethicorum	1971
49	Super L. De causis, Super L. Dionysii De divinis nominibus	in preparation
50	Super L. Boethii De Trinitate et De hebdomadibus	1992

3.112 *Opera Omnia.* 25 vols. Parma: Fiaccadori, 1852–1873; rpt. New York: Musurgia, 1948–1950.

3.113 *Opera Omnia.* 34 vols. Paris: Vivès, 1871–1882.

3.12 Interim Latin Editions and English Translations Tabulated according to Leonine Tome (Actual or Projected): Note that most of the following translations did not have the benefit of the critical editions published by the Leonine Commission; indeed many were based on defective Latin texts and will require retranslation. Publication data will be supplied only for complete versions. If no English version exists at all, three asterisks will be supplied (***); otherwise, a reference will be given to Weisheipl's Catalogue for further details. New translations based on the Leonine text are indicated when they are known to me.

1 *Aristotle on Interpretation: Commentary by St. Thomas and Cajetan,* trans. John T. Oesterle. Milwaukee, WI: Marquette, 1962. Aquinas' comments stop at II, lect. 14.
Thomas Aquinas, *Commentary on the Posterior Analytics of Aristotle,* trans. F. R. Archer. Albany, NY: Magi, 1970.

2 *Commentary on Aristotle's Physics,* trans. R. J. Blackwell et al. New Haven: Yale, 1963.

3 De caelo ***
De generatione ***
Meteorologicorum Weisheipl, p. 378, n. 41.

4–12 Summa theologiae cum Supplemento et commentariis Caietani
English Dominicans, trans. *Summa Theologica,* 22 vols. London: Burns, Oates and Washbourne, 1912–1936; rpt., 3 vols. New

York: Benziger, 1947–1948; rpt., 5 vols. Westminster, MD: Christian Classics, 1981.

Gilby, Thomas (ed.). *Summa Theologiae,* Latin-English bilingual ed., 60 vols. <Blackfriars Edition.> London: Eyre and Spottiswoode; New York: McGraw-Hill, 1964–1974. General Index, vol. 61 (1981).

13–15 Summa contra Gentiles cum commentariis Ferrariensis

Eng. trans. by A. C. Pegis, J. F. Anderson, V. J. Bourke, and C. J. O'Neil, 5 vols. *On the Truth of the Catholic Faith (Summa contra Gentiles).* New York: Doubleday, 1955–1957; rpt. as *Summa contra Gentiles,* Notre Dame, IN: Notre Dame University Press. The commentaries of Sylvester of Ferrara are not translated into English.

16 Indices in tomos IV–XV

17–20 Super IV Sententiarum ***

Scriptum super libros Sententiarum, ed. P. Mandonnet and M. F. Moos. 4 vols. Paris: P. Lethielleux, 1929–1947.

21 Quaestiones disputatae de potentia

English Dominican Fathers (L. Shapcote). *On the Power of God,* 3 vols. London: Burns, Oates and Washbourne 1932–1934; rpt., Westminster, MD: Newman, 1952.

22 Mulligan, R. W., J. V. McGlynn, and R. W. Schmidt, trans. *On Truth,* 3 vols. Chicago: Regnery, 1952–1954. Rpt. Hackett.

23 Oesterle, John and Jean, trans. *Disputed Questions on Evil.* South Bend, IN: Notre Dame University Press, 1983.

24 Quaestiones disputatae de immortalitate anime de spiritualibus creaturis, etc.

Fitzpatrick, M. C. and J. J. Wellmuth, trans. *On Spiritual Creatures.* Milwaukee, WI: Marquette, 1951.

25 Quaestiones quodlibetales ———

Edwards, Sandra, trans. *Quodlibetal Questions 1 and 2.* Toronto: Pontifical Institute of Mediaeval Studies, 1983.

26 Yaffe, Martin and Anthony Damico, trans. *The Literal Exposition on Job: A Scriptural Commentary concerning Providence.* Classics in Religious Studies 7. Atlanta, GA: Scholars Press, 1989.

27 Super Psalmos ***

28 Expositio super Isaiam ad litteram ***

29 Super Ieremiam ***

et Threnos ***

30 Super Matthaeum ***

31 Super Ioannem

Cai, P. R., ed. *Lectura super Evangelium S. Iohannis.* 5th ed. Turin & Rome: Marietti, 1954.

Weisheipl, James A. and F. R. Larcher, trans. *Commentary on the Gospel of John, Part I.* Albany, NY: Magi Books, 1980.

32–35 Super Epistolas Pauli Apostoli

Cai, P. R., ed. *Lectura super epistolas S. Pauli.* 2 vols. Turin & Rome: Marietti, 1953.

Lamb, M. L., trans. *Commentary on St. Paul's Epistle to the Ephesians.* Albany, NY: Magi Books, 1966.

Larcher, F. R., trans. *Commentary on St. Paul's Epistle to the Galatians.* Albany, NY: Magi Books, 1966.

Larcher, F. R. and Michael Duffy, trans. *Commentary on St. Paul's First Letter to the Thessalonians and the Letter to the Philippians.* Albany, NY: Magi Books, 1981.

36–39 English trans. *Catena aurea,* 4 vols. Oxford, 1841–1845.

40 Contra errores Graecorum ***

De rationibus fidei

De forma absolutionis

De substantiis separatis

Lescoe, Francis J. *Treatise on Separate Substances.* A Latin-English edition of a newly-established text based on 12 mediaeval manuscripts, with introduction and notes. West Hartford, CT: St. Joseph College, 1963.

Super Decretales ***

41 Contra impugnantes . . .

De perfectione . . .

Contra doctrinam retrahentium a religione

Proctor, J., trans. *An Apology for the Religious Orders.* London, 1902; Westminster, MD: Newman, 1950.

42 Compendium theologiae

Vollert, C., trans. *Compendium of Theology.* St. Louis, MO: B. Herder, 1947.

De articulis fidei

De 108 art.

De 43 art.,

De 36 art.

De 6 art.

Ad ducissam Brabantiae

De emptione

Ad Bernardum abbatem

De regno

Phelan, G. B. and I. T. Eschmann, trans. *On Kingship*. Toronto: Pontifical Institute of Mediaeval Studies, 1949.

—De secreto

43 De principiis naturae

In Bourke, Vernon J., trans. *The Pocket Aquinas*. New York: Pocket Books, 1960.

Goodwin, Robert P. *Selected Writings of St. Thomas Aquinas: The Principles of Nature*.. .. Indianapolis, IN: The Liberal Arts Press, 1979; rpt. of 1965.

De aeternitate mundi contra murmurantes***

De motu cordis

De mixtione elementorum

Larkin, V. R., trans. "*On the Combining of the Elements*." *Isis* 51 (1960) 67–72.

De operationibus occultis naturae

McAllister, Joseph Bernard. *The Letter of Saint Thomas Aquinas 'De Occultis Operibus Naturae Ad Quemdam Militem Ultramontanum'*. Ph.D. Dissertation. Washington, DC: The Catholic University of America Press, 1939.

De iudiciis astrorum

De sortibus

De unitate intellectus contra Averroistas

Brenan, R. E., trans. *The Trinity and the Unicity of the Intellect*. St Louis, MO: St. Louis University, 1946.

Zedler, Beatrice H., trans. *On the Unity of the Intellect Against the Averroists (De Unitate Intellectus Contra Averroistas)*. Milwaukee, WI: Marquette University Press, 1968.

De ente et essentia

Bobik, Joseph, trans. *Aquinas on Being and Essence*. Notre Dame, IN: Notre Dame Univeristy Press, 1965.

Maurer, Armand, trans. *On Being and Essence*, with an introduc-

tion and notes, 2d rev. ed. Toronto: Pontifical Institute of Mediaeval Studies, 1968.
Roland-Gosselin, M.-D., ed. *Le "De ente et essentia" de s. Thomas d'Aquin.* 2ème éd. Paris: J. Vrin, 1948. This edition contains many useful notes and valuable essays on sources, but no translation.
—De fallaciis ***
De propositionibus modalibus
44 *The Commandments of God,* trans. L. Shapcote. London 1937.
The Three Greatest Prayers, trans. L. Shapcote. London: Burns, Oates, and Washbourne, 1937.
Spiazzi, R., ed. *Expositio in symbolum apostolorum, scilicet "Credo in Deum."* In *Opuscula theologica,* v. 2 Rome: Marietti, 1954.
Sermones
Principia
45, 1 *Aristotle's De anima with the Commentary of St. Thomas Aquinas,* trans. K. Foster and S. Humphries. New Haven: Yale, 1951. Rpt. with intro. by R. McInerny, Dumb Ox Books.
45, 2 Sentencia libri De Sensu (K. White, forthcoming)
De memoria (E. M. Macierowski, forthcoming)
These items are to appear in a single volume published by The Catholic University of America Press.
46 Rowan, J. P., trans. *Commentary on the Metaphysics of Aristotle,* 2 vols. Chicago: Regnery, 1964. Rpt., with intro. by R. McInerny, Dumb Ox Books.
47 Sententia libri Ethicorum (2 volumes) 1969
Commentary on the Nicomachean Ethics, trans. C. I. Litzinger, 2 vols. Chicago: Regnery, 1964. Rpt. with foreward by R. McInerny, Dumb Ox Books.
48 Sententia libri Politicorum (E. Fortin, forthcoming)
Tabula libri Ethicorum
49 Super L. De causis ***
Commentary on the Book of Causes. Tr. Vincent A. Guagliardo, O.P., Charles R. Hess, O.P., and Richard C. Taylor. Washington, DC: The Catholic University of America Press, 1996.
Super L. Dionysii De divinis nominibus ***
50 Super L. Boethii De Trinitate
Faith, Reason and Theology: Questions I–IV of his Commentary on

the De Trinitate *of Boethius,* trans. with Introduction and Notes, Armand Maurer. Toronto: Pontifical Institute of Mediaeval Studies, 1987.

The Division and Methods of the Sciences: Questions V and VI of his Commentary on the De Trinitate *of Boethius,* trans. with introduction and notes, 4th rev. ed. Armand Maurer. Toronto: Pontifical Institute of Mediaeval Studies, 1986.

et De hebdomadibus

Unclear:

Robb, J. H., ed. *Quaestiones de anima.* Toronto: Pontifical Institute of Mediaeval Studies, 1968.

Robb, J. H., trans. *Questions on the Soul.* Milwaukee, WI: Marquette, 1984.

3.2 Ancient and Medieval Sources Cited

3.21 An Index to Authorities Cited by Peter Lombard Himself (Mandonnet pages 187–93). The explicit citations to sources quoted by Peter Lombard are noted here, with the assistance of the Quarrachi editors' *apparatus fontium;* they are quoted in the body of the text. Abbreviations and sigla are explained in §3.23.

Abelard, Peter. 189–90: *Theologia "Scholarium"*, II, 10: "Cum sit itaque tanta divinae substantiae unitas, simplicitas, puritas atque identitas, ut in ea videlicet nulla sit partium aut accidentium seu quarumlibet formarum diversitas, . . . variatio, . . . rerum multitudo" (*PL* 178, 1059 B). The text of Peter Lombard here offers not even an allusion to Peter Abelard. The secondary *apparatus fontium* of the Quarrachi editors discloses much more of the Lombard's dependence on Abelard.

Apostle, The: see **Paul**.

Augustine.

Contra Maximinum 189: *Contra Maximinum,* lib. II, cap. 12, n. 2 (*PL* 42, 768).

De Civitate Dei 192: *De civitate Dei,* XI, cap. 10, nn. 1–2 (PL 41, 325f.; *CSEL* 40–I, 526; *CCL* 48, 330).

De fide et symbolo 192: The Augustine citation given by the Lom-

bard to a book called *De fide ad Petrum* is corrected in the Quarrachi note to the *De fide et symbolo*, cap. 9, n. 20 (*PL* 40, 193; *CSEL* 41, 26).

De Trinitate

187: *De Trinitate*, V, cap. 2, n. 3 (*PL* 42, 912; *CCL* 50, 207f.); cf. also *De civitate Dei*, XII, cap. 2 (*PL* 41, 350: *CSEL* 40–I, 568f.; *CCL* 48, 356f.).

188: Lombard cap. 22: *De Trinitate*, V, cap. 2, n. 3 (*PL* 42, 912; *CCL* 50, 208).

189 (Two citations):

a. *De Trinitate*, I, cap. 1, n. 2 (*PL* 42, 821; *CCL* 50, 29).

b. *De Trinitate*, I, cap. 1, n. 3 (*PL* 42, 821; *CCL* 50, 30).

190 (Four citations):

a. Lombard cap. 23: *De Trinitate*, VI, cap. 6, n. 8 (*PL* 42, 928; *CCL* 50, 236f.).

b. Lombard cap. 24: ibid.

c. ibid. (*PL* 42, 929; *CCL* 50, 237).

d. ibid., cap. 7 (*PL* 42, 929; *CCL* 50, 237).

191 (Three citations):

a. Lombard cap. 25: *De Trinitate*, VI, cap. 4, n. 6 (*PL* 42, 927; *CCL* 50, 234).

b. Lombard cap. 26: *De Trinitate*, V, cap. 1, n. 2 (*PL* 42, 912; *CCL* 50, 207).

c. Lombard cap. 27: *De Trinitate*, VII, cap. 4–5, nn. 9–10 (*PL* 42, 942; *CCL* 50, 260f.).

192: *De Trinitate*, XV, cap. 17, n. 28 (PL 42, 1080f.; *CCL* 50A, 503).

Super Joannem 188: Lombard cap. 21: *Super Joannem*, Tract. 99, nn. 4–5 (*PL* 35, 1887f.; *CCL* 36, 584f.).

Super Genesim ad litteram 189: *De Genesi ad litteram*, lib. VIII, cap. 20, n. 39 (*PL* 34, 388; *CSEL* 28–I, 259).

Boethius. 192: Opusculum I: *De sancta Trinitate*, cap. 2 (*PL* 64, 1250 C, where the text seems to be corrupt; see the text used in the Middle Ages in N. M. Häring, *The Commentaries on Boethius by Gilbert of Poitiers*, Toronto 1966, p. 373).

David. 189: Psalm 101, 28.

Exodus. 187: Ex. 3, 14.

Hilary. De Trinitate

188: *De Trinitate*, VII, n. 11 (*PL* 10, 208 B–C).

192 (Two citations in Lombard cap. 28):
De Trinitate, VII, n. 27 (*PL* 10, 223 A–B).
De Trinitate, VIII, n. 43 (*PL* 10, 269 A).

Isidore. De summo bono 192: The Quarrachi editors modify the reference from *De summo bono* to *Sententiae*, I, cap. 1, n. 6 (*PL* 83, 540 A); *Etymologiae*, VII, cap. 1, n. 26 (*PL* 82, 262 C).

James 189: James 1, 17.

Jerome 187: The Quarrachi editors explain trace things thus: *Glossa Ordinaria* on Exod. 3, 14 (apud Lyranum, I, 128a); from Rhabanus (*PL* 108, 21 C–D), who drew it from Isidore, *Etymologiae*, VII, cap. 1, nn. 10–13 (*PL* 82, 261 A–B). He in turn gathered it from Jerome, *Epistola* 15 (*ad Damasum*), n. 4 (*PL* 22, 357; *CSEL* 54, 65), from Augustine, *De civitate Dei*, VIII, cap. 11 (*PL* 41, 236; *CSEL* 40–I, 373; CCL 47, 228) and *De fide et symbolo*, cap. 4, n. 6 (*PL* 40, 185; *CSEL* 41, 10f.) and from Gregory, *Moralia*, XVIII, cap. 50, n. 81 (*PL* 76, 87 B).

John. 188: Jo 16, 13.

Malachi. 189: Malachi 3, 6.

Paul. 189: 1 Timothy 6, 16.

Prophet, The: see **Malachi**.

3.22 An Index to Sources Cited by Aquinas in his Remarks on the *Sentences* (Mandonnet pages 193–236). Aquinas's citations here will be distinguished from those of the Lombard by prefixing a blank page icon '□' before Aquinas's key terms; in the body of the text, the asterisk will be placed after Aquinas's key terms but before the Lombard's key words. Wherever the relevant source is both not normally available in a good undergraduate library and I was able to get access to it, it will be quoted here.

□**Aristotle.** (The spelling of the Latin editions is retained in the following Aristotelian quotations without any effort to standardize it.)

De anima: 214, 227, 233, 234, 235

214: q. 3, a. 2, sol.—De anima, III, text 12, 429b22: (Crawford ed., p. 426: "Et dubitabit homo quod intellectus est simplex, non patiens . . ."). The response to this *aporia* is taken up at text 14, 429b29 (Crawford ed., p. 428: "Dicamus igitur quod passio, secundum quod prius videbatur, est universalis, et quod intellectus est in potentia quoquo modo intellecta, in perfectione autem non,

quousque intelligat."); Averroes's comment, however, is verbally closer to Aquinas's formulation (Crawford, p. 428. 12: "intelligere est aliqua passio.").
227: q. 5, a. 2, obj. 1—De anima, II, text 4. Aristotle does say that the soul is the form of the body at text 4, 412a20 (Crawford ed., p. 133: "Unde necesse est ut anima sit substantia secundum quod est forma corporis naturalis habentis vitam in potentia."). The claim that form is neither matter nor the composite can be justified textually in two ways: (a) from text 2 of Aristotle, 412a6 (Crawford ed., pp. 129–30: "Dicamus igitur quod substantia est unum generum entium. Substantiarum autem quedam est substantia secundum materiam, et ista non est per se hoc; et quedam est forma per quam dicitur/ in re quod est hoc; est autem tertia, et est illud quod est ex ambobus.") and Averroes's comment on it (Crawford, p. 130. 23–28: "Idest, et omnia de quibus dicitur substantia sunt tribus modis; quorum unus est ut sit materia prima, que per se non est formata neque aliquid per se in actu, ut dictum est in primo Phisicorum; secundus autem est forma per quam individuum fit hoc; tertius est illud quod fit ex istis ambobus."); and (b), from Averroes's specific comment on text 4, regarding that form which is soul (Crawford, p. 133. 7–12: "Cum declaravit quod corpus vivum est substantia secundum quod est compositum ex substantia que est secundum materiam et ex substantia que est secundum formam, incepit querere de anima utrum est substantia composita, scilicet corpus, aut secundum formam; dicere enim animam esse materiam inopinabile est, et hoc est manifestum per se." and p. 133. 13–14: "anima non est substantia secundum compositionem.").
233: q. 5, a. 3, sol.—De anima, II, text 9, 412b17 (Crawford ed., p. 143: "Et considerandum est quod dicitur de hoc in membris etiam. Oculus enim si esset animal, tunc visus esset anima eius; iste enim est substantia oculi, que est secundum suam intentionem. Et corpus oculi est materia visus, qui cum deficit, non dicetur oculus nisi equivoce, sicut dicitur de oculo lapideo. Et accipiendum est illud quod dicitur de parte in toto corpore; proportio enim partis ad partem est sicut totius sensus ad totum sensibile.").
234: q. 5,a. 3, ad 3—in *De anima* <Book> II, text 37, 415b13 (Crawford ed., p. 185–86: "Et esse vivi est vivere, et anima est causa et

principium istius. Et etiam endelechia est intentio eius quod est in potentia ens. Et manifestum est quod anima est causa secundum propter quid, quoniam, quemadmodum intellectus nichil agit nisi propter aliquid, ita Natura; et hoc est finis eius. Et similiter anima in animalibus et in omnibus;/ omnia enim naturalia sunt organa anime, sicut in animalibus, sic et in plantis, ita quod est etiam causa animati. Et propter quid dicitur duobus modis, quorum unus est illud propter quod, et alius cuius est hoc. Et anima est etiam illud ex quo primo fit motus in loco, sed ista virtus non invenitur in omnibus vivis. Et alteratio etiam et augmentum fiunt per animam; sensus enim existimatur esse alteratio aliqua, et nichil sentit nisi habeat animam. Et sic de augmento et diminutione; nichil enim augetur aut diminuitur naturaliter nisi nutritur, et nichil nutritur nisi habeat partem in vita."

235: Exposition of the second part of the text—*De anima,* I, text. 12, 403a3 (Crawford ed., p. 16: "Et est dubium de passionibus anime, utrum omnes sint communes, et sint cum hoc ei in quo sunt, aut quedam etiam approprientur anime. Hoc enim necesse est scire, sed non est facile. Et nos videmus quod plures earum impossibile est ut sint neque actio neque passio extra corpus, v. g. iracundia et desiderium, et audacia, et universaliter sentire. Quod autem videtur proprium ei est intelligere. Sed si hoc etiam est ymaginatio, aut non potest esse sine ymaginatione, impossibile est ut sit neque hoc etiam extra corpus.").

Metaphysics: 198, 201, 212–13, 220, 221 (twice), 224, 235

198: q. 1, a. 2, ad 3—"The diverse is absolute, but the different is relative" because the former need not be diverse by some thing, whereas the latter is different with reference to some common thing, a genus or a form.

See *Metaphysics* X, texts 12 (1054b23–31) and 13, 1054b31–1055a16, especially the Latin version from the Arabic (Junctas ed., fo. 260 E–F: t. 12 "Diuersitas autem & alietas alio modo. diuersum enim & illud, cuius est diuersum, non est necesse vt sit diuersum a re. omne enim ens aut est diuersum, aut idem: quod autem differt ab aliquo per aliquid differt: ergo est necesse vt sit aliquid idem, per quod non differt. & hoc est genus, aut forma. omne enim differens differt per genus, aut formam. secundum genus autem illa, quae nonhabent materiam communem, neque generan-

tur ex inuicem, vt omnia, quorum figura praedicamenti est alia: per formam vero illa, quorum est genus idem. & dicitur genus illud, quod est idem per substantiam omnia diuersa." Junctas ed., fo. 261 A–D: t. 13 "Quoniam autem & contrarietas est aliqua diuersitas, manifestum est ex sequentibus, quod bene fuit hoc positum. omnia enim videntur esse differentia, & non illa, quae sunt diuersa tantum. sed quaedam sunt diuersa secundum genus, & quaedam per ordinem vnius praedicamenti. ergo sunt in eodem genere, & sunt eadem secundum genus. & determinatum est in aliis locis, quae sunt secundum genus idem, aut diuersa. Cum igitur possibile est ut differant abinuicem differentia maiori et minori, manifestum est, quod aliqua differentia maxima est. Quoniam illa, quae differunt secundum genus, impossibile est vt sint ex inuicem, sed distant magis, & non conueniunt.illa autem, quae differunt secundum formam, generantur ex contrariis, quia sunt maiora: & distantia aliarum rerum est maxima distantia: ergo distantia contrariorum est. Sed maximum in quolibet genere est perfectum. Maximum enim est illud, cui non est additio. Perfectum vero, extra quod nihil est. diuersitas enim habet perfectionem. sicut alia etiam dicuntur perfecta, quae habent complementum. & complementum est, extra quod nihil est. vltimum enim est in ente, & est continens. & ideo nihil est extra complementum, & complementum nullo indiget omnino.").

Here the Latin term *contrarietas* corresponds to the Greek *enantiôsis; diuersitas,* to *diaphora; alietas,* to *heterotês.*

201: q. 2, a. 1, obj. 3—*Metaphysics* X, text 3, 1052b24–1053a8, especially 1052b33–35 (Junctas ed., fo. 252 C–D: "quia quaerunt mensuram in omnibus rebus aliquod indiuisibile. & hoc est simplex, aut qualitas, aut quantitas.").

212–13: q. 3, a. 2, obj. 1—That there are immaterial substances, given that there are eternal ones, see *Metaphysics* XII, text 30, 1071b12–37, especially 1071b20–22: "*eti toinyn tautas dei tas ousias einai aneu hylês; aïdious gar dei, eiper ge kai allo ti aïdion.*" (Junctas ed., fo. 314 E–I: "Sed, si fuerit substantia mouens, aut agens, & nihil agit, non erit motio. possibile est enim, vt illud, quod est in potentia, non agat. & si non, nihil prodest cum posuerimus substantias aeternas, aut dicentes formas, nisi in eis sit principium, quod potest transmutare. Sed hoc non sufficit, neque aliud extra

formam. Si enim non fuerit, non erit motus. neque si egerit, & substantia eius fuerit in potentia. non enim erit motio aeterna. Possibile enim est, vt quod est in potentia, non sit ens./ necesse est igitur vt tale principium sit substantia, quae est actio. *Et oportet etiam vt istae substantiae sint existentes extra materiam, cum necesse est vt sint aeternae. si etiam aliud fuerit aeternum,* actio est. Quamuis hic sit quaestio. Existimatum est enim, quod omne agens habet potentiam, qua potest, & non omne, quod potest per potentiam, agit. vnde potentia videtur prior. Sed quamuis ita sit, nullum quidem entium erit ens, cum sit possibile vt sit, & non sit ens. sed si secundum Loquentes in Diuinis generantes mundum ex nocte dicunt, & Naturales dicentes, quod omnia fuerunt insimul, impossibile est vt sint eadem omnibus. Et si non, quomodo mouentur, si non habent in actu causam? materia enim substantia carpentarii impossibile est vt moueatur per se, sed carpentarietas. neque sanguis menstruus, neque terra, sed semina & sperma. Et ideo quidam ponunt separationem, vt Plato, & Leucippus. dicunt enim motum semper esse aliquid. sed quare, non dicunt causam. nihil enim mouetur, sed oportet vt semper sit aliquid. sicut modo est, aut naturaliter, aut violente<r>, aut ex alio & post, qui est primus, multum enim differt." My italics.)

220: q. 4, a. 1, ad 3—*Metaphysics* V, text 20, 1020b24–1021b11, especially 1021a26 ff. (Ponzalii ed., p. 171. 39–47: "Omnia igitur relativa quae dicuntur modo numeri et potentiae sunt relativa quia essentia eorum dicitur ad aliquid, et non quia illud aliud dicitur ad illa. Mensuratum autem et intellectum et scitum dicitur relativum quia ad illud dicitur aliud aliquid. Intellectum enim significat habere intellectum, et intellectus non est relativus ad illud quod est intellectus, quoniam si hoc dicatur, tunc idem dicetur bis. <Et similiter> si visus est visus ad aliquid, non est visus illius quod est (et si iste sermo est verus) sed dicitur in respectu coloris aut ad aliud aliquid tale; per illud autem idem dicitur bis: illud cuius est visus." The angle brackets here are Ponzalli's.).

221: (Twice)

a. q. 4, a. 2, obj. 3—According to the Philosopher, each and every thing is measured by the least <element> of its kind: *Metaphysics* X, texts 3–7, 1052b24–1054a13 (fo. 251L–257B). See Averroes* for his comment on text 7 for the principal reference.

b. q. 4, a. 2, contra 2—The chapter on perfection in *Metaphysics* Book V, text 21, 1021b12–1022a3, especially 1021b30–1022a1 (Ponzalli ed., p. 180. 22–25: "Et quae dicuntur perfecta per se secundum hos modos dicuntur. Quaedam quia non diminuitur ab eis aliquid de bonitate neque in eis est magis etiam et nihil invenitur extra illa; et quaedam modo universali ita quod non est in eis nobilitas in unoquoque generum et nihil extra illa."). See Averroes* at his comment on text 21 for the principal reference.

224: q. 4, a. 3, obj. 2—I have not found the exact formulation in *Metaphysics* IV, text 4, 1004a1–34 (Junctas ed., fo. 68 B–I); Aristotle does argue, however, that the other, the dissimilar, and the unequal (1004a18) can be used by way of contrariety to find corresponding senses of unity (Junctas ed., fo. 68 D–F: "Et, cum vnius scientiae est consyderatio de substantiis secundum oppositionem aequalem, & aequaliter oppositum vni in situ est multitudo, manifestum est igitur quod vnius scientiae est consyderatio de negatione & priuatione. consyderatio enim de utroque est vna, & vnius aut erit negatio, aut erit priuatio, quae dicitur simpliciter, quod non est hoc, aut alicui generi. inter igitur vnum, & negationem est differentia, quia negatio est ablatio vnius, priuatio autem habet naturam subiectam sibi, de qua dicitur priuatio. Cum igitur fuerit oppositum in situ vnum multo, manifestum est, quod opponetur in loco diuersum, & dissimile, & non aequale, & alia, quae dicuntur hoc modo, aut modo multitudinis. Et, cum scientiae, quam diximus, est cognitio vnius, & contrarietas est vnum istorum, & vnum dicitur multis modis, manifestum est, quod haec contraria dicuntur etiam de multis speciebus."). The different meanings of 'one' are also discussed in *Metaphysics* V, texts 7–12, 1015b16–1017a6 (Ponzalli ed., pp. 104–25), but with less appropriateness to the point in question.

235: Expos. second part of the text. *Metaphysics,* XII, text. 39, 1072b16–30 (Junctas ed., fo. 321L–322A: "Voluptas enim est actio illius etiam. Et ideo vigilia, & sensus, & intellectus sunt voluptuosa. spes autem, & rememoratio sunt propter ista. Intellectus autem per se est eius, quod est nobilius per se. & quod est magis, est illius, quod est magis. & quod intelligit se, est intellectus per acquisitionem intellecti. fit enim intellectum, quando admiscetur,

& intelligit. intellectus igitur, & intellectum sunt idem. recipiens enim intellectum, & substantiam eius est intellectus, & non intelligitur, nisi cum habet. Intellectus igitur ille diuinus est maior isto. desideratio autem est aliquid valde nobile, & voluptuosum. Si igitur Deus semper est, sicut not in aliqua hora, hoc est mirum. & si magis, magis est mirum. est autem sic. Et habet vitam, quia actio intellectus est vita. & ille est intellectus per se, & habet vitam no/bilem, & semper aeternam. Deus igitur est vnus, aeternus, in fine nobilitatis. Ergo est vita, & est continuum aeternum. hoc quidem est Deus.")

Nicomachean Ethics 235: Exposition of the second part of the text—that there is pleasure or delight even in the divine nature. *Ethic.*, VII, cap. 17, 1154b25. The Latin Averroes was not available to me for tracing this source.

Perihermeneias 204: q. 2, a. 2, obj. 5—Though I have not found the explicit formulation "everything necessary is eternal," but *De interpretatione* 23a21–26 argues so as to associate necessity with eternity by way of the priority of actuality. The Latin Averroes was not available to me for this source.

Physics: 206, 210–11, 212, 215 (twice), 216 (thrice), 228, 234

206: q. 2, a. 3, obj. 2—The dependence of time on motion and motion on continuous magnitude is discussed in *Physics* IV, text 99, 219a10–21 (Junctas ed., fo. 179L–M: "Et, quia motum mouetur de aliquo in aliquid, & omnis mensura est continua, ideo motus sequitur mensuram. &, quoniam mensura est continua, ideo motus est continuus. &, quia motus etiam est continuus, tempus etiam erit continuum: quoniam secundum motum existimatur semper tempus esse. & Prius, & Posterius sunt primo in quantitate. sed his sunt in situ. Et, quia prius, & posterius sunt in quantitate, necesse est vt prius, & posterius sint in motu et, secundum quod illic. Et in tempore etiam sunt prius, & posterius, quoniam sequuntur se adinuicem semper. Et etiam prius, & posterius sunt in motu: secundum quidem quod sunt in aliqua hora sunt motus, in essentia autem sunt aliud a motu.")

210–11: q. 3, a. 1, obj. 4—That whatever gets from rest to act is being moved is shown in *Physics* III, text 16, 202a3–8 (Junctas ed., fo. 91 I–K: "Et omne, quod mouet naturaliter, mouetur vt diximus, cum in potentia fuerit mouens, & cessatio eius a motu fuerit quies. cessatio enim eius, cuius est motus, est quies ei. actio enim eius est versus

hanc intentionem, & secundum quod est tale est mouere: & facit hoc per contactum: ergo necesse est vt patiatur cum sua actione, & ideo etiam Motus est perfectio moti, secundum quod est motum.")

212: q. 3, a. 1, ad 3—The first mobile object was said to be "moved out of itself *(ex se)*" in *Physics* VIII, text 34, 256a13–21 (Junctas ed., fo. 372 L–M: "Si igitur est necessarium, vt omne motum moueatur ab alio, & vt motus eius sit ab alio, aut ita, quod non sit motum, aut ita, quod sit motum: et si motus eius fuerit ex alio moto, necesse est hic esse primum motorem, qui non mouetur ab alio. Et, si non, sequitur, si primum fuerit huiusmodi, vt postremum sit necessario. impossibile enim est hoc procedere in infinitum, hoc, quod motus sit motum semper ex alio. infinita enim non habent principium omnino. Si igitur omne motum moueatur, sed non mouetur ab aliquo, sequitur necessario vt moueatur ex se.").

215: (Twice).

a. q. 3, a. 3, obj. 1—That motion does not exist in <the category* of> 'when' can be inferred from *Physics* V, text 9, 225a34–225b9 (Junctas ed., fo. 214 A–B: "Et, quia omnis motus est transmutatio aliqua, & modi transmutationum sunt tres praedicti, & istorum trium modorum illud, quod est secundum generationem, et corruptionem, non est motus, in quo est contradictio, est necesse vt transmutatio sola, quae est de subiecto in subiectum, sit motus. Et duo subiecta sunt aut contraria, aut media. quoniam nos ponemus priuationem etiam contrarium. quoniam per illam significatur nudum per affirmationem, vt album, & nigrum. Et, cum praedicamenta diuidantur in substantiam & qualitatem, & vbi, & ad aliquid, & quantum, & agere, & pati, necesse est vt motus sint motus qualitatis, & motus quantitatis, & motus in loco."). More explicit is Averroes's comment on text 9 (Junctas ed., fo. 214 I–K: "cum sit declaratum quod motus est de subiecto in subiectum contrarium, & est declaratum etiam in alia scientia quod praedicamenta sunt decem, necesse est vt motus sit in tribus tantum, in qualitate, & est Alteratio, in quantitate, & est Augmentum, & Diminutio, & in loco, & est Translatio.").

b. q. 3, a. 3, obj. 3—ibid.

216: q. 3, a. 3 (Three citations)

a. sol.—*Physics* Book IV, text 99: quoted above in the note to p. 206.

b. sol.—The requirements for continuity of motion are discussed in *Physics* V, texts 39–42, 228a20–b15 (Junctas ed., fo. 231 F–233 G). Text 39, 228a20–26 (Junctas ed., fo. 231 F–G) reads thus: "Et, quia omnis motus est continuus: ideo motus, qui est simpliciter vnus, debet esse continuus: cum/ omnis motus est diuisibilis. &, si motus fuerit continuus, erit vnus. quoniam non omnis motus est continuus cum omni motu, quemadmodum in aliis non quilibet continuatur cum quolibet, sed illa, quorum vltima sunt vnum. & quaedam non habent vltima, & quaedam habent, sed in forma sunt aequivoca. quoniam impossibile est vt vltimum lineae tangat vltimum ambulationis, et fiant vnum."

c. ad 4.— *Physics* IV, texts 101–02, 219a30–b9 (Junctas ed., fo. 181B: text 101 "Cum igitur senserimus aliquid, quasi in eodem instanti, & non perceperimus in motu prius, & posterius, aut senserimus ipsum vnum vnius, non ita, quod sit prius, & posterius, non reputabimus ipsum fieri in tempore, cum non habeat notum. et, cum senserimus prius, & posterius, tunc dicemus tempus esse. secundum hoc igitur Tempus est numeratio motus secundum prius, & posterius. Tempus igitur non est motus, sed quodammodo est numerus motus"; fo. 181 I–K: text 102 "Et signum eius est hoc, quod narrabo. quoniam nos determinamus per numerum magis, & minus: & per tempus determinamus motum magis, & minus: tempus igitur est aliquis Numerus. Et, cum numerus est duobus modis: dicimus enim numerum illud, quod numeratur, & numeratum, & illud, per quod numeratur, non illud, per quod numeratur. et illud, quod numeratur, est aliud ab illo, per quod numeratur.").

228: q. 5, a. 2, obj. 5—That a mover is already perfect in itself is reported in *Physics* VIII, text 40, 257a31–b13 (Junctas ed., fo. 379 K–380 A: "Oportet igitur nos consyderare nunc de hoc, incipiendo alio modo, scilicet, si aliquid mouet se, qualiter mouet, & quo modo. Dicamus igitur, quoniam necesse est vt omne motum diuidatur in diuisibilia. hoc enim declaratum est prius in nostro sermone de summis de natura. omne enim motum per se est continuum. Et impossibile est vt illud, quod mouet se, moueat se secundum totum.quoniam tunc secundum totum transferret, & transferretur eodem modo translationis, & est vnum indiuisibile in sua specie, & tunc idem alterabitur, & alterabit: & sic sciet, et addiscet insimul, et sanabit, &

sanabitur eadem sanatione. Et iam determinauimus etiam quid intendimus, cum dicimus, quod aliquid mouetur, secundum quod mouetur: et est quod in potentia mouetur, & non in actu: & illud quod mouetur, semper nititur ad perfectionem. & motus est perfectio non completa ei, quod innatum est moueri: & motor autem iam exiuit in actu: verbi gratia, quod calefaciens est calidum, & vniversaliter est illud, quod iam habet for-/mam. & sic idem in eodem modo erit calidum, & non calidum insimul. & secundum hunc modum est de qualibet aliarum rerum motarum, quarum motor est vniuocum secundum formam."). The objector's explicit conclusion that the form of fire is not a mover is not found in this text, nor in the corresponding comment of Averroes, which is principally concerned with showing that Plato's notion of a self-moving soul employs 'motion' equivocally as compared with bodies.

234: q. 5, a. 3, ad 1—The reference reported in Mandonnet to the "whole" as perfect (*Physics* III, text. 61) should be corrected to III, text 63, 207a7–12 (Junctas ed., fo. 115 E–F: "Infinitum igitur est illud, ex quo, cum aliquid accipitur, possibile est semper accipere aliquid extra illud in quantitate. Et illud, extra quod nihil est, illud est perfectum totale. sic enim definimus Totum, scilicet quia est illud, ex quo nihil est separatum ab eo: vt dicimus totus homo, & tota arca. & sicut est de particularibus, ita est in rei veritate, scilicet quod totum est illud, extra quod nihil est. & illud, extra quod aliquid est separatum, non est totum, quodcunque sit illud separatum, siue extraneum, siue non extraneum.")

Posterior Analytics 213: q. 3, a. 2, obj. 4— *Posterior Analytics,* I, texts 7–8, 73a 21–a34 (fo. 64 A and 65 E: "Quoniam autem impossibile aliter se habere, cuius est scientia simpliciter, necessarium vtique fuerit scibile, quod est secundum demonstratiuam scientiam: demonstratiua autem est, quam habemus, eo quod habemus demonstrationem: ex necessariis igitur syllogismus est demonstratio. Accipiendum igitur ex quibus, & qualium demonstrationes sunt./ Primum autem determinemus, quid dicimus de omni, & quid per se, & quid vniversale. De omni quidiem igitur hoc dico, quod sit vtique non in aliquo quidem, in aliquo autem non: neque aliquando quidem, aliqando autem non. vt si de omni homine animal, si verum hunc dicere hominem, verum & animal: & si nunc alterum, & alterum. & si in omni linea punctum consimiliter. signum autem, etenim instantias ita ferimus, tanqua de omni interrogati,

aut si in aliquo non, aut si aliquando non.")
□**Augustine.**
Confessiones 213: q. 3, a. 2, obj. 4—That prime matter does not have successions of time is asserted using the technical term *informitas* or 'formlessness' to stand in for 'prime matter': *Confessions* XII, cap. 19 (M. Skutella ed., 312. 4–24, especially 14–15: "verum est informitatem, quae prope nihil est, vices temporum habere non posse.")
Contra Maximinum 202–03: q. 2, a. 1, ad 2—*Contra Maximinum,* lib. II, cap. 12, n. 2 (PL 42, 768).
De Civitate Dei 201: q. 2, a. 1, obj. 4—*On the City of God,* XI, cap. 6 (*CSEL* 40.1: 519. 4–10).
De Trinitate: 204, 224, 233
204: q. 2,a. 2, obj. 5—*De Trinitate* IV, cap. 18 (*CCL* 50: 191–93).
224: q. 4, a. 3, contr.—*De Trinitate* V, cap. 8 (*CCL* 50: 215. 1–6).
233: q. 5, a. 3, sol.—*De Trinitate,* VI, cap. 6 (*CCL* 50: 237. 20–34).
Super Genesim ad litteram: 210, 212
210: q. 3, a. 1, obj. 2—*De Genesi ad litteram,* lib. VIII, cap. 20, n. 39 (*PL* 34, 388; *CSEL* 28–I, 259).
212: q. 3, a. 1, ad 2—ibid.
in Littera: 214, 215, 216, 217, 224 (Allusions to Augustinian texts quoted by the Lombard; cf. §3.21, above.)
214: q. 3, a. 2, sol.
215: q. 3, a. 2, ad 3.
216: q. 3, a. 3, ad 3.
217: Division of the Second Part of the Text.
224: q. 4, a. 3, contr.
□**Averroes.**
Aristotelis opera cum Averrois commentariis. Venice: Junctas, 1562–1574; rpt. Frankfurt: Minerva, 1962.
Metaphysics: 212, 221 (twice), 224
212: According to the Junctas edition the Commentator's remarks on Book XII are found in three 'Summae': I (texts 1–28) on sensible substance; II (texts 29–51) on immobile substance; III (texts 52–55) on the goodness of the universe. The claim that God moves Himself obviously pertains to Summa II, where I have found no explicit mention of the *Parmenides* of Plato. Aristotle does mention Plato in text 31, 1071b37–1072a3 (Junctas ed., 315 L: "Neque etiam

possibile est Platoni dicere quod multotiens existimabat, quod principium est illud, quod mouet se. anima enim, sicut dixit, est in postremo cum coelo."); Averroes's comment (315 L–M) is simply a gloss. Plato's most famous treatment of self-motion is found in *Laws,* Book X, but St. Thomas could have had only indirect testimony deriving from it, since that text was translated into Latin only in the Renaissance. I have not found the connection.

As to the claims that God understands Himself and wills Himself, Aristotle is explicit on the former point in text 51, 1074b 13–1075a10 (Junctas ed., fo. 334K–335D), especially 1074b33–35: "hauton ara noei, eiper esti to kratiston, kai estin hê noêsis noêseôs noêsis" (Junctas ed., 335 A: "Ergo intelligit se, cum est fortius, & ipse intelligit intelligere.") The closest text I could find to justify the latter point is Averroes's introductory remark on text 51 (Junctas ed., fo. 335 D: "Quia ista quaestio est nobilissima omnium, quae sunt de Deo, scilicet scire quid intelligit, & est desyderata ab omnibus naturaliter. . . ."); if God Himself is among "all things" that desire Him "naturally," the latter point also follows.

221: Twice.

a. Averroes shows that the first mover or God is the measure of all substances in his comments on *Metaphysics* Book X, texts 3–7, especially comment on text 7 (fo. 257 A–B: "Deinde dicit 'sed sicut in coloribus', etc. id est, quod est principium esse substantiarum est principium numeri eorum, quae existunt in substantia. Et intendit quod, cum huic fuerit iunctum quod declaratum est in Physicis <I, textus 78–79>, scilicet hoc esse primum motorem aeternum, et absolutum ab omni materia, et declarauit post, quod hoc non solummodo est principium tanquam motor, sed tanquam forma et finis, declarabitur, quod illud est vnum, de quo declaratum fuit hoc, quod est principium substantiae: sicut est declaratum, quod est actus vltimus, cui non admiscetur potentia omnino.").

b. on *Metaphysics* Book X, text 21, 1021b30–1022a1 (Ponzalli ed., p. 182. 71–79: "Deinde dicit: *Et quae dicuntur perfecta per se,* etc., idest: illa igitur quae dicuntur perfecta per se sunt a quibus nihil diminuitur in bonitate et quibus nihil est nobilius in illo genere, sed sunt in summo nobilitatis per se. Et dixit hoc quia ista sunt perfecta in quantitate et qualitate primo et essentialia-

ter." By way of contrast, the divine being contains neither intrinsic nor extrinsic imperfections: "Deinde dicit: *Et quaedam modo universali*, etc., idest: et diffinitio eorum universaliter est talis: perfecta sunt illa quorum nihil invenitur per quod dicuntur imperfecta in eis aut extrinsecus. Et ista est dispositio primi principii, scilicet Dei.").

224: The claim that relation has the weakest *being* among all beings cannot be found in Averroes's commentary on Book XI (Kappa), since he seems not to have had the Arabic text of that book to comment upon. If one skips Kappa and continues the enumeration, Book Lambda will count as XI. Aristotle's text 11, 1069b26–32 there does not explicitly make the point (Junctas ed., fo. 297 B-C: "Et dubitandum est in hoc & dicendum ex quo non ente fit generatio. non ens enim tripliciter dicitur. Si igitur fuerit in potentia: sed non ex qualibet potentia, sed alterum ex altero. Et non sufficit etiam, vt omnia sint insimul, nam sunt diuersa secundum materiam. & si non, qua de causa sunt infinita, non vnum intelligentia enim vna est? si autem materia fuerit vna, & illud erit in actu, cuius materia fuit in potentia."), but distinguishes three types of non-being. Averroes' comment on text 11 does introduce the notion of relation in this context under the technical term *habilitas* (Junctas ed., fo. 297 D–F: "Vult narrare, quod quamuis materia prima sit vna, tamen multa est in potentia, & habilitate, & quod quodlibet ens cum materia communi habet naturam propriam. & incoepit ponere quaestionem, quam dissoluit, & est quod ens non fit ex ente, sed ex non ente, & dicit &, si aliquis posuerit, quod generatio fit ex non ente, habet dubitare & dicere ex quo non ente fit generatio. Non ens enim dicitur tripliciter. Et intendit, quorum vnum est non ens simpliciter, quod non habet esse, neque imaginationem. Secundum est non esse, quod est in materia, scilicet priuatio formarum. Tertium est ens in potentia. Ens enim in potentia dicitur non ens, scilicet non ens in actu. Et, cum posuit haec tria, incoepit breuiter ponere intentionem,qua dissoluitur quaestio, & dicit. Si igitur fuerit in potentia, &c. idest & si quaestio dissoluitur, ponendo quod ens fit ex non ente in actu, & ente in potentia. non enim quodlibet ens fit ex qualibet potentia, sed vnumquodque entium fit ex eo quod est in potentia illud, quod fit, idest ex potentia propria, ita quod numerus potentiarum sit

sicut numerus specierum entium generabilium. Et dicit hoc, quia opinatur, quod prima materia est vnum secundum subiectum, & multa secundum habilitates. Primo enim habet habilitates ad recipiendum primas contrarietates, scilicet formas omnium quatuor elementorum. Secondo vero habet potentias consimilium partium mediantibus formis quotuor elementorum. & istae potentiae diuersantur secudum diuersitatem mixtionis quatuor elementorum, ita quod ex hoc diuersantur formae generabilium. . . ."), but does not explicitly make the claim alluded to. If, however, prime matter has no actual being in itself and yet certain relations are based upon it, these relations should have, at best, a very weak degree of being indeed; the reference could then be justified.

Physics: 216, 229

216: q. 3, a. 3, ad 3. The reference to text 53 ought to be corrected to text 54. *Physics* VIII, Summa Tertia, cap. 1, texts 54–60, 260a20–261a26 argues that there is a continuous motion, namely local motion; cap. 2, texts 61–63, 261a27–262a12, shows that motions other than local motion are not continuous. Aristotle's text 61, 261a27–31 (Junctas ed., fo. 400 C–D: "Apparet igitur ex hoc quod translatio est primus motuum. Quae autem translatio sit prima, declaratum erit nunc. & manifestabitur cum hoc per hanc eandem viam illud, quod posuimus positione in hoc loco, & prius, scilicet quoniam possibile est vt aliquis motus sit continuus, & aeternus.") argues tersely for the primacy of local motion; Averroes's comment is more expansive (Junctas ed., 400 D–F: "Declaratum est igitur ex omnibus istis demonstrationibus, quod translatio est primus motuum natura, & tempore. & ista propositio erat prius accepta pro vera, & declarauit ipsam hic. Et, quia translatio est duobus modis, recta, & circularis, & fuit declaratum quod motus aeternus est continuus, & accepit pro vero quod motus continuus est motus localis, ex quo declarauit quod motus localis est primus motuum secundum tempus, incoepit hoc declarare, & quaerere in quo motu inuenitur continuatio, per quid declarabitur quod translatio sit continua, & quae translatio in rei veritate et prima. Et ideo dicit Quae autem translatio, & c., & dicit hoc, quia, nondum est declaratum, nisi hoc, scilicet, quod translatio simpliciter est prior. Deinde dicit & manifestabitur cum hoc per hanc eandem viam, idest per hunc modum consyderandi. & intendit per prius,

illud quod dixit in Sexto, scilicet quod motus circularis solus potest esse aeternus: sed illic non compleuit perscrutationem de hoc. In initio vero tractatus istius, & ante hunc sermonem non solummodo declarauit possibile esse, vt sit hic motus continuus, sed declarauit quod necesse est vt sit hic motus continuus. Ex hoc ergo sermone, quem nititur declarare, apparent duo. Quorum vnum est illud, quod prius posuit. scilicet quod possibile est vt sit hic motus continuus, aeternus. Secundum autem est quis motus sit motus continuus, quem declaratum est esse aeternum necessario. & hoc declarabitur, quando declarabit quod motum impossibile est esse continuum.").

229: That "the first form that is received in matter is corporeity, from which <matter>is never denuded." Aristotle's text I *Phys.* text. 63, 190b5–10 is rather austere (Junctas ed. 37 K: "Et illa, quae generantur vniueraliter, generantur quaedam per transmutationem figurae, vt idolum ex cupro:& quaedam per additionem, vt illa, quae augmentantur: & quaedam per diminutionem, vt ex lapide humus: & quaedam per compositionem, vt domus: & quaedam per alterationem, vt illa, quae mutantur secundum materiam. manifestum est igitur quod generation secundum istos modos est ex subiectis."). Averroes, however, expands the discussion eightfold (Junctas ed., fo. 37L–38F: "Dicit: Et apparet per inductionem quod generatio indiget necessario subiecto, non solummodo in naturalibus, sed & in artificialibus. generatio enim aut est in qualitate, vt idolum ex cupro: aut in quantitate, vt augmentum, & diminutio: aut secundum compositionem, vt domus ex lateribus, & lapidibus: aut secundum transmutationem, quae est in ipsa substantia. & hoc intendebat, cum dixit: & quaedam per alterationem, vt illa, quae mutantur secundum materiam, idest quorum materia transmutatur & omnia ista videntur esse in subiecto: & necessarium est vt omne generatum sit ex subiecto, & in subiecto, & verificat hoc inductione. Et hae duae transmutationes, scilicet quae est in accidentibus rei, & quae est in substantia, conueniunt in hoc, quoniam sunt alteratio eiusdem rei de vna qualitate in aliam, & de vna dispositione in aliam. sed quia viderunt quod, quando res transmutatur in quibusdam istis dispositionibus, statim nomen, & definitio eius transmutabuntur, & in quibusdam non, vocauerunt primum modum transmutationem in substan-

tiam, & alterationem substantialem, vocaue-/runt istas dispositiones substantiales: secundam vero transmutationem, in qua neque nomen rei, nec eius definitio transmutatur, vocauerunt alterationem accidentalem. Et, cum consyderauerunt illud, quod defert vtramque transmutationem, inueniunt ipsum idem numero, & est corpus demonstratum. videmus enim idem corpus in eodem loco transferri de carneitate in terrestreitatem, & de terrestreitate in vegetabilitatem, & mutabitur nomen eius, & definitio: & videmus etiam ipsum transferri de albedine in nigredinem, sed non amittit nomen, & definitionem. & ex hoc scitur, quod corpus, quod est subiectum isti transmutationi, permanet in nomine, & definitione, & quod est eius dispositio substantialis, qua fit vnum numero. corpus autem, cuius nomen, & definitio mutantur per transmutationem dispositionum, non est vnum per dispositionem existentem in ipso, dantem ei nomen, & definitionem propriam. vnde necesse est vt istud subiectum sit vnum quia non habet formam dantem nomen, & definitionem vnam. Et est necesse etiam vt tres dimensiones, quae videntur inseparabiles ab ipso, & eaedem numero, quae dicuntur corpus, sint accidentia, & vnum, quia subiectum eorum non habet nomen, neque definitionem vnam numero. non enim est subiectum habens formam substantialem: quoniam, si essent de dispositionibus substantiae, non mutaretur nomen istius subiecti, neque eius definitio per mutationem alicuius dispositionis eius, & esset tota transmutatio in accidentibus. Et, cum ita sit, est igitur vnum subiectum numero, non habens dispositionem substantialem, sed habens naturam recipiendi istas dispositiones substantiales. est igitur in potentia ens omnes dispositiones substantiales, & accidentales, & haec dicitur prima materia, & prima hyle. Et manifestum est *quod ista materia non denudatur a corporeitate,* quoniam tunc haberet dispositionem substantialem, & haberet nomen, & definitionem." My italics.

"Et ex hoc patet quod qui ponit hance naturam esse corpus peccat: & similiter qui ponit illud, quod defert dimensiones, subiectum habe<n>s formam in actu, vt existimat Auicenna."

□**Avicenna.**

De anima 232: q. 5, a. 2, ad 6—*De anima,* Part V, cap. 3 shows (a) that the individuation of souls depends upon their bodies to start with: (ed. Van Riet 105.40–106.62: "Dicemus autem quod anima

humana non fuit prius existens per se et deinde venerit in corpus: animae enim humanae unum sunt in specie et definitione; si autem posuerimus quod prius habuerunt esse per se et non inceperunt cum corporibus, impossibile est tunc ut animae in ipso esse habeant multitudinem. Multitudo enim rerum/ aut est ex essentia et forma, aut est ex comparatione quae est ad materiam et originem multiplicatam ex locis quae circumdant unamquamque materiam secundum aliquid aut ex temporibus propriis uniuscuisque illarum quae accidunt illis accidentibus, aut ex causis dividentibus illam. Inter animas autem non est alteritas in essentia et forma: forma enim earum una est. Ergo non est alteritas nisi secundum receptibile suae essentiae cui comparatur essentia eius proprie, et hoc est corpus. Si autem anima esset tantum absque corpore, una anima non posset esse alia ab alia numero. Et hoc generaliter est in omnibus; ea enim quorum essentiae sunt intentiones tantum et sunt multa, quorum multiplicatae sunt species in suis singularibus, non est eorum multitudo nisi ex sustentibus tantum et receptibilibus et patientibus ex eis, aut ex aliqua comparatione ad illa aut ad tempora eorum. Cum enim nudae fuerint omnino, non different per id quod diximus; ergo impossibile est inter illas esse alteritatem et multitudinem. Ergo destructum est iam animas priusquam ingrederentur corpora fuisse multas essentialiter."—and (b) that this individuation does not end with death: (ed. Van Riet 109.96–110.01: "Dicemus ergo quod postea animae sine dubio habuerunt esse et essentiam/ per se, propter diversitatem materiarum quas habebant et propter diversitatem temporis suae creationis et propter diversitatem affectionum suarum quas habebant secundum diversa corpora sua quae habebant."

Metaphysica: 195, 195, 213, 222, 228, 229

195: q. 1, a. 1, sol.—*Metaphysics* VIII, chap. 1 shows that there is a First Principle of the being of the universe and some of Its properties. *Metaphysics* Treatise VIII, cap. 1 (ed. Van Riet 376.10–15): "Primum . . . incumbit nobis . . . ut ostendamus quod causae omnibus modis finitae sunt, et quod in unoquoque ordine earum est principium primum, et quod principium omnium illorum est unum, et quod est discretum ab omnibus quae sunt, ipsum solum ens necesse esse, et quod ab ipso est principium sui esse omnis quod est."

195: q. 1, a. 1, sol.— *Metaph.* II, chap. 1. I have not found in Avi-

cenna any explicit text to the effect that the name *ens* ('a being' or 'that which is') is derived from the act of *being* ('ab actu essendi') or that *mawjûd* is derived from *wujûd;* cf. A.–M. Goichon, *Lexique de la langue philosophique d'Ibn Sina (Avicenne)* §754, pp. 421–23 on *mawjûd* and §748, pp. 418–19 on *wujûd*. The closest texts I have seen are the passages Peter Lombard quotes from Augustine in ch. 21 of the *Sentences* saying: "Just as 'essence' is named from *being* (*esse*), so also do we say 'substance' from subsisting. . .'; and in ch. 27 "For just as wisdom was named from being wise, and knowledge was named from knowing, so too is essence named from 'esse'—*being* or *to be*.'

The closest text in Avicenna that I have been able to find answering to Aquinas's 'in everything that is, it is possible to consider its quiddity, through which it subsists in a determinate nature' is *Metaphysics* I, 5 (Van Riet ed., 34.50–35.64: "Dico ergo quod intentio entis et intentio rei imaginuntur in animabus duae intentiones; ens vero et aliquid sunt nomina multivoca unius intentionis nec dubitabis quin intentio istorum non sit iam impressa in anima legentis hunc librum. Sed res et quicquid aequipollet ei, significat etiam aliquid aliud in omnibus linguis; unaquaeque enim res habet certitudinem qua est id quod est, sicut triangulus habet certitudinem qua est tri-/angulus, et albedo habet certitudinem qua est albedo. Et hoc est quod fortasse appellamus esse proprium, nec intendimus per illud nisi intentionem esse affirmativi, quia verbum *ens* significat etiam multas intentiones, ex quibus est certitudo qua est unaquaeque res, et est sicut esse proprium rei." The Arabic original omits the *nisi*. Accordingly the Latin identifies and the Arabic separates *esse proprium* and *esse affirmativum*. In post-Thomistic Scholasticism the Avicennian expression *esse proprium* will be changed to *esse essentiae,* and *esse affirmativum* to *esse existentiae*. The Latin term *certitudo* renders the Arabic *haqîqah;* cf. Goichon, *Lexique* §171, pp. 82–84.

The text continues: "Redeamus igitur et dicamus quod, de his quae manifesta sunt, est hoc quod unaquaeque res habet certitudinem propriam quae est eius quidditas." The Latin term *quidditas* literally renders the Arabic *mâhîyyah;* cf. Goichon, *Lexique* §679, pp. 386–87. The term *mâhîyyah* names the answer to the Arabic question *'mâ huwa?'*—What is it? Likewise the Latin *quidditas* names

the principle answering to the question *'quid est?'* The English analogue would be the word 'whatness'.
213: q. 3, a. 2, sol.—*Metaphysics* Treatise VIII, cap. 4 (ed. Van Riet 401.33–34): "Item dico quod, quicquid habet quidditatem praeter anitatem, causatum est." For evidence to line up Avicenna's *quidditas* (Arabic 'mâhiyya') with Aquinas's *essentia* and Avicenna's *anitas* (Arabic, 'anniyya') with Aquinas's *esse,* see E. M. Macierowski, "Does God Have a Quiddity according to Avicenna?" in *The Thomist* 52 (1988) 79–87. See also Goichon, *Lexique* §27, pp. 9–12 on *anniyyah.*
222: q. 4, a. 2, <sol.>—The third, subtler argument is that of Avicenna <in his> *Metaphysics,* Treatise V, chap. 4 and Treatise IX, chap. 1. I have not found the like argument in either passage cited.

Aquinas himself, however, in the contemporary early *De ente et essentia,* cap. 4 offers a strikingly similar argument, without attribution (Roland-Gosselin ed., p. 34. 4–32, with my normalized spelling, punctuation and typographical emphasis: "Huiusmodi <simplices> autem substantiae, quamuis sint formae tantum sine materia, non tamen in eis est omnimoda simplicitas naturae ut sint actus purus, sed habent permixtionem potentiae, et hoc sic patet: Quicquid enim non est de intellectu essentiae uel quidditatis hoc est adueniens extra et faciens compositionem cum essentia, quia nulla essentia sine his quae sunt partes essentiae intelligi potest. *Omnis autem essentia uel quidditas potest intelligi sine hoc quod aliquid intelligatur de esse suo;* possum enim intelligere quid est homo uel phoenix et tamen ignorare an esse habeat in rerum natura. *Ergo patet quod esse est aliud ab essentia uel quidditate, nisi forte sit aliqua res cuius quidditas sit ipsum suum esse. Et haec res non potest esse nisi una et prima,* quia impossibile est quod fiat plurificatio alicuius nisi per additionem alicuius differentiae, sicut multiplicatur natura generis in species; uel per hoc quod forma recipitur in diuersis materiis, sicut multiplicatur natura speciei in diuersis indiuiduis; uel per hoc quod est unum absolutum et aliud in aliquo receptum, sicut si esset quidam calor separatus, esset aliud a calore non separato ex ipsa sua separatione. *Si autem ponatur aliqua res quae sit esse tantum ita ut ipsum esse sit subsistens,* hoc esse non recipiet additionem differentiae quia iam non esset

esse tantum sed esse et praeter hoc forma aliqua; et multo minus recipiet additionem materiae quia iam esset esse non subsistens sed materiale. Unde relinquitur quod talis res quae sit suum esse non potest esse nisi una. Unde oportet quod in qualibet alia re praeter eam aliud sit esse suum et aliud quidditas uel natura seu forma sua.").

Allowing for the fact that Avicenna uses the modal expression *necesse esse* rather than Aquinas's mere *esse,* we find a suggestive parallel passage in Avicenna's *Metaphysics* VIII, 4 (Van Riet ed., 399.00–400.19: "Dico igitur quod necesse esse non potest esse eiusmodi ut sit in eo compositio, ita ut sit hic quidditas aliqua quae sit necesse esse et illi quidditati sit intentio aliqua praeter certitudinem eius, quae intentio sit necessitas essendi; verbi gratia, si illa quidditas esset homo, tunc hominem esse aliud esset quam ipsum esse necesse esse, et tunc non/ posset esse quin hoc quod dicimus necessitas essendi, vel esset haec certitudo, vel non esset. Absurdum est autem ut huic intentioni non sit certitudo <. . .> quae sit praeter ipsam quidditatem, si autem illi necessitati essendi fuerit hoc ut pendeat ab illa quidditate et non est necesse esse sine illa, tunc intentio de necesse esse, inquantum est necesse esse, est necesse esse propter aliud quod non est ipsum. Igitur non erit necesse esse inquantum est necesse esse. Ipsum enim in se, inquantum est necesse esse, considerare esse necesse esse propter aliquid quod est ei propter quod est necesse esse, est absurdum, <. . .> si autem fuerit ut discrepet ab illa re, tunc illa quidditas non erit necesse esse ullo modo absolute nec accidet ei necessitas essendi absolute: ipsa enim non sit necesse esse aliquando, sed necesse esse absolute semper est necesse esse. Non est autem sic dispositio entis cum accipitur absolute sequens quidditatem, non ligatum cum necessitate pura." The ellipses in the angle brackets mark lacunae in the Arabic.).

Avicenna then considers and replies to an objection at *Metaphysics* VIII, 4 (Van Riet ed., 400.20–401.32: "Nec obest si quis dixerit quod illud ens causatum est quidditati hoc/ modo vel alii rei; possibile est enim ut ens sit causatum et necessitas absoluta quae est per essentiam non sit causata; restat ergo ut necesse esse per essentiam absolute certificatum, inquantum est necesse esse per se, sit necesse esse sine illa quidditate. Ad quod respondeo

quod tunc illa quidditas esset accidentalis ad necesse esse quod est certificatae existentiae per se, si illud esset possibile; igitur necesse esse esset designatum in intellectu in hoc, et esset certificatum necesse esse, quamvis non esset quidditas illa accidentalis. Illa igitur non est quidditas rei designatae in intellectu quae est necesse esse, sed est quidditas alterius rei sequentis eam; iam autem posita fuerat quidditas sua non alterius rei, et hoc est inconveniens. Igitur necesse esse non habet quidditatem nisi quod est necesse esse, et haec est *anitas*.") See the note to Avicenna on p. 213 for evidence that *anitas* is a term for being or *esse*.

The argument continues by showing that whatever has a quiddity other than being (*anitas*) is caused. *Metaphysics* VIII, 4 (Van Riet ed., 401.33–402.47: "Item dico quod, quicquid habet quidditatem praeter anitatem, causatum est. Tu autem iam nosti quod ex anitate et esse non constat quidditas quae est praeter anitatem ad modum quo aliquid constat ex constituente; erunt igitur de comitantibus; et tunc non potest esse quin vel comitentur quidditatem ex hoc quod est ipsa quidditas, vel comitentur eam propter aliquid aliud. Intentio autem de hoc quod dicimus *comitantur* est sequi esse et quod esse sequitur non esse. Si autem fuerit hoc quod anitas sequatur quidditatem et comitetur eam/ per se, tunc erit hoc quod anitas in suo esse sequetur esse; quicquid autem in suo esse sequitur esse, id post quod sequitur, habet esse per essentiam prius eo; igitur quidditas per essentiam erit prior suo esse, quod est inconveniens. Restat igitur ut esse sit ei ex causa. Igitur one habens quidditatem causatum est; et cetera alia, excepto necesse esse, habent quidditates quae sunt per se possibiles esse, quibus non accidit esse nisi extrinsecus."

The argument concludes that the First has no quiddity (Van Riet ed., 402.48) and therefore no genus (Van Riet ed., 402.61).

228: q. 5, a. 2, sol.—<*Metaphysics*> Treatise III, chap. 8 (Van Riet ed., 160.98–02: "Sensus enim nostrae dictionis quod ipsae <substantiae separatae> per se intelliguntur hic est scilicet quod ipsae intelligunt se, quamvis alia non intelligant eas, et etiam quia per se se sunt spoliatae a materia et ab eius appendiciis non quod ad intelligendum eas necesse sit animae eas exspoliare."). Avicenna seems also to suggest that there are degrees of immateriality corresponding to degrees of abstraction by various powers of the

soul in De anima, II, 2 (Van Riet ed., 114.50–115.62: "Loquamur nunc de virtutibus sensibilibus et apprehendentibus, sed loquamur de eis verba generalia, dicentes quia videtur quod apprehenere non sit nisi apprehendere formam apprehensi aliquo modorum; sed, si apprehendere est apprehendere rem materialem, tunc apprehendere est apprehendere formam alicuius abstractam a materia aliqua abstractione. Species autem abstractionis diversae sunt et gradus earum multum distantes. Formis etenim materialibus propter materiam accidunt dispositiones et alia quae non habent ex sua essentia ex hoc scilicet quod ipsae sunt formae. Ergo illarum abstractio a materia aliquando est abstractio non sine illis appendiciis/ vel aliquibus illarum, aliquando illa est perfecta abstractio quae abstrahit intellectam rem a materia et ab aliis appendiciis propter materiam.") Avicenna distinguished several such levels (Van Riet ed., 116.85: "visus"; 117.88: "imaginatio"; 118.6: "aestimatio"; and finally at 120.26–29: "Sed virtus in qua formae existentes non sunt materiales ullo modo nec accidit eis esse materiatas, nec sunt formae rerum materialium, sed denudatae ab omni colligatione cum materia, constat quia apprehendit formas apprehensione nuda a materia omni modo."). Earlier, Avicenna had identified the contemplative power with the power of being informed by a universal form denuded of matter: *De anima,* I, 2 (Van Riet ed., 94.15–95.19: "Sed virtus contemplativa est virtus quae solet informari a forma universali nuda a materia. Si autem fuerit nuda in se, apprehendere suam formam in se facilius erit; si autem non fuerit nuda, fiet tamen nuda quia ipsa denudabit eam, ita ut de omnibus affectionibus eius/ cum materia nihil remaeat in ea.")

229: q. 5, a. 2, sol.—The Thomistic terms *forma totius* and *forma partis* (which play a major role in Aquinas's contemporary opusculum *De ente et essentia,* chapter 2) do not occur explicitly in Avicenna.

In a chapter explaining the difference between genus and matter, Avicenna suggests that a whole can be predicated of a whole and explicitly stantes that a part cannot be predicated of a whole. Metaphysics V, 3 (Van Riet ed., 247.15–20: "Dicemus ergo quod corpus dicitur genus hominis et dicitur materia hominis. Cum autem fuerit materia hominis, sine dubio erit pars esse eius;

impossibile est autem ipsam partem praedicari de toto. Consideremus ergo quomodo est differentia inter corpus consideratum ut genus et ipsum consideratum ut materia, et hinc erit nobis via ad cognoscendum quod volumus patefacere."

Further, according to Avicenna, the distinction between quiddity (the whole) and form (the part) properly applies only to substances composed of form and matter, in contrast to simple substances. In composite substances the substantial form cannot be simply identified with the definition or quiddity of the whole composite: *Metaphysics* V, 5 (Van Riet ed., 274.57–276.82: "Quidditas autem omnis simplicis est ipsummet simplex: nihil enim est ibi receptibile suae quidditatis. Si enim ibi esse aliquid receptibile suae quidditatis, illud non esset quidditas recepta quae habetur in eo, immo ipsum receptum esset forma eius; forma autem eius non est idem quod/ adaequatur definitioni, sed nec composita sunt ex forma tantum id quod sunt. Definitio enim compositorum non est ex sola forma: definitio enim rei significat omne id ex quo constituitur eius essentia: unde continguit ut contineat materiam aliquo modo, et per hoc cognoscitur differentia inter quidditatem et formam. Forma enim semper est pars quidditatis in compositis; omnis vero simplicis forma est ipsum simplex, quoniam non est ibi complexio. Compositorum vero forma non est ipsa composita, nec est eorum quidditas ipsa composita; non est forma, ideo quia constat quod pars est eorum; quidditas vero est id quod est quicquid est, forma existente coniuncta materiae, quod quidem amplius est quam intentio formae; composito etiam non est haec intentio quia composita est ex forma et materia; haec enim est quidditas compositi et quidditas est haec compositio. Ergo forma est unum eorum quae conveniunt in hac compositione, quidditas vero est ipsa compositio complectens formam et materiam, unitas autem quae fit ex illis duobus est ad hoc unum. Et generi quidem ex hoc quod est genus est quidditas, et speciei ex hoc quod est species est quidditas, et singulari et particulari ex hoc quod est singulare et particulare est quidditas, cum accidentibus et comitantibus ex quibus constituitur. Cum igitur quidditas praedicatur de eo quod est genus, et de/ eo quod est species, et de eo quod est singulare individuum, fit hoc sola communione nominis, quoniam haec quidditas non est discreta ab eo quod per ipsam est

quicquid est, alioquin, non esset eius quidditas.").

In contrast to Avicenna, Aquinas here explicitly extends the scope of the term 'quiddity' so as to allow it to cover not merely composites of matter and form but also simple substances, if there are any.

□**Bernard.** 198: q. 1, a. 2, sol.—*Serm. IV super Cant.* in S. Bernardi Opera vol. I: Sermones super Cantica Canticorum 1–35, ad fidem codicum recensuerunt J. Leclercq, O.S.B., C. H. Talbot, H. M. Rochais, O. S. B. Romae: Editiones Cistercienses, 1957, p. 20. 2–18: "Sed enim et os habet Deus quo docet hominem scientiam, et manum habet qua dat escam omni carni, et pedes habet quorum terra scabellum est, ad quos nimirum peccatores terrae conversi atque humiliati satisfaciant. Haec, inquam, habet Deus omnia per effectum, non per naturam. Invenit profecto apud Deum et verecunda confessio, quo se humiliando deiciat, et prompta devotio, ubi se innovando reficiat, et iucunda contemplatio, ubi excedendo quiescat. Omnia omnibus est qui omnia administrat, nec quidquam est omnium proprie. Nam quod in se est LUCEM HABITAT INACCESSIBILEM, et PAX EIUS EXSUPERAT OMNEM SENSUM, ET SAPIENTIAE EIUS NON EST NUMERUS, ET MAGNITUDINIS EIUS NON EST FINIS, nec potest eum videre homo ut vivat. Non quod longe ab unoquoque sit qui esse omnium est, sine quo omnia nihil, sed, ut tu plus mireris, et nil eo praesentius, et nil incomprehensibilius. Quid nempe cuique rei praesentius quam esse suum? Quid cuique tamen incomprehensibilius quam esse omnium? Sane esse Deum omnium dixerim, non quia illa sunt quod est ille, sed quia EX IPSO ET PER IPSUM ET IN IPSO SUNT OMNIA. Esse est ergo omnium quae facta sunt, ipse factor eorum, sed causale, non materiale."

□**Boethius.**

Consolation of Philosophy 201, 203, 207

201: q. 2, a. 1, obj. 1—*De Consolatione Philosophiae,* V, prosa 6 (*CSEL* 67, 122.12–13): "Aeternitas igitur est interminablis vitae tota simul et perfecta possessio."

203: q. 2, a. 1, ad 6—ibid.

207: q. 2, a. 3, sol.—*De Consolatione Philosophiae,* V, prosa 2 (*CSEL* 67, 109.22–24): "Quare, quibus in ipsis inest ratio, inest etiam volendi nolendique libertas, sed hanc non in omnibus aequam esse constituo."

De Hebdomadibus: 218, 226, 235

218: q. 4, a. 1, obj. 2—*De hebdomadibus* (*PL* 64, 1311 C): "Omne quod est, participat eo quod est esse, ut sit; alio vero participat, ut aliquid sit."

219–20: a. 1, ad 2m—ibid.

226: q. 5, a. 1, obj. 2—ibid.

235: Exposition of the second part of the text—ibid.

De Trinitate: 213, 226, 228

213: q. 3, a. 3, obj. 3—*De Trinitate,* cap. 2 (*PL* 64, 1250 D): "Forma vero, quae est sine materia, non poterit esse subjectum, nec vero inesse materiae. . . ."

226: q. 5, a. 1, contra—ibid. *De Trinitate* I, chap. 2*, "In all that is this side of the First, <that>-which-is* and <that>-by-which-it-is* differ."

228: q. 5, a. 2, obj. 4—ibid., 1250 A–D.

□**Book of Causes.**

197: Prop. 20: "The first cause rules all things without being commingled with them." O. Bardenhewer, ed. *Die pseudo-aristotelische Schrift über das reine Gute, bekannt unter dem Namen Liber de Causis.* Freiburg im Breisgau: Herder, 1882, § 19: "Causa prima regit res creatas omnes praeter quod commisceatur cum eis." (Latin, pp. 181–82; Arabic and German, pp. 95–97).

199: Prop. 4: "The first of created things is *being.*" Bardenhewer, § 4: "Prima rerum creatarum est esse, et non est ante ipsum creatum aliud." (Latin, pp. 166–68; Arabic and German, pp. 65–69).

□**Commentator**: (see **Averroes** regarding Aristotle; see **Maximus** regarding Dionysius.)

□**Damascene**: (see John of Damascus).

□**Daniel** 204: q. 2, a. 2, obj. 2—Daniel 12, 3.

□**Dionysius.**

Caelestial Hierarchy 197, 198, 211

197: q. 1, a. 2, obj. 1—*De caelesti hierarchia,* cap. I, n. 1 (*PG* 3, 119–22): "*Omne datum bonum, et omne donum perfectum deursum est, descendens a Patre luminum* (James 1, 17): quin et omnis a Patre motae illustrationis emanatio, in nos benefice exundans, denuo ceu unifica vis, ad supera nos revocando simplificat, et convertit ad congregantis Patris unitatem, et ad deificam sim-/ plicita-

tem. Quoniam *ex ipso et in ipsum sunt omnia* (Romans 11, 36), ut sermo sacer ait."

198: q. 1, a. 2, ad 1—allusion to *De caelesti hierarchia,* Chap, IV, sect. 1 (*PG* 3, 177/178): "Primum omnium id dictu verum, superessentialem deitatem per bonitatem cunctas rerum essentias subsistere faciendo, in lucem produxisse." The first truth of all worth telling is that Superessential Deity (*hê hyperousios thearchia*) brought into being (*pros to einai parêgagen*) by rendering subsistent (*hypostêsasa*) all the essences of beings (*tas tôn ontôn ousias*).

211: q. 3, a. 1, ad 1: same text as 197.

Divine Names: 195, 197, 198, 199 (thrice), 200 (twice), 202, 207, 224

195: q. 1, a. 1, sol.—De divinis nominibus, cap. V, sect. 1 (*PG* 3, 815 B): "Siquidem nomen boni de Deo declarat omnes emanationes auctoris omnium, et porrigitur haec nominatio Dei a bono tum ad ea quae sunt, tum ad ea quae non sunt, estque supra ea quae sunt, et supra ea quae non sunt. Nomen autem entis ad omnia quae sunt extenditur, ac supra essentias ipsas eminet. Nomen vero vitae ad omnia viventia tenditur, et supra viventia est. Nominatio Dei a sapientia, porrigitur ad omnia quae intelligunt, quae ratiocinantur, quae sentiunt, et supra omnia ista est."

197: q. 1, a. 1 ad 4 "tenebra ignorantiae"—*De div. nom.,* cap. VII, sect. 3; *PG* 3, col. 870. *Myst. theol.,* capp. 1 & 2: *PG* 3, col. 998 ff with annotation. *Epist. V ad Doroth.; PG* 3, col. 1074.

199: q. 1, a. 3, contr.—(Three Times)

a. q. 1, a. 3, obj. 1—"Dionysius in the *Divine Names* treats the good <chap. IV> prior to the existent <chap. V>." There is also an implicit reference to Dionysius in obj. 2 'the good is more common than the being'—De div. nom., cap. V, sect. 1; *PG* 3, 815/ 816 Greek: "Siquidem nomen boni de Deo declarat omnes emanationes auctoris omnium, et porrigitur haec nominatio Dei a bono tum ad ea quae sunt <*eis ta onta*>, tum ad ea quae non sunt <*kai eis ta ouk onta ekteinetai*>, estque super ea quae sunt, et super ea quae non sunt. Nomen autem entis ad omnia quae sunt extenditur <*eis panta ta onta ekteinetai*>, ac super essentias ipsas eminet." Compare the more explicit gloss of Maximus* cited in obj. 2.

b. q. 1, a. 3, contr.—*De div. nom.*, cap. I, sect. 4; *PG* 3, col. 590–94: "Modo autem, ut valemus, ad divina capienda signis utimur, quibus scilicet ad simplicem et unicam illam intelligibilium spectaculorum veritatem pro captu nostro adducimur, et post omnem nostram rerum deiformium intelligentiam, sedantes nostras intellectiles operationes, in superessentialem istum radium, quantum fas est, intendimus, in quo cuncti fines omnium cognitionum ineffabili modo praeexstiterunt/ 594A quemque nec mente concipere, nec oratione proloqui valemus, neque visu quomodolibet intueri, eo quod sit omnibus exemptus, et eminenter ignotus <*hyperagnôston*>, ut qui simul omnes omnium cognitionum essentialium virtutumque terminationes superessentialiter in semetipso anticiparit, cunctis coelestibus intelligentiis eminentior incomprehensa virtute collocatus. Etenim cum notiones omnes sint entitatum, et ad entitates terminentur, is qui omni entitate sublimior est, omnem quoque effugit cognitionem <*hê pasês ousias epekeina kai pasês gnôseôs estin exêirêmenê*>."

c. *De div. nom.*, cap. V, sect. 6; *PG* 3, col. 819: "Primum igitur donum per se esse cum per se illa supraquam bonitas producat, merito ab antiquiore et prima omnium participationum laudatur <*Prôtên oun tên tou autoeinai dôrean hê autouperagathotês proballomenê, têi presbyterâi prôtêi tôn metochôn hymneitai*>; et est ex ipsa et in ipsa ipsum per se esse, et rerum principia, et omnia quaecunque sunt, et quae quomodocunque sunt; idque incomprehense, et copulate, et singulariter." (Reading *oun* for *hou* and *autoeinai* for *hauto einai* in the Greek text.)

200: q. 1, a. 3 ad 2 (Twice): "For Dionysius calls matter a non-being because of its associated privation; hence, too, in *On the Divine Names*, chap. IV, sect. 3, he says that a non-existent itself desires the good."

a. *De divinis nominibus* cap. IV, sect. 28; *PG* 3, col. 730 A: "Sed neque tritum illud: 'In materia malum, ut aiunt, quatenus materia est.' nam et ipsa pulchritudinis et ornatus formaeque fit particeps. Si autem seorsum ab his suapte natura materia qualitatem nullam speciemque obtinet <*Ei de toutôn ektos ousa hê hylê, kath' heautên apoios esti kai aneideos*>, quonam pacto materia quidquam agat, quae nec id ipsum a se habet ut pati possit?"

b. *De divinis nominibus* cap. IV, sect. 3, Migne, *Patrologia Graeca,* vol. 3, col. 698 A: "et, si dictu fas sit, illud ipsum quod non est *<auto mê on>*, illius quod supra res omnes est, doni desiderio tenetur, quin etiam in bono vere supersubstantiali per omnium ablationem esse contendit." The notion of 'removal' (*ablatio*) is expressed by the Greek term *aphairesis,* which is also Aristotle's regular term for 'abstraction'. Etymologically, it suggests 'taking away' or 'subtraction'; against this background, Aquinas's notion of *separatio* as a negative judgment that one thing is not another can reasonably be called an abstraction, albeit by way of the second act of the intellect (judgment) rather than by the first (conceptualization).

202: q. 2 a. 1 ad 1: *De divinis nominibus,* cap. VII, sect. 3 (*PG* 3, 885/886 C): "negationes vero etiam in nobis ponentur, quoniam supra omnia ista Deus est; et non potest ex his a nobis intelligi." Negations (*hai apophaseis*) will be set up (*tachthêsontai*) for us (*eph' hêmin*), since God is above all that we can sense or understand and cannot be understood by us.

207: q. 2, a. 3, sol.: *De divinis nominibus,* cap. V, sect. 4 (*PG* 3, 818 C–D): "Qui est . . . . <e>st ea quae sunt, in iis quae sunt, et quae quocunque modo existunt, et quae per se existunt. Deus enim non quovis modo est <e>ns, sed simpliciter et infinite totum esse in se pariter complexus et anticipans; quamobrem etiam Rex saeculorum nominatur, ut in quo et penes quem cujuslibet esse et sit et constet, et in quo nec erat, neque erit, neque factum est, neque fit, neque fiet, imo nec est; sed ipse est esse rebus; et non tantum ea quae sunt, sed ipsum esse rerum, ex praeaeterno ente; ipse enim est aevum aevorum, existencs ante omne aevum."

224 (q. 4, a. 3, sol.): *On the Divine Names* cap. VII, sect. 3 (*PG* 3, 870 C–871 A): "An non potius vere dicatur, quod Deum non cognoscimus ex natura ejus (id enim quod natura ejus est incognitum est, et omnem rationem ac mentem superat) sed ex ordine omnium rerum, tanquam ab ipso proposito, et imagines quasdam ac similitudines exem-/ plarium ejus divinorum in se habente, ad cognoscendum illud summum bonum et omnium bonorum finem, via et ordine pro viribus ascendimus in ablatione et in superlationes omnium, et in omnium causa." The

last phrase might be rendered "within the removal and overcoming of all things, and within the cause of them all." Removal is expressed by the Greek *aphairesis,* and overcoming or excess by *hyperochê.*

□**Exodus.** 194: q. 1, a. 1, contra—Exodus 3,14.

□**Gregory the Great.** 208, 209, 214

208: q. 2, a. 3 ad 4—*Moralia,* XXIX, c. 1 (Migne, *Patrologia Latina,* vol. 76, col. 477B commenting on Job 38, 12): "Dominus Deus Iesus, in eo quod virtus et sapientia Dei est, de Patre ante tempora natus est, vel potius, quia nec coepit nasci nec desiit, dicamus verius 'semper natus'. Non autem possumus dicere 'semper nascitur,' ne imperfectum esse videatur. At vero, ut aeternus designari valeat et perfectus, et semper dicamus et natus, quatenus et 'natus' ad perfectionem perineat et 'semper' ad aeternitatem; quamvis per hoc ipsum quod 'perfectum' dicimus, multum ab illius veritatis expressione deviamus, quia quod factum non est, nec potest dici proprie perfectum." This passage is quoted by Master* Peter Lombard at Liber I, Distinctio IX, Capitulum IV in the 1971 Grottaferrata edition, p. 106. 6–14.

209: Exposition of the first part of the text—the *Moralia,* Book XVI, chap. 37 (PL 76, col. 1143) This text is not quoted by Lombard in Distinction 8 (Chapters 21–28) of the *Sentences.*

214: q. 3, a. 2, sol.: ibid.

□**Hilary.** 209, 236: VII lib. *De Trinit.,* § 11, col 208; t. II

209: An allusion to Lombard 188 (see 3.21)

236: An allusion to Lombard 192

□**James** 211: James 1, 17

□**Jerome** (see 3.21).

□**John of Damascus.**

De Fide Orthodoxa: 194 (thrice), 195, 213, 214, 225

194: q. 1, a. 1, obj. 2—A word as messenger or angel of the intellect: *De fide orthodoxa* I, 13 (*PG* 94, 858A/ 857 Greek: "*Verbi ac sermonis acceptationes variae.*—Verbum est, quod cum Patre substantialiter semper est. Rursus verbum est naturalis mentis agitatio, qua movetur, et intelligit, et cogitat; veluti lux ipsius et splendor exsistens. Est praeterea verbum intimum, quod in corde tantum eloquimur. Est denique verbum intelligentiae nuntius <*angelos noêmatos*>, quod sci-

licet ore profertur. Deus itaque Verbum substantivum est et subsistens: tria vero reliqua animi sunt facultates, nec considerantur in propria subsistentia. Quorum primum, naturlais est mentis fetus, naturaliter ex ipsa semper ut ex fonte manans: secundum, internum dicitur: tertium, prolatitium.").

194: q. 1, a. 1, obj. 4—That "He Who is" signifies an infinite sea of substance: *De fide orthodoxa* I, 9 (PG *94*, 835). See next note.

194: q. 1, a. 1, contra—On the special propriety of being as a name of God: *De fide orthodoxa* I, 9 (*PG* 94, 835 A–B, my transliteration of the Greek 836 A: "Ex omnibus porro nominibus quae Deo tribuntur, nullum aeque proprium videtur, atque *ho ôn* (id est, *Qui est*): quemadmodum ipsemet cum Moysi in monte responderet, ait: *Dic Filiis Israel: Qui est, misit me.*). Nam totum esse, velut immensum quoddam ac nullis terminis definitum essentiae pelagus complexu suo ipse continet: ut autem Dionysio placet, primarium ipsius nomen est; prius esse, tum bonum esse." The scriptural dictum *'Say to the sons of Israel, He Who IS sent me'* is from Exodus 5, 14. Migne cites Gregory Nazianzen, *Oratio* 36 on the sentence "For He Himself contains all being <*holon . . . to einai*> grasping it within Himself like a boundless and infinite sea of entity <*hoion ti pelagos ousias apeiron kai ahoriston*>." Migne also calls attention to Dionysius, *Divine Names,* chapters 2, 3, and 4.

195: q. 1, a. 1, sol.—ibid.

213: q. 3, a. 2, contra 2—on vertibility: *De fide orthodoxa* I, 3 (*PG* 94, 795 A–C Latin/796 Greek: First proof that there is a god, based on the mutability of things. "Omnia quae sunt, aut creata sunt aut increata. Si creata, utique et mutabilia < *treptá* > sunt. Quorum enim esse a mutatione incepit, ea mutationi quoque subsint necesse est, sive intereant, sive per voluntatis actus alia atque alia fiant. Sin autem increata, sequitur profecto ut et mutari omnino nequeant. Quorum enim esse contrarium est, horum etiam modus quo sunt, proprietatesve contrariae sunt. Ecquis ergo hoc nobis non assentiatur, omnia quae sunt mutabilia esse, nec ea tantum quae sub sensum nostrum cadunt, sed et angleos mutari, alios ex aliis fieri, multiplici modo moveri, ac transmutari: sic nimirum, ut intelligibilia, angelos dico, animas, et daemones, ratione voluntatis, sive progredientis in bono, sive rursus ab eo recedentis, seque vel intendentis, vel remittentis; reliqua vero secundum generationem et corruptionem, aug-

mentum et decrementum, aut secundum qualitatem, et secundum motum de loco in locum immutentur? Cum ergo mutabilia sint, sane etiam creata esse oportet. Si vero creata, haud dubium quin ab aliquo opifice sint condita. Atqui creatorem increatum esse necessem est. Nam si ipse quoque creatus est, a quodam profecto creatus erit, sicque donec ad aliquod increatum venerimus. Increatus igitur cum sit ille conditor, omnino nec mutabilis est. Hoc autem quid aliud, nisi Deus fuerit?" The Greek term *treptá,* from the Greek verb *trepô* 'turn' and here rendered as *'mutabilia'*, is more literally translated *'vertibilia'*, i.e., 'able to be turned' from the Latin verb *verto.*).

Neither the last text nor the second argument for God's existence (based on the conservation and governance of things) literally says "All that is from nothing can be turned back into nothing; for whatever began from a mutation is necessarily subject to mutation." If dissolution be taken as equivalent to annihilation, the reference holds true. *De fide orthodoxa* I, 3 (*PG* 94, 795 C–D Latin/796 Greek: "Porro ipsa quoque rerum creatarum compages, conservatio, atque gubernatio, nos docent Deum esse, qui universum hoc coagmentarit, sustentet, et conservet, eique provideat. Qui enim fieri potuisset, ut inter se pugnantes naturae, ignis, inquam, et aquae, aeris et terrae, ad unius mundi constitutionem coirent, tenacique adeo nexu cohaerent, ut nulla ratione solvi possint; nisi omnipoterns vis aliqua ea compaginasset, ac perpetuo a dissolutione servaret <*kai aei têrei adialyta*>."). That such an identification is plausible may be gathered from *De fide orthodoxa* I, 12 (*PG* 94, 843 C–D: Addam etiam, eorum qui ab ipso facti sunt, Pater. Etenim, si proprie loquamur, Deus Pater noster verius est, qui ex nihilo nos produxerit <*ho ek mê ontôn eis to einai paragagôn*>, quam qui nos genuerunt <*hoi gennêsantes*>. . . ."), where the Greek text speaks of God's producing us 'out of non-beings' and the Latin 'out of nothing' in contrast to the natural generation involved in fathers 'begetting' their children.

214: q. 3, a. 2, sol.—ibid.

225: q. 4, a. 3, ad 2—The closest text that I have found does not explicitly address qualitative or quantitative features applied to God, but anything expressed 'in a bodily manner': *De fide orthodoxa* I, 11 ad finem (*PG* 94, 843 B: "Denique, ut uno verbo dicam, in iis omnibus quae de Deo corporeo modo enuntiantur, abstrusus quidam sensus inest, quo per illa quae nobis congruunt, ea quae supra nos

sunt edocemur: nisi forte quidpiam de corporeo Dei adventu dictum est. Nam ipse totum hominem salutis nostrae causa suscepit; hoc est animam intelligentem, et corpus, atque humane naturae proprietates, necnon naturales, nullique reprehensioni obnoxias passiones."). Then the following chapter continues, I, 12 (*PG* 94, 843 C: "Enimvero haec ex acris, ut divinus ait Dionysius <Div. nom, cap. 1>, coemur oraculis; quod nempe Deus omnium causa ac origo sit; eorum quae sunt, essentia; viventium, vita; rationalium ratio; intelligentium, intellectus; ac eorum quidem qui ab eo labuntur, revocatio et erectio; eorum autem quid id quod naturae consentaneum est, corrumpunt et vitiant, renovatio et instauratio; eorum qui profanis quibusdam fluctibus jactantur, sacra stabilitas; stantium tutum praesidium; assurgentium ad ipsum via et manuductio, qua in altum subvehuntur." The text then continues as given at the end of the note to p. 213.

☐**Liber de Causis**: (see *Book of Causes).

☐**Malachi** (3, 6).

☐**Master**, The: (see **Peter Lombard**).

208 (Exposition): An honorific title. When used without a name, it often refers to the principal authority in the field. Thus, in canon law, "Magister" refers to Gratian; here, in theology, it refers to Peter Lombard, the "Magister Sententiarum" (b. ca. 1095–1100 at Lumellogno in Italy; d. 20 July 1160 as bishop of Paris). For his life, see Grottaferrata 1971 ed., Tomus I, Pars 1, pp. 8*–45*; for a discussion of the *Sentences* proper, see pp. 117* ff.

☐**Matthew** (25, 41)

☐**Maximus of Chrysopolis** (580–662 AD), the Commentator on Dionysius: 199 (q. 1, a. 3, obj. 2), remarking on *De Div. Nom.* cap. V (*PG* 4, 309 A–B Greek/ 310 Latin A: "Quomodo Deus dicitur bonus. Vide autem quomodo dicit *bonum* seu divinum eius nomen extendi ad omnia quae sunt et quae non sunt, atque supra ea quae non sunt esse; *unum* vero esse supra ea quae sunt, ipsumque ulterius protendi: *vitam* autem superare omnia quae vivunt, et *sapientiam* supra omnia quae intelligunt, et quae ratione et quae sensu utuntur extendi, ita ut manifestum sit quod *bonum,* id est Deus, sit causa et ejus quod est, et vitae et sapientiae; illud autem quod est, vitae et sapientiae causam, intellige ad res accommodate." Latin B: "Atque ad ea quae non sunt extenditur bonum <*kai eis ta ouk onta ekteinetai to agathon*>, tanquam ipsa ut sint vocans

<*hôs eis to einai kaloun auta*>, aut juxta illud, quod Pater alibi dixit, quaia etiam id quod non exsistit est bonum, cum in Deo propter essentiae excessum consideratur. *Onta* vero vocat ea quae non sunt materialia, sicut saepe superius declaravimus; aut sic, quoniam Deus loco non circumscribitur, merito ait eum etiam supra ea quae non sunt esse, ut ostendat illum minime circumscribi posse.")

Here "the good extends even into the non-beings, as though calling <*kaloun*> them into *being*.") There is, in Greek, no etymological connection between the good (*to agathon*) and the verb to call (*kaleô*) whose present participle (*kaloun*) figures in Maximus's observation; a more plausible verbal connection could be made between the beautiful (*to kalon*) and that which calls (*to kaloun*) for our attention. Accordingly, Maximus is making a substantive point, not a mere pun.

□**Moses Maimonides.** Guide of the Perplexed: 194.

Rabi Mossei Aegyptii. *Dux seu Director dubitantium aut perplexorum.* Ed. Augustinus Justinianus, O.P. Parisiis 1520; rpt. Frankfurt am Main: Minerva, 1964. This Latin edition of Justinianus, not the more literal translation of Johannes Buxtorf the Younger (Basel 1629), is based on the medieval textual tradition according to J. Perles*. Liber I, capitulum LXII: De hoc nomine Sum qui sum (fol. 25v–26r): "Remittam tibi quoddam stramentum: & dicam quod quia dixit Moyses, Dicent ad me quid est nomen eius: quid respondebo eis: ideo fuit ipsa ratio conueniens illi quaestioni: vt quaereret quae esset responsio quam diceret eis. Quid autem dixit: ecce non credent & non audient vocem meam: quia dicent: Non apparuit tibi dominus. hoc manifestum est: quia sic debet dici omni qui se iactuauerit prophetam, donec adducat signa et portenta propter quae credatur ei. Si autem res se habet sicut apparet. quod illud nomen simplex sit & loquantur in eo sicut consuetum est loqui in quocumque alio nomine, necesse erit alterum de duobus contingere, scilicet quod vel Israelitae sciebant hoc nomen vel nunquam audierant illud. Si sciebant illud, non suberat ratio ad narrandum illis: quia scientia ipsius erat sicut & ipsorum. Si vero nunquam audierant illud: quae erit probatio, quod illud est nomen Creatoris, si fuerit scientia nominis sui probatio? Postquam autem Creator fecit ipsum scire hoc nomen, dixit ei, Vade & congregabis seniores Israel. Et dixit ei, audient vocem tuam. & postea dixit ei Moyses. Ecce non credent, nec audient vocem meam. Et postea dixit ei. Quid habes in manu tua? Et respondit virgam. Quod autem scire

debes & deteget tibi omnia occulta est quid dicam tibi. Iam scis opinionem gentis & aliorum quae fuit temporibus antiquis. quoniam omnes idolis seruiebant paucis exceptis: hoc est credebant in virtute stellarum, & faciebant opera: vel opera coelorum & imagines cuilibet stellae. In temporibus autem illis, omnis considerator asserebat alterum de duobus: vel dicebat quod consideratio sua & intellectus ostendebat ei quod vniuersus mundus habebat Creatorem: sicut Abraham. vel dicebat quod transierat per ipsum spiritus stellae, vel angelus, vel istis similia. Ante tempus autem Moysis non fuit scitum quod aliqus disceret se prophetam, & quod Dominus locutus fuisset cum eo: & quod misisset eum. Nec inducat te in errorem quid legitur de Patriarchis: quia Dominus loquebatur cum eis: & ostendebat se ipsis: quia non inuenies in illis modum prophetiae Moysi, scilicet vt aliquis institueret homines: vel quod redderet eos cautos: vel quod Abraham, vel Isaac, vel Iacob, vel alius qui praecessisset eos dixerit hominibus. Dominus dixit mihi facite hoc: vel non faciatis istud: vel misit me ad vos. Istud nunquam accidit ante: sed loquebatur cum eis in his quae ipsis erant necessaria, scilicet in sua perfectione & ostensione eorum quae facere debebant, & in promittendo ad quid perueniret finis generationis ipsorum. Ipsi vero reddebant homines cautos per viam considerationis & disciplinae sicut notum est apud nos, scriptura testante quae dicit animabus quas fecerunt in Pharaonem. Quando vero Dominus apparuit Moysi: et praecepit vt conuocaret homines: & quod diceret eis nuncium suum, dixit: quid primo quaerent a me, erit vt ostendam eis vere quod Creator est in mundo. Et postea dicam eis: quia ipse me misit. tunc etenim omnes homines paucis exceptis ignorabant Creatorem esse: & finis considerationis ipsorum non transcendebat coelum, vel opera ipsius, vel potentiam: quia non recesserunt a sensu nec fuerunt perfecti perfectione intellectus. Et idcirco ostendi ei Creator tunc scientiam quam faceret eos intelligere: per quam firmaretur eis essentia Creatoris: & hoc quid dixit Sum qui sum. Sum vero est verbum substantiuum: cuius expositio est essentia: quia verbum sui significat praeterisse: nec refert si dixerit fuit vel fuit ens in lingua hebraea. Secretum autem est in repetitione verbi quid significat super essentiam in modo agnominationis: quia verbum quid dicit quid inducit rememorationem agnominationis quae coniungitur ei quid hoc nomen, est imperfectum & eget perfectione rationis. Et idcirco posuerunt ver-

bum primum: & illud est agnominatum sum: & verbum secundum quid est agnominator sum & ipsum est per se: & est ac diceres quod agnominatum est ipsamet agnominatio: & eius expositio est: quia est non in essentia, et hoc est deputatio ipsius rationis: scilicet ens qui est ens: ac si diceret necesse esse. Hoc autem est sicut ostendemus probatione. Cum autem Creator fecit scire probationes per quas astrueretur essentia sua apud sapientes illorum, postea dixit ei. Vade & congregabis seniores Israel. & promisit quod intelligerent quod diceret eis & reciperent illum. & hoc est quod dixit, audient vocem tuam. Conuersus autem Moyses dixit ad eum. Ecce non credent mihi: quia Deus est propter/xxvi/ ista signa intelligibilia quae erunt probatio mea quod ipse Deus misit me ad eos: & idcirco dedit ei probationem. Iam autem patet quod huius dicti quid est nomen eius, non est sua ratio: quis est de quo dicis quod misit te: Sed eius expositio est sublimitas & honor dicti: hoc est dicere quod non est qui ignorat quod tua substantia & veritas sint inuenta. Si quaesierint a me de nomine tuo quam rationem de rationibus dicam quid significat hoc nomen? quia remotum erat ab ipso vt diceret quod aliquis erat ibi qui ignoraret hunc entem: & posuit ignorantiam ipsorum in secreto nominis, non eius quid nominatur per ipsum. Similiter nomen duarum literarum quid est sumptum a nomine quatuor literarum, est de ratione firmitudinis essentiae: & saday est decisuma day: quid est sufficientia & sin quid est, scilicet & ponitur pro qui: et ratio saday hoc est qui sufficit hoc est qui non eget essentia alicuius entis, nec eget alio extra se ad firmitatem essentiae suae, sed sua essentia sufficit sibi: & omnia nomina sunt istius modo. Nullum autem nomen conuenit Creatori, quid non sit sumptum ab opere vel dictum in participatione praeter nomen quatuor literarum quid scibitur & non legitur: quid est nomen separatum: quia non significat agnominationem sed super essentia simplici tantummodo de communi conditione essentiae praedictae est: quia debet esse in sempiternum permanens hoc est necesse esse: & nunc intellige finem verbi."

Paul: 189

Peter Lombard. 215,

□**Philosopher**, The: (see **Aristotle** and also the **Book of Causes**): q. 1, a. 2, contra. The Scholastic nickname for Aristotle. It should be noted, however, that Aristotle did not write the *Book of Causes,* which con-

sists largely of quotations from Proclus's *Elementatio Theologica*.

□**Plato.** *Parmenides:* 212. I have found no explicit reference; cf. Averroes* note to p. 212.

□**Proverbs** (16, 4): 235—Exposition of the second part of the text.

□**Psalms** 204, 213

204: q. 2, a. 2, obj. 3—Psalm 75, 5.

213: q. 3, a. 2, contr.—Psalm 101, 28.

□**Wisdom** 210: q. 3, a. 1, obj. 1—Wisdom 7, 24.

3.23 A Bibliography of Ancient and Medieval Sources Cited in sections 3.21 and 3.22

Sigla and Abbreviations

< >	Angle brackets are used to mark proposed additions to the original text.
[ ]	Square brackets are used to mark proposed deletions from the original text.
CCL	*Corpus Christianorum, Series Latina.*
CSEL	Corpus *Scriptorum Ecclesiasticorum Latinorum.* Vienna.
DTC	*Dictionnaire de théologie catholique,* ed. Vacant-Mangenot-Amann. Paris: Letouzey et Ané, 1903– .
PG	*Patrologia Graeca,* ed. Migne. Patrologiae cursus completus, Series Graeca, with Latin trans., 162 vols. Paris 1844–1866.
PL	*Patrologia Latina,* ed. Migne. Patrologiae cursus completus, Series Latina, 221 vols. Paris 1844–1864.

Aristotle. *Opera graece ex recensione I. Bekkeri.* Ed. Academia Regia Borussica. 5 vols. Berlin: 1831–1870. Ever since the publication of this work it has been scholarly standard practice to cite the works of Aristotle according to the page, column ('a' for left, 'b' for right), and lines of Bekker's edition. In the Middle Ages and Renaissance, citation was by Book and the Text of the Commentator Averroes*.

———. *The Works of Aristotle.* Ed. W. D. Ross. 12 vols. London: Oxford University Press, 1908–1952.

Augustine. *Confessiones.* Ed. M. Skutella (1934), ed. corr. H. Jürgens and W. Schaub. Stuttgart: B. G. Teubner, 1981.—Ed. L. Verheijen. *CCL* 27. Turnhout: Brepols, 1981.

———. *Contra Maximinum. PL* 42: 709–814.

———. *De civitate Dei*, Ed. B. Bombart and A. Kalb. *CCL* 47–48. Turnhout: Brepols, 1955. —Ed. E. Hoffmann. *CSEL* 40. Partes I et II. Vienna: Tempsky: 1898–1900.

———. *De fide et symbolo*. Ed. J. Zycha. *CSEL* 41: 1–32. Vienna: F. Tempsky, 1900.

———. *De Trinitate*. Ed. W. J. Mountain. *CCL* 50 & 50 A. Turnhout: Brepols, 1968.

———. *Super Joannem*, Tract. 99, nn. 4–5 (*PL* 35, 1887f.; *CCL* 36, 584f.).

———. *De Genesi ad litteram* (imperfectus liber). Ed. J. Zycha. *CSEL* 28–I. Vienna: Tempsky, 1894.

Averroes. *Aristotelis opera cum Averrois commentariis*. Venice: Junctas, 1562–1574. 11 vols. Rpt.: Frankfurt: Minerva, 1962.

———. *Commentarium magnum in Aristotelis de Anima libros*. Ed. F. S. Crawford. Corpus Commentariorum Averrois in Aristotelem, Versionum Latinarum Volumen VI, 1. Cambridge, MA: The Mediaeval Academy of America, 1953.

———. *In Aristotelis librum II (Alpha elatton) Metaphysicorum Commentarius: Die lateinische Übersetzung des Mittelalters auf handschriftlicher Grundlage mit Einleitung und problemgeschichtlicher Studie*, ed. Gion Darms. Thomistische Studien XI. Freiburg (Switzerland): Paulusverlag, 1966.

———. *Averrois In Librum V (Delta) Metaphysicorum Aristotelis Commentarius: Edizione condotta su manoscritti scelti con introduzione, note ed uno studio storico-filosofico*, ed. Ruggero Ponzalli. Bern (Switzerland): Edizioni Francke, 1971.

———. *Das neunte Buch (Theta) des lateinischen grossesn Metaphysik-Kommentars von Averroes: Text-Edition und Vergleich mit Albert dem Großen und Thomas von Aquin*, ed. Bernhard Bürke. Bern (Switzerland): Francke Verlag, 1969.

Avicenna. *Liber de anima seu sextus de naturalibus*. Ed. S. Van Riet. 2 vols. Louvain-Leiden: E. J. Brill, I–III 1972; IV–V 1968.

———. *Liber de philosophia prima sive scientia divina*. Ed. S. Van Riet. 3 vols. Louvain-Leiden: E. J. Brill, I–IV 1977; V–X 1980; I–X Lexiques 1983.

———. *Opera*. Venice, 1508. Rpt. Frankfort: Minerva, 1962.

Bernard of Clairvaux. *Sermones super Cantica Canticorum*. Ed. J. Leclercq, C. H. Talbot, and H. M. Rochais. S. Bernardi *Opera*. Rome: Editiones Cistercienses, 1957– . Volumes 1 and 2 contain the 86 Sermons on the Song of Songs, left incomplete at Bernard's death in 1153. The

task was later taken up by John, Abbot of Ford, and Gilbert of Hoyland, Abbot of Swineshead.

———. *On the Song of Songs*. Trans. Kiliam Walso, O.C.S.O. and Irene Edmonds. 4 vols. Cistercian Fathers Series, nn. 4, 7, 31, 40. Kalamazoo, MI: Cistercian Publications, 1971–1980.

Boethius. *The Theological Tractates and the Consolation of Philosophy*. Ed. and trans. H. F. Stewart, E. K. Rand and S. J. Tester. The Loeb Classical Library. Cambridge, MA: Harvard University Press, 1973.

———. Also in N. M. Häring, *The Commentaries on Boethius by Gilbert of Poitiers*. Toronto: Pontifical Institute of Mediaeval Studies, 1966.

———. *Opera*. *PL*: 63–64.

Book of Causes:

Bardenhewer, O., ed. *Die pseudo-aristotelische Schrift über das reine Gute, bekannt unter dem Namen Liber de Causis*. Freiburg im Breisgau: Herder, 1882. prop. 20

Dionysisus the pseudo-Areopagite. *Opera*. *PG*: 3–4.

Glossa ordinaria. Biblia sacra cum glossa ordinaria ... et postilla Nicolai Lyrani. Paris, 1590. (Not seen.)

Gregory the Great. *Moralia in Job*. Ed. M. Adriaen. *CCL* 143AB. Turnhout: Brepols, 1979–1985. *Opera*. PL: 75–79.

Hilary of Poitiers. *De Trinitate*. Ed. P. Smulders. *CCL* 62–62A. Turnhout: Brepols, 1979–1980.

Jerome. *Epistolae*. Ed. I. Hilberg. *CSEL* 54 and 56. Vienna: Tempsky, 1910–1918.

John of Damascus. *PG* 94–96. *De fide orthodoxa*, PG 94: 782–1228.

Liber de Causis. See *Book of Causes*.

Maimonides. *The Guide of the Perplexed*. Trans. Shlomo Pines. Introd. essay by Leo Strauss. Chicago: University of Chicago Press, 1963.

———. Rabi Mossei Aegyptii. *Dux seu Director dubitantium aut perplexorum*. Ed. Augustinus Justinianus, O.P. Parisiis 1520; rpt. Frankfurt am Main: Minerva, 1964.

Maximus, Saint <of Chrysopolis>. *Commentaria in Sancti Dionysii Areopagitae Opera*. PG 4.

Peter Lombard. Magistri Petri Lombardi, Pariensis Episcopi, *Sententiae in IV Libris Distinctae*. Editio tertia. Spicilegium Bonaventurianum IV. Grottaferrata (Romae): Editiones Collegii S. Bonaventurae ad Claras Aquas, Tom. I, Pars I: Prolegomena, 1971; Tom. I, Pars II: Liber I et II, 1971; Tom. II: Liber III et IV, 1981.

3.3 Select Modern Works on Being, God, and Thomism; Other Works Mentioned Incidentally.

Adler, Mortimer J. *Ten Philosophical Mistakes.* New York: Collier Books, 1985.

———. and Charles Van Doren. *How to Read a Book,* 2d ed. New York: Simon & Schuster, 1972; orig. ed., 1940.

Aertsen, Jan A. "Aquinas's philosophy in its historical setting," pp. 12–37 in *The Cambridge Companion to Aquinas,* edd. Norman Kretzman and Eleonore Stump. Cambridge: University Press, 1993.

Alvira, Tomás, Luis Clavell, and Tomás Melendo. *Metafísica.* Pamplona: Editorial de Universidad de Navarra (EUNSA), 1986.

Anawati, Georges C. "Saint Thomas d'Aquin et la *Métaphysique* d'Avicenne," vol. 1, pp. 449–65 in Maurer (ed.) *St. Thomas Aquinas 1274–1974: Commemorative Studies,* 2 vols. Toronto: Pontifical Institute of Mediaeval Studies, 1974.

Arnou, R. "Platonisme des Pères." *DTC,* XII, 2258–2392.

Bourke, Vernon J. *Aquinas' Search for Wisdom.* Milwaukee, WI: Marquette University Press, 1965.

Burns, Robert M. "The Divine Simplicity in St. Thomas." *Religious Studies* 25 (1989) 271–93. This revisionist article offers to correct Aquinas in the light of Friederich Schelling; the author seems to be unaware of Fabro's critique of Schelling in *God in Exile* (see below).

Burrell, David B. *Knowing the Unknowable God: Ibn-Sina, Maimonides, Aquinas.* Notre Dame, IN: University of Notre Dame Press, 1986.

Chenu, M.-D. *Toward Understanding Saint Thomas,* translated and revised by A.-M. Landry and D. Hughes. Chicago: Henry Regnery, 1964.

Chossat, M. "Dieu I. (Connaissance naturelle de)." *DTC,* IV, 756–874.

———. "Dieu II. (Son existence)." *DTC,* IV, 874–948.

———. "Dieu V. (Sa nature selon les scolastiques)." *DTC,* IV, 1152–1243. See also Mangenot, Le Bachelet, and Moisant for the other contributions to this massive, seven-part article.

Clark, Mary T. *An Aquinas Reader.* New York: Fordham University Press, 1988; orig. Doubleday 1972.

Davies, Brian. "The Shape of a Saint," pp. 1–20 in *The Thought of Thomas Aquinas.* Oxford: Clarendon Press, 1992.

De Ghellinck, J. "Pierre Lombard." *DTC,* XII (1933) 1941–2019.

Dewan, Lawrence. "Saint Thomas, Alvin Plantinga, and the Divine Sim-

plicity." *The Modern Schoolman* 66 (1989) 141–53. A critique of Plantinga's 1980 Aquinas Lecture, *Does God Have a Nature?* alleging Plantinga's failure "to enter into serious philosophical discussion with the historical Thomas . . . on the issue of divine simplicity" and attempting "to suggest what such serious discussion would have required" (141), namely an analogical rather than a "fundamentally homogenizied or univocal" conception of being and goodness (150).

———. "St. Thomas and the Ground of Metaphysics." *Proceedings of the American Catholic Philosophical Association* 54 (1980) 144–54.

Dienstag, Jacob I. (ed.). *Studies in Maimonides and St. Thomas Aquinas, selected with an Introduction and Bibliography*. ([New York]: Ktav Publishing House, 1975.

Elders, Leo. *The Philosophical Theology of St. Thomas Aquinas*. Leiden: E. J. Brill, 1990.

———. *Autour de Saint Thomas d'Aquin: Recueil d'études sur sa pensée philosophique et théologique I: Les Commentaires sur les oeuvres d'Aristote. La Métaphysique de l'être*. Paris: FAC-ditions, 1987.

———. *Faith and Science: An Introduction to St. Thomas'* Expositio in Boethii De Trinitate. Rome: Herder, 1974.

———. *De Metafysika van St. Thomas van Aquino in historisch perspectief*, I: *Het gemeeschappelijk Zijnde*. Brugge: Uitgeverij Tabor, 1982. German version: *Die Metaphysik des Thomas von Aquin in historischer Perspective, I: Das ens commune*. Trans. Klaus Hedwig. Salzburg & München: Anton Pustet, 1985.

———. *De Metafysika van St. Thomas van Aquino in historisch perspectief*, II: *Filosofische Godsleer*. Brugge: Uitgeverij Tabor, 1987. *Die Metaphysik des Thomas von Aquin in historischer Perspective, II*. Salzburg & München: Anton Pustet, 1987.

Eschmann, I. T. "A Catalogue of St. Thomas's Works: Bibliographical Notes," in Étienne Gilson, *The Christian Philosophy of St. Thomas Aquinas*, trans. L. K. Shook, pp. 381–439. New York: Random House, 1956.

Fabro, Cornelio. *God in Exile: A Study of the Internal Dynamic of Modern Atheism from Its Roots in the Cartesian* Cogito *to the Present Day*. Trans. & ed. Arthur Gibson. Westminster, MD: Newman Press, 1968. A massive, superbly documented diagnosis of modern and contemporary intellectual trends by an eminent Italian Thomist; interesting also as a 'cryptologie dévoilée'. The new Part VIII on Anglo-American developments is not in the Italian original.

———. *Introduzione a San Tommaso: La Metafisica tomista e il pensiero moderno*. Milano: Ares, 1983.
———. *La nozione metafisica di partecipazione secondo S. Tomaso d'Aquino*, 3 ed. Turin, 1963.
———. *Participation de causalité selon S. Thomas d'Aquin*. Louvain, 1961.
Foster, Kenelm, trans. and ed. *The Life of Saint Thomas Aquinas: Biographical Documents*. London: Longmans, Green, 1959.
Gardet, Louis. "Saint Thomas et ses prédécesseurs arabes," vol. 1, pp. 419–48 in Maurer (ed.) *St. Thomas Aquinas 1274–1974: Commemorative Studies*, 2 vols. Toronto: Pontifical Institute of Mediaeval Studies, 1974.
Geiger, L.-B. *La participation dans la philosophie de saint Thomas d'Aquin*, 2 ed. Paris, 1953.
Gilson, Étienne. *Being and Some Philosophers*, 2d ed. Toronto: Pontifical Institute of Mediaeval Studies, 1952. Since Canadian books are not normally listed in U.S. Books in Print, and are therefore difficult for most American bookshops to acquire, it will be useful to supply this important publisher's address here:

Publications Department
Pontifical Institute of Mediaeval Studies
59 Queen's Park Crescent East
Toronto, Ontario M5S 2C4 Canada.

———. *Christian Philosophy*, trans. Armand Maurer. Toronto: Pontifical Institute of Mediaeval Studies, 1993.
———. *The Christian Philosophy of St. Thomas Aquinas*, trans. L. K. Shook. New York: Random House, 1956.
———. *God and Philosophy*. New Haven, CT: Yale University Press, 1941; rpt. 1969. A clear, brief, and well-focused introduction to the most important issues.
———. *A History of Christian Philosophy in the Middle Ages*. New York: Random House, 1955. A scholarly standard for over a generation with a superb bibliography, this text is suitable for advanced undergraduates and the educated public.
———. *Introduction à l'étude de saint Augustin*. Paris: J. Vrin, 2ème éd., 1943.
———. *La théologie mystique de saint Bernard*. Paris: J. Vrin, 1934.
———. "Quasi Definitio Substantiae," vol. 1, pp. 111–29 in Maurer (ed.) *St. Thomas Aquinas 1274–1974: Commemorative Studies*, 2 vols. Toron-

to: Pontifical Institute of Mediaeval Studies, 1974.
———. *Le Thomisme*, 6ème éd., rev. Paris: J. Vrin, 1965.
———. *Thomistic Realism and the Critique of Knowledge*, trans. Mark A. Wauck. San Francisco: Ignatius Press, 1986.
Glorieux, P. "Sentences and Summae." *The New Catholic Encyclopedia*, vol. 13. New York: McGraw-Hill, 1967.
———. "Sentences (Commentaires sur les)." *DTC*, XIV (1941) 1860–1884.
Grabmann, Martin. *Gesammelte Akademieabhandlungen*. Veröffentlichungen des Grabmann-Instituts, Neue Folge 25.2. Paderborn: Ferdinand Schöningh, 1979.
———. *The Interior Life of St. Thomas Aquinas*, trans. N. Aschenbrener. Milwaukee, WI: Bruce, 1951.
———. *Thomas Aquinas: His Personality and Thought*. Engl. trans. of 1926 edition. London: Longmans, Green, 1928.
Johnson, Mark F. "St. Thomas' *De Trinitate*, Q. 5, A. 2, Ad 3: A Reply to John Knasas." *The New Scholasticism* 63 (1989) 58–65.
Jordan, Mark D. "The Names of God and the Being of Names." *The Existence and Nature of God*. Ed. Alfred J. Freddoso. Notre Dame, IN: University of Notre Dame Press, 1983, pp. 161–90.
Jugie, M. "Jean Damascène." *DTC*, VIII, 2258–2393.
Kantorowicz, Ernst. *Frederick the Second 1194–1250*, trans. E. O. Lorimer. New York: Frederick Ungar, 1957; orig. London: Constable, 1931. A strongly statist and anti-ecclesiastical biography of the major political figure in the first half of Aquinas's life. The English translation does not include the volume containing the notes to sources found in the German original (vol. 2, Berlin: Georg Bondi), but gives only a summary of sources (pp. xxv–xxvii). It is useful as a treatment of what the Popes were fighting.
Kluxen, Wolfgang. "Die Geschichte des Maimonides im lateinischen Abendland als Beispiel einer christlich-jüdischen Begegnung." In Paul Wilpert (ed.) *Judentum im Mittelalater: Beiträge zum christlich-jüdischen Gespräch*. Berlin: Walther De Gruyter, 1966, pp. 146–66.
———. "Literargeschichtliches zum lateinischen Moses Maimonides." *Recherches de théologie ancienne et médiévale*, 21 (1954) 23–50.
Knasas, John F. X. "*Esse* as the Target of Judgment in Rahner and Aquinas." *The Thomist* 51 (1987) 222–45.
———. "Transcendental Thomism and the Thomistic Texts." *The Thomist* 54 (1990) 81–95.

Kovach, Francis J (ed.). *Scholastic Challenges to Some Mediaeval and Modern Ideas*. Stillwater, OK: Western Publications, 1987.
Kretzmann, Norman, et al. *The Cambridge History of Later Medieval Philosophy: From the Rediscovery of Aristotle to the Disintegration of Scholasticism 1100–1600*. New York: Cambridge University Press, 1982.
Le Bachelet, X. "Dieu IV. (Sa nature d'après les Pères)." *DTC*, IV, 1023–1152.
———. "Hilaire." *DTC*, VI (1925) 2388–2462.
Lobkowicz, Nicholas. "What Happened to Thomism? From *Aeterni Patris* to *Vaticanum Secundum*." *American Catholic Philosophical Quarterly*, vol. 69, n. 3 (Summer 1995), pp. 397–423.
Lohr, Charles H. *St. Thomas Aquinas: Scriptum Super Sententiis: An Index of Authorities Cited*. Amersham, Buckingshire: Avebury Company, 1980. Not seen.
Lukasiewicz, Jan. *Aristotle's Syllogistic*. Oxford: 1951.
MacDonald, Scott. "The *Esse/Essentia* Argument in Aquinas' *De Ente et Essentia*." *Journal of the History of Philosophy* 22 (1984) 157–72.
Macierowski, E. M. "Does God Have a Quiddity according to Avicenna?" *The Thomist* 52 (1988) 79–87. An analysis of Avicenna's *Metaphysics* VIII, 4, from the *Kitâb al-Shifâ'*, Aquinas's chief source for the arguments for the divine simplicity in his *Scriptum super libros Sententiarum*, I, dist. 8.
Mangenot, E. "Dieu III. (Sa nature d'après la Bible)." *DTC*, IV, 948–1023.
———. "Dieu VII. (Sa nature d'après les décisions de l'Église)." *DTC*, IV, 1296–1300.
Maritain, Jacques. *Les Degrés du savoir*. In Jacques et Raissa Maritain. *Œuvres Complètes*, v. 4. Paris: 1983. The final section, animated by St. John of the Cross, is concerned with mystical knowledge of God.
———. *Existence and the Existent*, trans. Lewis Galantiere and Gerald B. Phelan. New York: Pantheon Books, 1948; rpt. Lanham, MD: University Press of America, 1987.
———. *A Preface to Metaphysics: Seven Lectures on Being*. New York: Sheed and Ward, 1939.
———. *St. Thomas Aquinas*. Tr. J. F. Scanlan. New York: Sheed and Ward, 1931; new translation by Joseph W. Evans and Peter O'Reilly. New York: Medridian, 1958.
Maurer, Armand A. Maurer, Armand. *Medieval Philosophy*. Toronto: Pontifical Institute of Mediaeval Studies, 2d ed. 1982. This very

clearly written undergraduate textbook has the additional merit of exhibiting how other medieval philosophers converge with or depart from the thought of Aquinas.

———, ed. *St. Thomas Aquinas 1274–1974: Commemorative Studies,* 2 vols. Toronto: Pontifical Institute of Mediaeval Studies, 1974.

———. "St. Thomas on the Sacred Name *Tetragrammaton.*" *Mediaeval Studies* 34 (1972) 275–86; reprinted in *Being and Knowing: Studies in Thomas Aquinas and Later Medieval Philosophers.* Papers in Mediaeval Studies 10. Toronto: The Pontifical Institute of Mediaeval Studies, 1990, pp. 59–69.

McCool, Gerald A. "The Tradition of Saint Thomas in North America: At 50 Years." *The Modern Schoolman* 65 (1988) 185–206.

McGrath, Margaret. *Etienne Gilson: A Bibliography/Une Bibliographie.* Toronto: Pontifical Institute of Mediaeval Studies, 1982. Gilson (1884–1978) was one of the central figures in the 20th-century study of medieval philosophy.

McInerny, Ralph. "Aquinas" art. in *Dictionary of the Middle Ages,* ed. Joseph R. Strayer, vol. 1, pp. 353–66. New York: Charles Scribner's Sons, 1982.

———. *A First Glance at St. Thomas Aquinas: A Handbook for Peeping Thomists.* Notre Dame, IN: University of Notre Dame Press, 1990.

———. *Boethius and Aquinas.* Washington, DC: The Catholic University of America Press, 1990.

———. *Thomism in an Age of Renewal.* Notre Dame, IN: University of Notre Dame Press, 1968.

Moisant, X. "Dieu VI. (Sa nature d'après la philosophie moderne)." *DTC,* IV, 1243–1296.

Mondin, Battista. *St. Thomas Aquinas' Philosophy in the Commentary to the Sentences.* The Hague: Martinus Nijhoff, 1975.

Montagnes, Bernard, O.P. *La Doctrine de l'analogie de l'être d'après saint Thomas d'Aquin.* Louvain: Publications Universitaires, 1963.

Oesterle, John A. *Logic: The Art of Defining and Reasoning.* 2d. ed. Englewood Cliffs, New Jersey: Prentice-Hall, 1963.

O'Rourke, Fran. *Pseudo-Dionysius and the Metaphysics of Aquinas.* Leiden: E. J. Brill, 1992. Bibliography, pp. 277–97.

Owens, Joseph. *The Doctrine of Being in the Aristotelian Metaphysics: A Study in the Greek Background of Mediaeval Thought,* 3d rev. ed. Toronto: The Pontifical Institute of Mediaeval Studies, 1978. Counter-

ing a tendency to divide Aristotle's *Metaphysics* into a 'general metaphysics' or 'ontology' and a 'special metaphysics' or 'theology', Owens argues that it is not an ontology (or study of being) because it is a theology (a study of divine being).
———. "Common Nature: A Point of Comparison between Thomistic and Scotistic Metaphysics." *Mediaeval Studies* 19 (1957) 1–40. The two authors are compared against the common background of Avicenna's *Metaphysics* V.
———. *An Elementary Christian Metaphysics*. Houston, TX: <University of St. Thomas> Center for Thomistic Studies, 1990; orig. 1963. Bibliography of suggested readings at the end of each chapter; valuable notes throughout.
———. *An Interpretation of Existence*. Milwaukee, WI: Bruce, 1968; rpt. Houston, TX: The Center for Thomistic Studies, 1990.
———. *Towards a Christian Philosophy*. Studies in Philosophy and the History of Philosophy 21. Washington, DC: The Catholic University of America Press, 1990.
Pegis, Anton C. *St. Thomas and the Greeks*. Milwaukee, WI: Marquette University Press, 1939.
———. "Penitus Manet Ignotum." *Mediaeval Studies* 27 (1965) 212–26.
Perles, J. "Die in einer Münchener Handschrift aufgefundene erste lateinische Übersetzung des Maimonidischen 'Führers.'" *Monatschrift für Geschichte und Wissenschaft des Judenthums* (Breslau) 24 (1875) 9–24, 67–86, 99–110, 149–59, 209–18, 261–65.
Pieper, Josef. *Guide to Thomas Aquinas*, trans. Richard and Clara Winston. New York: Octagon Books, 1982; orig. 1962.
———. *Leisure, the Basis of Culture*. New York: Pantheon, 1952.
Portalié, E. "Augustin (saint)." *DTC*, I, 2268–2472.
Ross, W. D. (ed.) *Aristotle's Prior and Posterior Analytics*. Oxford: Clarendon, 1949.
Sladek, F. P. *Gott und Welt nach dem Sentenzenkommentar des heiligen Thomas von Aquin*. Würzburg, 1941. Not seen.
Stump, Eleonore and Norman Kretzmann. "Simplicity Made Plainer: A Reply to Ross's 'Absolute Simplicity.'" *Faith and Philosophy* 4 (1987) 198–201. This article provides a point of entry to a discussion on the divine simplicity in Aquinas among contemporary philosophers in the Anglo-American tradition.
Synan, Edward A. "Saint Thomas Aquinas: His Good Life and Hard

Times," in *Thomistic Papers III*, ed. Leonard A. Kennedy, pp. 35–53. Houston, Texas: Center for Thomistic Studies, 1987.

———, "Aquinas and his Age," in *Calgary Aquinas Studies*, ed. Anthony Parel, pp. 1–25. Toronto: Pontifical Institute of Mediaeval Studies, 1978.

Torrell, Jean-Pierre. *Initiation à Saint Thomas d'Aquin: sa personne et son oeuvre.* Fribourg (Suisse): Éditions Universitaires, 1993. Bibliography pp. [529]–67. An English translation by Robert Royol appeared in the summer of 1996 from The Catholic University of America Press. I had been unable to set eyes on either the French original or the English translation until after this book was already in press; among other valuable points is the suggestion that Aquinas travelled by sea in at least some of his trips to Paris from Italy.

Tugwell, Simon (trans., ed., intro.). *Albert & Thomas: Selected Writings.* Classics of Western Spirituality. Mahwah, NJ: Paulist Press, 1988. The introductions on Albert (pp. 3–129) and Aquinas (pp. 201–351) are valuable. He translates Albert's Commentary on Dionysius' Mystical Theology and an anthology of thomistic texts on prayer, the contemplative life, and religious life.

Wallace, William A. and James A. Weisheipl. "Thomas Aquinas, Saint," vol. 14, pp. 102–15. *The New Catholic Encyclopedia.* New York: McGraw-Hill, 1967.

Weisheipl, James A. *Friar Thomas d'Aquino: His Life, Thought & Works, with* Corrigenda *and* Addenda. Washington, DC: The Catholic University of America Press, 1983; orig. Doubleday, 1974. See especially "A Brief Catalogue of Authentic Works," pp. 355–405, which updates Eschmann on editions and English translations, when they exist; students, professors and librarians alike will find it indispensable. It provided the materials for our sketch of the life of Aquinas.

Wippel, John F. *Metaphysical Themes in the Philosophy of Thomas Aquinas.* Washington, DC: The Catholic University of America Press, 1984.

———. "The Latin Avicenna as a Source of Thomas Aquinas' Metaphysics." *Freiburger Zeitschrift für Philosophie und Théologie,* 37 (1990) 51–90.

Zum Brunn, Émilie. "La Métaphysique de l'*Exode* selon Thomas d'Aquin," pp. 245–69 in *Dieu et l'être: Exégèse d'Exode 3, 14 et de Coran 20, 11–24.* Ed. Études Augustiniennes. Paris: Centre National de la Recherche Scientifique, 1978.

Glossary of Technical Terms

English to Latin (The forms given in the original Latin text have been reduced wherever possible to the nominative singular of nouns and adjectives and the first person present tense of verbs, so as to facilitate access to Latin dictionaries). Some effort has been made to index the key terms noted in this glossary. The page references given refer to the Latin edition by Pierre Mandonnet (1927), which we have also employed in the body of our translation in bold print between slashes for ease of reference. Bold-faced type is used in this indexing of this glossary to point out pages on which either definitions of the term or discussions in which it figures prominently are to be found.

Since all passages of our translation fall within Book I, Distinction 8 of the *Sentences,* we shall here omit redundant references to the Book and Distinction (1, d. 8) and shall specify, in the case of unique or unusually interesting occurrences, only its subdivisions into Question and Article, along with further internal locators to Objection ('obj.' with the appropriate number), Solution ('sol.'), or Reply to Objection ('ad' followed by the appropriate number). The glossary is intended chiefly to indicate the range of terms in the translation and the corresponding Latin originals. It has sometimes been helpful to classify terms according to part of speech as noun, verb, or adverb, for example; further precisions, such as the degree of adverbs (e.g., *proprie, proprius, propriissime* for positive, comparative, and superlative degree of 'properly') have generally been avoided.

When Peter Lombard in his *Sentences* cites an author, see Bibliography §3.21: An Index to Authorities Cited by Peter Lombard Himself (Mandonnet pages 187–93).

When St. Thomas cites an author, see Bibliography §3.22: An Index to Sources Cited by Aquinas in his Remarks on the *Sentences* (Mandonnet pages 193–236).

English	**Latin**	**Mandonnet** Page	**Internal** Reference
absolute	absolutus, -a, -um	220	q. 4, a. 1 ad 2
accident	accidens, (gen.) accidentis	188, 189, 191, 198, 209, 215, 216, 217, 219, 221, 222, 224, 227, 230, 231.	
accidental	accidentalis, -e	214, 228, 230.	
accidental, be	accido, -ere	188, 192, 209, 222, 235.	
according as	secundum quod	195, 196, 200, 213, 216, 229, 235.	
according to which	secundum quod	202, 217	
acquire	***		
act	actus, -ûs	195	q. 1, a. 1, sol.
a. of *being*	actus essendi	229	q. 5, a. 2, sol.
action	actio, -nis	225	q. 4, a. 3, sol.
actually	(in) actû	195	q. 1, a. 1, sol.
adverb	adverbium, -ii, n.	203	
aevum *eternity	eviternity	205	q. 2,a. 2, sol. Compare and *time. The Latin term 'aevum' seems to be used to render the Greek term *aiôn.*
affected, being	patî (present passive infinitive of *patior*)	214	q. 3, a. 2, sol.See *passive.
agent	agens, (gen.) agentis	198	q. 1, a. 2, contr. 2.
allow	patior, pati, passus sum	226	See *passive.
almost	quasi	234	q. 5, a. 3, ad 2.
always	semper	187, 188, 198, 202, 213, 214, 219.	
analogously	analogicê	198	q. 1, a. 2, sol.
		222	q. 4, a. 2, ad 1.
		See also *equivocally and *univocally.	
analysis	resolutio, -nis	199	q. 1, a. 3, contr.2.
angel	angelus, -î, m.	189, 194, 205, 209, 213, 214, 230.	
animal	animal, -is, n.	209, 212, 219, 232, 233, 234. See also *soul.	
animate	animatus, -a, -um	232.	
Apostle, the	Apostolus, -î, m.	189	
appurtenance	appenditium, -iî	228	q. 5, a. 2, sol.
article	articulus, -î A subdivision of a question*.	194	q. 1, a. 1.
as	quasi	202	
as	secundum quod	194, 198, 222, 225, 231.	
as it were	quasi	195	

aspect	ratio, -nis, f.	196	q. 1, a. 1 ad 4.
assert	pono, -ere	231, 233, 235.	See *posit.
assign	assigno, -are, -avi, -atum		See *signify.
Augustine	Augustinus, -î, m.		
authenticity	sinceritas, -atis, f.	192	
Avicenna	Avicenna, -ae, m.		
axiom	dignitas, -âtis, f.	200	q. 1, a. 3, sol.
badness	malitia,ae, f.	226	q. 5, a. 1, sol.
being	êns, (gen.) entis		
	(present participle	195	q. 1, a. 1, sol.
	of sum)	196	a. 1, sol.
		197	a. 2, contr. 2.
		199	a. 3, obj. 2.
			a. 3, obj. 3.
			a. 3, contr. 2.
		200	a. 3, sol.
		201	a. 3, ad 2.
			a. 3, ad 3.
		202	q. 2, a. 1, sol.
		218	q. 4, a. 1, obj. 1.
			a. 1, obj. 2.
		219	a. 1, ad 1.
		221	a. 2, obj. 2.
		222	a.2, ad 1.
			a. 2, ad 2.
		223	a. 2, ad 2.
		224	a. 3, obj. 4.
		226	q. 5, a. 1, obj. 2.
		228	a. 2, obj. 3.
			obj. 5.
		230	a. 2, ad 3.
being	esse		
	(infinitive of *sum*)	195	q. 1, a. 1, sol.
		198	a. 2, sol.
			ad 1.
			ad 2.
			ad 3.
		199	a. 3, obj. 2.
			contr. 1.
			contr. 2.
		200	a. 3, sol.
		201	q. 2, intro.
			q. 2, a. 1, obj. 2.

202	sol.
203	ad 2.
	ad 3.
	ad 4.
	ad 5.
	ad 6.
204	a. 2, contr.
	sol.
205	sol.
	ad 1.
206	a. 3, obj. 3.
	obj. 4.
	obj. 6.
207	sol.
	ad 1.
	ad 3.
208	ad 4.
	Expos. first part of text.
209	Expos. first part of text.
210	Expos. first part of text.
213	q. 3, a. 2, sol.
214	sol.
215	ad 3.
	ad 4.
218	q. 4, a. 1, obj. 1.
218	q. 4, a. 1, obj. 2.
	obj. 3.
	contr. 2.
219	contr. 2.
	contr. 3.
	ad 1.
220	ad 2.
222	a. 2, sol.
	ad 1.
223	ad 2.
	ad 3.
224	a. 3, obj. 4.
225	ad 4.
226	q. 5, a. 1, contr. 1.
	contr. 2.
	sol.
227	sol.
	a. 2, obj. 2.
228	obj. 3.

			obj. 5.
			sol.
		229	sol.
		230	sol.
			ad 1.
			ad 2.
			ad 3.
			ad 4.
		231	ad 4.
			ad 6.
		232	ad 6.
		233	a. 3, sol.
		234	ad 3.
		235	Expos. second part of text.
		236	Expos. second part of text.
being	(verbal noun, nominative wanting) essendî (gerund of *sum*, genitive singular)	195	q. 1, a. 1, sol.
		219	q. 4, a. 1, contr. 3, Item.
		223	q. 4, a. 2, ad 2.
		229	q. 5, a. 2, sol.
being-in (verbal noun)	inesse	224	q. 4, a. 3, sol.
Bernard	Bernardus, -î, m.		
body	corpus, corporis, n.	190, 191, 193, 206, 212, 216, 217, 225, 227, 228, 229, 230, 231, 232, 233, 234, 235, 236.	
Boethius	Boethius, -iî		
bodily	corporalis, -e	196, 205, 206, 207, 215, 216, 217, 228, 235.	
book	liber, librî, m.	1. A literary unit. 197, 199. 2. The main division of a literary unit. 187, 201 (3 instances), 203, 204, 207, 209, 210, 212, 213, 214, 215, 216, 221, 224, 225, 226, 227, 228. (For the *Sentences*, cf. *distinction.)	
Book of Causes	*Liber de Causis*		
chapter	capitulum, -î, n.	194, 195, 197, 199, 200, 201, 202, 203, 204, 207, 209, 210, 212, 213, 214, 222, 224, 225, 226, 228, 229, 232, 233.	
categorically	sicut genus	221	q. 4, a. 2, obj. 1.
category	genus, generis, n.	202	q. 2, a. 1, obj. 6.
		209	Expos. first part of the text.
		209	Expos. first part of the text.
		215	q. 3, a. 3, obj. 3.

		216	q. 3, a. 3, ad 1.
		218	q. 4, intro.
		221	q. 4, a. 2
			obj. 1.
			obj. 2.
			obj. 3.
		223	ad 3.
		224	a. 3, sol.
		225	ad 3.
	praedicamentum, -î	191	
		218	q. 4, intro.
		221	q. 4, a. 2, obj. 1.
		223	a. 3, obj. 1.
		224	obj. 4.
			contr.
			sol.
		225	ad 3.
cause	causa, -ae, f.	188, 189, 197, 198, 200, 207, 210, 214, 216, 219, 222, 224, 228, 233.	
c., agent	causa agens	198	q. 1, a. 2, sol.
			ad 2.
c., intrinsic formal	c. formalis intrinsecus	198	ad 2.
c., effective	c. effectiva	198	ad 2.
		200	q. 1, a. 3, sol.
c., exemplar	c. exemplaris	200	q. 1, a. 3, sol.
			ad 2.
c., final	c. finalis	200	q. 1, a. 3, sol.
cause (v.)	causo, -are, -avi, -atum	197, 219, 224.	
cease	desino, -ere	187, 188, 189.	
change	mutatio, -onis, f.	188, 189, 191, 203, 210, 211, 212, 213, 214, 215, 216.	
change (v.)	muto, -are	188, 189, 190, 213, 214, 215, 216.	
changeable	mutabilis, -e	191, 193.	
character	ratio, -nis	196, 198, 201, 203, 204, 211, 229.	
Commentator	Commentator, -is	1. When connected with the works of Aristotle, this is the nick-name of the Muslim scholar Ibn Rushd known to the Latin West as *Averroes (d. 1198). 2. When connected to the works of pseudo-Dionysius the Areopagite, this title refers to *Maximus of Chrysopolis (d. 662).	
common	communis, -e	199, 200, 202, 218, 219, 222, 226, 228.	

communicate* to	communico, -âre, -avi, -atum + cum	204, 205, 222	
community	communitas, -âtis, f.	199	
compare	comparo, -âre, -âvî, -âtum	187, 193, 199, 209, 220, 233.	
comparison	comparatio, -onis, f.	212.	Cf. *relation, s.v. *comparatio.
complete	compleo, -ere, -evi, -etum	211, 215, 225, 226, 227, 228, 230.	
completely		214	
completing difference	differentia completiva	224	
component	componens, -entis	218, 219, 226, 227, 235, 236.	
compose	compono, -ere, -sui, compositum	212, 219, 224, 226, 227, 228, 229, 230, 232, 235. See also *posit.	
composed, able to be	componibilis, -e	227	
composite	compositum, -î	192, 197, 215, 218, 219, 226, 227, 229, 230, 235.	
composition	compositio, -nis, f.	196, 217, 218, 219, 220, 226, 227, 228, 229, 230, 234, 236.	
concrete	concretus, -a, -um	196, 226,	
concreteness	concretio, -nis, f.	195	q. 1, a. 1 ad 3.
conjunct	conjunctum, -î, n.	227, 230.	
conjunction	conjunctio, -nis, f.	227, 229, 230.	
connatural		207	
connote	connoto, -âre, -avi, -atum	196.	
connotation	vis, f.	222.	
consider	accipio, -ere	191, 202, 205 (q. 2, a. 2 ad 2), 207 (q. 2, a. 3, sol.), 232, 233.	
	animadverto, -ere	190.	
	considero, -are	193, 195, 200, 201, 203, 205, 213, 214, 215, 224, 225, 228, 233, 235.	
constitution	commixtio, -nis	233.	
continuous	***		
convert with	converto, -ere + cum	199, 200, 201. In logic, when subject and predicate terms are interchanged in a proposition, the terms are said to be converted. When the subject and predicate terms stand for individual entities of a given nature, simply interchanging subject and predicate terms	

		does not preserve the truth of the original cate-gorical proposition. For example, "Every man is an animal" converts into "Every animal is a man," which is obviously false. For an elementary treatment of the rules of conversion, see a standard textbook like John Oesterle, *Logic: The Art of Defining and Reasoning,* 2d ed. (Englewood Cliffs, New Jersey: Prentice-Hall, 1963), pp. 141–46.	
corruption			
corporeal	corporalis, -e	190, 227, 228, 230.	
corporeity	corporeitas, -âtis, f.	228, 229.	
co-signify	consignifico, -are, -avi, -atum	See *signify.	
creature	creatura, -ae, f.	189, 190, 191, 194, 196, 197, 198, 199, 200, 202, 203, 204, 205, 206, 207, 209, 210, 211, 212, 213, 214, 215, 216, 217, 218, 220, 222, 224, 225, 226, 227.	
Damascene	Damascenus, -î		
defect	defectus (See *fall short)	206, 207.	
defective	defectivus, -a, -um	206.	
defectively	diminute	215	q. 3, a. 3, obj. 3.
define	definio, -ire	201, 202, 203.	
definition	definitio, -onis, f.	201, 202, 204, 222.	
denuded	nudus, -a, -um	228.	
	denudo, -âre, -avi, -atum (in passive)	229.	
deny	nego, -âre, -avi- -atum	196.	
designate	designo, -are, -avi, -atum	See *signify.	
desire	***		
determine	determino, -âre, -avi, -atum	195, 196, 200, 217, 219, 220, 221, 222, 223, 231.	
determination	determinatio, -onis, f.	193	Division of the first part of the text.
dialectic	dialectica, -ae, f.	191: The liberal art of reasoning or logic.	
difference	differentia, ae, f.	197, 198, 205, 219, 220, 224, 225.	
Dionysius	Dionysius, -iî, m.		
distinct			
distinction	distinctio, -nis	1. Generally, a sort of otherness between two notions or things. 193, 220, 232.	

		2. An editorial division of the Sentences of *Master Peter Lombard; he originally divided each of the four *books into *chapters (*capitula*). Later, someone else, not known, substituted the division of the books into *distinctiones,* which group the chapters into larger units for discussion; Alexander of Hales used the *distinctiones.* He and other com-mentators were then free to add further subdivi-sions as needed. Aquinas normally subdivides each distinction into quaestions* and them, in turn, into *articles. For a fuller discussion of the "distinc-tions," see Grottaferrata 1971ed., Tomus I, Pars 1, pp. 143*-44*. 187, 217.
distinguish	distinguo, -ere, -ui, distinctum	193, 218, 232, 234.
diverse	diversus, -a, -um	**198**, 201, 202, 209, 211, 212, 222, 228, 229, 230, 231, 232, 234. See also *various.
diversely	diversimode	223.
diversify	diversifico, -are	198.
diversity	diversitas, -tatis, f.	190, 191, 198, 217, 220, 226, 228, 234.
division	divisio, -nis, f.	193. Division of the first part of the text: What Aquinas here calls Distinction 8 comprises Peter Lombard's *Sentences,* Book I, chapters 21–28. The First Part of the text consists of Lombard's Chapters 21–22; see Grottaferrata 1971ed., Tomus I, Pars II, pp. 95–98. The text of ch. 21 (nn. 1–7) is divided into three bold-faced segments at n. 1 (**De proprietate et incommutabilitate et simplicitate Dei essentiae**), n. 4 (**Qualiter intelligenda sint verba Hieronymi quaerendum est**), and n. 6 (**Hic aperit qualiter sint intelligenda**). Chapter 22 (nn. 1–4) is divided into two such segments at n. 1 (**De incommutabilitate hic**) and n. 2 (**Quae sit vera immortalitas quae in solo Creatore est**). 217. Division of the second part of the text: The Second Part of the text deals with Lombard's Chapters 23–28; see Grottaferrata 1971ed., Tomus I, Pars II, pp. 98–103. Chapter 23 is an undivided unit **(Hic de**

simplicitate—Quare creatura sit multiplex et non simplex). Chapter 24 (nn. 1–3) is divided into two units at n. 1 (**Hic de corporali creatura ostendit quare sit multiplex**) and at n. **2** (**Hic de spirituali creatura ostendit quomodo sit multiplex et non simplex**). Chapter 25 consists of an undivided unit (**Qualiter Deus, cum sit simplex, tamen multipliciter dicatur**). Chapter 26 is again an undivided unit (**Tanta est Dei simplicitas quod nulli praedicamentorum subicitur**). Chapter 27 is an undivided section (**Quod Deus non proprie, sed abusive dicitur substantia**). Chapter 28 (nn. 1–3), the last of Distinction 8, is also taken under a single bold-face heading at n. 1 (**Quod non est in Deo aliquid quod non sit Deus**).

effect	effectus, -ûs, m.	196, 198, 211.
effectively	effectivê	198.
emotion	affectio, -nis, f.	189, 215, 216, 231, 235.
equivocally	aequivoce	198, 229. See also *analogously and *univocally.
essence	essentia, -ae, f.	187, 188, 189, 191, 193 (Division of the first part of the text.), 207, 208, 209, 210, 217, 218, 220, 221, 222, 226, 227, 229, 233, 234.
essentially	essentialiter	198, 220, 236.
eternity	aeternitas, -atis, f.	187, 193, 201 (Boethius's definition), 202, 203, 204, **205**, 206, 207, 212. Compare **aevum* and *time.
example, by way of	exemplariter	196, 198.
exist	exsisto, -ere	188, 197, 199, 200, 209, 211.
exposition	expositio, -nis, f.	208–10 (Exposition of the first part of the text*): Here Saint Thomas quotes portions of Distinction* 8 (Chapter 21) of the Master's* text and explains their sense. 1. p. 208: "One ought now to deal with the truth* or propriety* or incommutability* and simplicity* of the divine nature or substance* or essence." 2. p. 209: "Nature or substance or essence." A closer look at the latter part of text 1.

Here Aquinas omits Grottaferrata ed., Tomus I, pars 1, p. 95. 6–8, i.e. the sentence "Est itaque Deus, ut ait Augustinus in V libro *De Trinitate,* since dubitatione substantia vel, si melius hoc appellatur, essentia, quam Graeci usiam vocant."
3. p. 209: "For just as wisdom is so called from being wise (*sapere*)... so is essence so called from *being* (*esse*)." Grottaferrata ed., Tomus I, pars 1, p. 95. 8–10, omitting the phrase "et ab eo quod est scire dicta est scientia."
4. p. 209: "And who is greater than He Who said to His servant: 'I am Who AM?' " Grottaferrata ed., Tomus I, pars 1, p. 95. 10–11, omitting "et *Dices filiis Israel: Qui est misit me ad vos*".
5. p. 209: "God, however, Who did not know WAS or ABOUT TO BE merely IS." Grottaferrata ed., Tomus I, pars 1, p. 95. 18–19, omitting the rest of the passage quoted from *Jerome.
6. p. 209: "Our *being* compared with His essence is not." Grottaferrata ed., Tomus I, pars 1, p. 95. 19–20: "cuius essentiae comparatum, nostrum esse non est." Aquinas omits the main clause: "Solus igitur Deus vere est." The whole sentence, rendered more literally, reads: "Therefore God alone truly is, compared to Whose essence our *being* is not."
7. p. 209: "*Being* is not an accident to God." Here Aquinas skips paragraphs 4–6 of the Grottaferrata ed., Tomus I, pars 1, p. 95. 21–p. 96. 30, quoting only the first clause of a sentence from *Hilary's *De Trinitate* VII, n. 11 (PL 10, 208 B-C): "Esse non est accidens Deo, sed subsistens veritas, et manens causa, et naturalis generis proprietas."
8. p. 209: "But subsistent Truth." Here Aquinas cites the first three words of the rest of text 7 as its tag-line.

fall short	deficio, -ere, defeci, defectum	194, 196, 198, 206, 207, 208, 210, 214, 226, 227. See also *defect and *short-fall.

father	Pater, -tris, m.	189, 192, 193, 211,
finite, render	finio,—îre, -ivi, -itum	197, 202, 225, 226.
first		
form	forma, -ae, f.	189, 192, 200, 202, 207, 209, 213, 214, 215, 226, 227, 228, 229, 230, 231, 232, 233, 234, 235.
accidental f.	f. accidentalis	214.
substantial f.	f. substantialis	228, 229, 232, 233.
f. of the part	f. partis	229.
the f. consequent on a whole	f. consequens totum	209.
formally	formaliter	198, 236.
genus	genus, generis, n.	188, 202, 210, 212, 219, 221, 222, 223, 224, 225.
Gregory	Gregorius, -iî, m.	
habit	habitus, -ûs, m.	209, 211, 228, 235.
harmony	harmonia, -ae, f.	233.
(He) Who IS	qui est	187 See "*who is."
highest	summus, -a, -um	192, 205, 224, 226.
highly, most	summê	190, 217, 221.
Hilary	Hilarius, -iî, m.	
human (being)	homo, hominis, m.	203, 205, 209, 210, 222, 226, 227, 228, 230, 231.
humanity	humanitas, -atis, f.	195, 209, 222, 229, 236.
imagining	imaginatio, -nis, f.	233.
imagination	imaginatio, -nis, f.	200.
i. of the intellect	i. intellectûs	200. An echo of the Arabic phrase *tasawwur bi-l-'aql,* which is used in Book Lambda of Aristotle's *Metaphysics* to translate the Greek word *noêsis* "intellection" or "understanding." The Latin rendering is *imaginatio per intellectum.* In Avicenna, the verb *tasawwara* (SWR 5) is used to express the first operation of the intellect, simple conceptualization, in contrast to *saddaqa* (SDQ 2), which names the second operation, judgment, in which truth first appears; cf. Goichon, *Lexique* §371 (pp. 184–85) and §375 *tasawwur* (pp.

English	Latin	Pages / Remarks	Reference
		191–93) for the former, and §359 (p. 178) and §361 *tasdîq* (pp. 179–180) for the latter.	
imperfect	imperfectus, -a, -um	188, 198, 200, 203, 206, 208.	
imperfection	imperfectio, -onis, f.	196, 203, 205, 207, 208, 209, 224, 230.	
imperfectly	imperfectê	196.	
inasmuch as	secundum quo<d>	197, 205, 207, 208, 209, 211, 212, 214, 230, 231, 233. Remark on 212 (q. 3, a. 1 ad 2): The Latin text erroneously drops the final letter.	
	inquantum	197, 202, 205, 208, 211, 228, 230, 231.	
individual	individuum, -î, n.	209, 230, 231.	
individually	secundum individua	228.	
individuate	individuo, -âre	228	q. 5, a. 2, obj. 6
	(usu. in passive)	230	ad 4.
		231	ad 6.
individuation	individuatio, -nis	228, 231, 232.	
impose	impono, -ere, imposui, impositum		194. See also *posit.
infinite	infinitus, -a, -um	192, 193, 194, 196, 197, 209, 211, 226.	
intellect	intellectus, -ûs, m.	194, **200**, 202, 207, 217, 220, 226. See also *understand.	
intellective	intellectivus, -a, -um	228, 233, 235.	
intellectual	intellectualis, -e	196, 209.	
intelligible	intelligibilis, -e	228.	
intention	intentio, -nis, f.	1. A technical term in logic—a concept or the real foundation thereof, the meaning; cf. Goichon, *Lexique* §469 *ma'nà*, plur. *ma'ânî* (pp. 253–55): 199, 201, 216, 231. 2. What a person wants to do; the object of his will: 215.	
itself, of	de se	202, 228.	
itself, out of	ex se	212	q. 3, a. 1 ad 3.
itself, through	per se	197, 198, 210, 212, 213, 215, 216, 221, 227, 228, 230, 231, 232.	
Jerome	Hieronymus, -î, m.		
judgment			
j. of the intellect	credulitas intellectûs	200: An echo of the Arabic term *tasdîq*, the standard term in Avicenna's logic for the second operation of the intellect, judgment; cf. our gloss on "*imagination of the intellect" also on p. 200.	
justify	verifico, -âre	212	q. 3, a. 1, ad 2. Cf. *true.

kind	genus, generis, n.	221, 222.
lack	desum	188, 208.
lay down	pono, -ere	See *posit.
lay under	substerno, -ere, -ui, -stratum	214, cf. *substrate.
life	vita, -ae, f.	192, 196, 200, 201, 202, 203, 232, 234, 235, 236.
literally	ex litterâ	195: i.e., from the text itself.
	ad litteram	205: i.e., properly, not metaphorically.
living (verbal noun)	vivere (infinitive of *vivo*)	195, 203, 234.
live, to (infinitive)	vivere (infinitive of *vivo*)	189, 234.
living	vivêns (pres. participle of *vivo*)	192, 193, 196, 200, 202, 234, 235, 236.
Maimonides	Rabbi Moyses, gen. Moysis.	
man	homo, hominis, m.	Remark: The Latin term *homo* applies to any member of the human race, man, woman, or child. The term *vir* (also translated by the English word 'man') applies only to adult male human beings; the term *femina* (translated 'woman') by contrast applies to adult female human beings.
manner	modus, -î, m.	187, 188, 189, 190, 191, 192, 193, 195, 196, 197, 198, 200, 202, 203, 204, 205, 207, 208, 209, 210, 211, 212, 213, 214, 215, 216, 217, 218, 219, 220, 221, 222, 223, 224, 225, 226, 229, 230, 231, 233, 234, 235.
Master, the	Magister, -trî, m.	Peter Lombard: 201, 215.
matter	materia, -ae, f.	200, 213, 214, 215, 227, 228, 229, 231, 232, 234, 235.
meaning	intentio, -nis, f.	199.
	ratio, -onis, f.	219, 220, 221.
	significatio, -onis, f.	194.
measure (n.)	mensura, -ae, f.	193, 197, 201, 203, 206, 215, 223, 224, 231.
measure (v.)	mensuro, -are	201, 205, 216, 217, 221, 223.
mind	animus, -î, m.	191.
	intellectus, -ûs, m.	199.
	mens, mentis, f.	206.
mode	modus, -î, m.	198, 205, 207, 210, 215, 220, 222, 225, 230.

		Cf. *manner.
modeled	exemplatus, -a, -um	196.
motion	motus, -ûs, m.	188, 189, 202, 206, 208, 211, 212, 213, 214, 215, 216, 217, 225, 228.
move	moveo, -êre	189, 210, 211, 212, 213, 214, 216, 231.
mover	motor, -is, m.	210, 211, 221, 228, 233, 234.
	movens, moventis	228.
moving	movens, moventis	212.
mutability	mutabilitas, -tatis, f.	191, 210, 213, 214, 217.
mutable	mutabilis, -e	187, 189, 190, 191, 210, 212, 213, 214, 215.
mutation	mutatio, -onis, f.	191, 211, 212, 213, 214, 215, 216.
name (n.)	nomen, nominis, n.	190, 191, 192, 193, 194, 195 196, 198, 199, 200, 203, 207, 220, 221, 222, 223, 225.
name (v.)	nomino, -are, -avi, -atum	187, 191, 194, 195 (denominare),, 196, 209, 222.
nameable	nominabilis, -e	194.
natural	naturalis, -e	188, 205, 213, 215, 231.
naturally	naturaliter	199, 211.
naturally apt, be	natum esse	205, 213.
nature	natura, -ae, f.	195,200, 205, 208, 209, 211, 214, 217, 218, 219, 224, 226, 227, 228, 229, 230, 231, 234, 235, 236.
negation	negatio, -onis, f.	195, 200, 201, 202, 219, 222.
negate (v.)	nego, -are, -avi, -atum	218, 220.
notion	ratio, -nis, f.	200, 202, 203, 206, 222.
notionally	secundum rationem	220.
objection	objectum	227 Arguments presented as opposed to the proposition to be defended (cf. In Sent, 1, d. 8, q. 5, a. 1).
occur	potest esse	199 q. 1, a. 3, sol.
	advenio, -îre	230 q. 5, a. 2, sol.
one	unus, -a, -um	200, 204, 205, 211, 212, 216, 218, 220, 222, 223, 224, 227, 228, 232, 233, 234.
operation		
opinion	opinio, -nis, f.	228.
opposed,	oppositus, -a, -um	201 q. 2, a. 1, obj. 4. See also *posit.
opposite		
order	ordo, ordinis, m.	206, 209, 211, 212, 229.
orderly way,	secundum ordinem	211.

in an originally	de novô	212	q. 3, a. 2, ad 4. There may be an echo of the Arabic notion of comining into being (*hudûth*) sometimes referred to by the term *novitas*, as in "novitas mundi," the origination of the world; cf. Goichon, *Lexique*, §§132–138 (pp. 60–65).
paradigmatically	exemplariter	198	q. 1, a. 2, sol.
part	pars, partis, f.	193, 201, 202, 203, 204, 205, 208, 212, 214, 217, 218, 225, 227, 229, 230, 232, 233, 234, 235, 236.	
part of, on the	ex parte (+ gen.)	202, 204, 221. See also "from the *side of."	
participate	participo, -âre	197, 198, 199, 200, 202, 204, 205, 209, 218, 220, 231, 233: Aquinas uses this verb, as a technical philosophical term, with a direct object (to participate *something*) rather than with a prepositional construction (to participate *in* something). In this respect he follows the manner of speaking of such Platonic philosophers as Proclus, who, in the *Elementatio Theologica*, uses the corresponding Greek verb *metechein* with a similar construction. We follow that technical usage as employed by E. R. Dodds in his English rendition of Proclus. See the studies of participation in Aquinas by Fabro and Geiger.	
participation	participatio, -nis, f.	195, 199, 200, 205, 211.	
participatively	participative	204, 205.	
particular	particularis, -e	215, 227, 233.	
passion	passio, passionis, f.	235.	
passive, be	patior, pati, passus sum	191, 214, 226 (allow), 227 (undergo).	
perfect (v.)	perficio, -ere	232, 233.	
perfect(ed)	perfectus, -a, -um	188, 191, 192, 194, 195, 197, 201 (Boethius), 202, 203, 204, 205, 206, 208, 214, 215, 217, 219, 223, 228, 230, 234.	
	nobilis, -e	204, 211, 219, 234.	

perfectible	perfectibilis, -e	228, 234.
perfection	perfectio, -nis, f.	195, 201, 205, 206, 207, 208, 220, 221, 222, 223, 224, 228, 229, 231, 232, 233, 234, 235.
	nobilitâs, -âtis, f.	221, 222, 229, 231.
perfectly	perfectê	202, 207.
Philosopher, the	philosophus, -î, m.	1. (singular) The scholastic nickname for Aristotle. 2. (plural) Certain philosophers taken collectively.
phrase-by-phrase	ad litteram	210: Augustine means to stay close "to the *text."
place	locus, -î, m.	210, 211, 213, 215, 216, 232, 233, 234.
place (v.)	ponô, -ere	See *posit.
Plato	Plato (gen. Platonis), m.	
pluperfect	pluperfectus, -a, -um	188.
posit	ponô, -ere, -posuî, -positum	199 (place), 201(posit), 202 (lay down), 203 (posit), 206 (suppose), 208 (posit), 214 (posit), 220 (posit), 221 (posit), 222 (posit), 223 (posit), 225 (posit), 229 (suppose), 231 (assert), 233, 235 (assert).
	compono, -ere	192, 197, 212, 215, 218, 219, 226, 227, 228, 229, 230, 232, 235, 236.
	dispono. -ere	229.
	impono, -ere	194, 195, 221, 225.
	oppono, -ere	201.
	praesuppono, -ere	214.
	propono, -ere	217.
	suppono. -ere	199. See also *supposit.
position	situs, -ûs, m.	191, 229, 233.
potency	potentia, -ae, f.	205, 208, 211, 212, 213, 215, 227, 230.
potentiality	potentialitas, -atis, f.	196, 208, 210.
potentially	in potentiâ	234.
	potentialiter	219.
power	potentia, -ae, f.	See *potency.
	virtûs, virtûtis, f.	190, 191, 192, 200, 223, 224, 234, 235, 236.
	vîs, f.	222 See *connotation.
predicate (n.)	praedicatum, -î, n.	195, 209, 221, 222.
predicate (v.)	praedico, -are, -avi, -atum	194, 201, 217, 218, 221, 222, 223, 224, 225.
predication	praedicatio, -onis, f.	200, 208, 217, 222, 224, 225.
prime(s)	primus, -a, um	198, 212, 213, 215, 224, 226, 227, 228.
principle	principium, -iî, n.	195, 196, 200, 209, 218, 219, 223, 228, 230,

		231.
privation	privatio, -nis, f.	196, 200, 208.
processive	processivus, -a, -um	211 q. 3,a. 1 ad 1.
proper	proprius, -a,-um	194, 195, 196, 200, 203, 206, 219, 224, 225,
properly	proprie	187, 188, 189, 191, 193, 194, 195, 198, 207, 208, 210, 211, 212, 214, 216, 217, 222, 223, 224, 232.
property	proprietas, -atis, f.	193, 195, 196, 210, 220, 231.
	proprium, -iî, n.	195.
Prophet*, the	Propheta, -ae, m.	189 Malachi.
proposition	propositio, -onis, f.	197, 199. Cf. *posit.
propriety	proprietas, -atis, f.	187, 188, 193, 208.
proportion	proportio, -nis, f.	209, 233.
proportioned, -ate	proportionatus, -a, -um	234.
Psalm	Psalmus, -î, m.	189, 204, 213.
pure	purus, -a, -um	192, 211, 213, 219, 231.
purity	puritas, -tatis, f.	193, 231.
question	quaestio, -nis, f.	193, 197, 201, 210, 218, 225.
quiddity	quidditas, -atis, f.	See second note to Avicenna's *Metaphysics* on p. 195.
rational		189, 197, 198, 209, 231,
real	realis, -e.	220. See also *thing (res).
reality		209.
really	realiter	203, 218, 220.
	secundum rem	225, 226.
reason	ratio, -nis, f.	189, 194, 195, 196, 200, 202, 203, 207, 212, 214, 215, 219, 220, 221, 222, 224, 225, 227, 228, 230, 231, 233.
receive	recipio, recipere, -cêpî, -ceptum	188, 197, **202**, 205, 219, 220, 222, 226, 229, 234. 233
receiver	recipiens, (gen.) recipientis	202, 205, 233.
received	receptus, -a, -um	202, 204, 219, 226, 229.
reception	receptio, -onis, f.	214 q. 3, a. 2 sol.
refer/relate	refero, -ferre, -tuli, -latum	198, 220, 224, 227.
regard		
with r. to	circa	193, 201, 210, 217, 218, 220, 225, 235.
relation	ad aliquid (literally "toward something")	224, 225, 227.

	comparatio, -onis, f.	187, 190, 209, 212, 217, 224.
	habilitas, -tatis, f.	Not used in the Thomistic text, but see the note to Averroes's *Metaphysics* cited on 224.
	habitûdo, habitûdinis, f.	226, 227.
	relatio, -onis, f.	196, 200, 206, 215, 216, **220**, 224, 225, 227, 233.
	respectus, -ûs, m.	194, 195
relationship	habitudô, habitûdinis, f. See *relation.	
relative	relativus, -a, -um	220,
relatively	relative	193, 220.
removal	remotio, -nis, f.	196, 202,
remove	removeo, removêre	193, 196, 199, 202, 206, 208, 215, 219, 220, 224, 227, 228, 230, 232.
re-present	repraesento, -âre	196 q. 1, a. 1, ad 2 & ad 3.
respect	respectus, -ûs, m.	195, 201, 219, 220, 222, 224, 225, 228, 229, 230, 232, 233, 234, 235, 236. (Cf. "*relation.")
with r. to		190 (de)(in comparatione + gen.)(nihil patiens), 193 (circa), 196 (secundum), 198 (secundum), 199 (secundum), 200 (secundum), 201 (secundum), 203 (secundum) (quantum ad), 204 (ex parte + gen.)(quantum ad), 206 (secundum), 207 (secundum) (quantum ad)(quantum), 208 (secundum) (quantum ad), 209 (quantum ad), 211 (secundum), 212 (secundum)(de), 213 (secundum), 214 (secundum)(ad)(secundum) (quantum ad), 216 (secundum), 217 (circa), 219 (secundum), 220 (secundum)(circa), 222 (secundum)(quantum ad), 223 (secundum), 224 (secundum), 225 (secundum), 228 (secundum), 232 (secundum), 233 (secundum), 234 (secundum), 235 (secundum)(quantum ad), 236 (quantum ad).
rest(ing)	quies, -etis, f.	203.
	otium, -ii, n.	210.
right, in its own	per sê	227, 228, 230, 231.
	secundum se	235.
ringed	annulôsus, -a, -um	234.
same	idem	188, 189, 190, 191, 192, 193, 194, 196, 197, 199, 203, 208, 209, 211, 212, 217, 222, 224, 227, 228, 229, 231, 232, 233, 234.

sentence	sententia, -ae, f.	A scholarly or authoritative judgment. Peter Lombard collected theological *sententiae* into a book that became the standard for professional theologians to comment upon in order to obtain their advanced degree. The text here being translated is a portion of *Aquinas's Scriptum super libros Sententiarum.*
short-fall	defectus, -ûs, m.	227 q. 5, a. 1, sol.
side of, from the	ex parte (+ gen.)	196, 225. See also "on the *part of."
signify	significo, -âre	190, 191, 194, 195, 196, 203, 206, 207, 208, 220, 222–23.
signification	significatio, -onis, f.	194. See also *meaning.
	signo, -are	208.
	assigno, -are	193, 201, 210, 215, 221.
	consignifico, -are	207.
	designo, -are	206, 208, 219, 234.
simple	simplex	189, 190, 191, 192, 193, 197, 201, 202, 207, 208, 212, 213, 217, 218, 221, 223, 225, 226, 227, 228, 229, 230, 231, 232, 233, 234.
simpler		191, 201, 218.
simplest		201, 221.
simplicity	simplicitas, -atis, f.	187, 189, 191, 192, 193, 199, 208, 217, 218, 225, 226, 227, 230, 233.
simply	simpliciter	188, 199, 200, 204, 205, 214, 215, 216, 222; "without qualification": 219, 221, 223.
solution	solutio, -nis, f.	194, 198, 199, 202, 204, 207, 211, 213, 215, 216, 221, 224, 226, 227, 228, 230, 232, 233.
some(thing)	aliquis, aliquid	187, 188, 189, 190, 191, 192, 193, 194, 195, 196, 197, **198**, 200, 201, 202 (also: aliquod) 203, 204, 205, 206, 207, 208, 209, 210, 211, 212, 213, 214, 215, 216, 217, **218**, 219, 220, 221, 222, 223, 224, 225, 226, 227, 228 (also: aliquod), 229, 230, 230 (also: aliquod), 231 (also: aliquod), 232, 233, 234, 235, 236.
	alicuius (gen.)	196, 202, 207, 209, 227, 235.
	alicui (dat.)	194, 195, 204, 209.
	aliqualiter	202.
	aliquando	208.
soul	anima, -ae, f.	189, 190, 193, 212, 215, 216, 217, 225, 227, 228, 229, 230, 231, 232, 233, 234, 235, 236.
span	palmus, -I, m.	223 q. 4, a. 2 ad 3.
species	speciês, specieî, f.	222, 223, 224, 225, 228, 231.

special	specialis, -e	225.	
specifically	specialiter	217.	
spirit	spiritus, -ûs, m.	188, 189, 192, 193, 236.	
spirit, vital	spiritus vitalis (pl. spiritûs vitalês), m.	233.	
	spiritualis, -e	190, 202, 204, 210, 219, 228, 236.	
Sabellians	Sabellianus, -a, -um	193.	
sea	pelagus, -i, n.	194, 196.	
son	filius, -ii, m.	187, 189, 192, 193, 194, 208.	
stand under	substo, -are	221, 222.	
starting-point	principium, -iî, n.	212	q. 3, a. 1, ad 4. See also *principle.
subject	subjectum, -î, n.	191, 192, 194, 195, 209, 213, 217, 220, 221, 222, 223, 224, 225, 228, 230.	
subject, be (vi)	subjacio, -ere	213, 216.	
subject (vt.)	subjicio, -ere, -jêcî, -jectum	191, 213, 215, 231.	
subsist	subsisto, -ere	191, 192, 194, 209, 215, 227, 229, 230, 235.	
subsistence	subsistentia, -ae, f.	193.	
subsisting	subsistêns, (gen.) subsistentis	188, 209, 210.	
substance	substantia, -ae, f.	187, 188, 189, 190, 191, 192, 193, 194, 196, 198, 208, 209, 212, 213, 215, 217, 218, **221**, 222, 223, 224, 225, 228, 229, 233.	
	substantialis, -e	214, 221, 228, 229, 232, 233.	
	substantialiter	235.	
	substantivus, -a, -um	188.	See "substantive *verb."
substrate	substratum, -î, n.	214	q. 3, a. 2 sol.: cf. "lay* under."
suddenly	de novô	218	q. 4, a. 1 obj. 3: The Latin "cum nulli rei substantia sua de novo adveniat" is easier to paraphrase than to translate; it may be rendered "since <a thing's> substance does not come to it as a novelty." There seems to be some echo of the Arabic notion of *hudûth,* i.e. 'generation' or 'coming into being'; see Goichon, *Lexique,* §§132–138 (pp. 60–65).
super-*being*	superesse	198	q. 1, a. 2 ad 1: Aquinas suggests that God is not what this or that creature is (i.e., its **being*), but is something above and beyond any crea-

		turely entity. Plato uses the Greek word *ousia* "being" in *Republic* VI 509Bff. to refer to the permanent intelligible essence of a thing (i.e., the form or *eidos* of a thing) with a principle still higher than *ousia,* namely "the idea of the Good" which is *epekeina tês ousias,* "above and beyond being." Here super-*being* is contrasted with *being.* If the term "*being*" were here taken in an existential sense, super-*being* by contrast would have to fall totally out of existence. To avoid this absurdity, we suggest that 'super-*being*' might be taken existentially and '*being*' essentially.
supposit	suppositum, -î, n.	199, 201, 202, 229. Cf . *posit.
take	sumo, -ere, sumi, sumptum	195 (+ ex)(+ a(b)), 196 (+ pro: 'taken to stand for'), 202 (+ ad), 205, 208 (+ pro), 209 (+ pro), 221 (+ ex), 229.
temporal	temporalis, -e	188, 189, 204, 206, 207.
tense	tempus, -oris, n.	188 (tense, time), 189 (time), 191 (time), 201, 202 (time), **205** (time), 206 (time, tense), 207 (time, tense), 209 (time), 211 (time), 213 (time), 215 (time), 216 (time), 217 (time), 218 (time), 220 (time). Compare *eternity and **aevum.*
text	1. textus, -ûs, m.	193: "Division of the First Part of the Text." 208: "Exposition* of the first part of the text."
	2. littera, -ae, f.	210: q. 3, intro.: "3∘ de modis mutationum, quos Augustinus assignat in *Littera.*" 213: q. 3, a. 2, obj. 4: Master* Peter Lombard *Sentences,* I, Chapter 22 (Grottaferrata 1971 ed., Tomus I, pars 1, p. 97. 20–22) quotes Augustine, *De Genesi ad litteram,* VIII, c. 20, n. 39 (PL 34, 388; CSEL 28–I, 259): "Ideo Augustinus, *Super Genesim,* dicit quod Deus nec per loca nec per tempora movetur, creatura vero per tempora et loca."
text of the comment	textus commentarii	See Bibliography §3.23, note on *Averroes.
that He is	quia est	195, 196. Contrast with "*what He is."
(that) which	(id) quod est	187, 191, **195**, 196, 197, 199, 202, 207, 208,

English	Latin	Pages	Reference / Notes
is		209, 210, 211, 212, 213, 214, 215, 218, 219, 220, 221, 222, 223, 226, **227**, 228, **229**, **230**, 232, 234.	
(that) by which it is	(id) quo est	209, 213, 218, **227**, **229**, **230**.	
the <word>	ly	203	q. 2, a. 1, ad 4: Latin does not have a definite article. Aquinas seems to have borrowed the colloquial French definite article "*le*" in some cases to mark quoted terms. See Ludwig Schütz, *Thomas-Lexikon,* p. 457. The Greek neuter singular article ' *to*' is used similarly.
themselves, through	per se	See "*itself, through."	
thing	res, rei, f.	188, 191, 193, **195**, 197, 198, 199, 202, 207, 208, 209, 211, 213, 214, 218, 219, 220 (also: 'really'), 223, 225 ('really'), **226**, 227, 228, 231, 235.	
this something	hoc aliquid	219	q. 4, a. 1 ad 2.
		231	q. 5, a. 2 ad 6.
time	tempus, -oris, n.	See *tense.	
tool	instrumentum, -î, n.	232.	q. 5, a. 2, ad 6.
transcendental(s) ***		200	q. 1, a. 3, especially the sol.: The term 'transcendentals' is not used in the text of Aquinas itself. Certain notions are confined to one of the ten Aristotelian categories* of being, e.g. the notion of color belongs to the category of quality; transcendental notions are not confined to just one category, e.g. both 'dog' and 'white' can be called by the name 'thing,' whose application cuts across categories, but, from a categorical point of view 'dog' belongs to the category of substance and 'white' to that of quality. For further explanation of transcendentals, see Joseph Owens, *An Elementary Christian Metaphysics.*
transmutation	transmutatio, -onis, f.	189, 211.	
treat	tracto, -are, -avi, -atus	200.	
	ago, -ere, egi, actum	187, 193, 199,	
treatise	tractatus, -ûs, m.	188, 195, 213, 222, 228, 229.	
true	verus,-a, -um	188, 189, 190, 196, 199, 200, 212, 228, 230.	
true, render	verifico, -are, -avi, -atus	212 (justify).	

truly	vere	187, 188, 189, 190, 191, 192, 193, 208, 217, 218, 224, 230.	
truth	veritas, -atis, f.	187, 188, 190, 193, 196, 204, 206, 208, 209, 210, 217, 223.	
turn back, able to be	vertibilis, -e	213. See *vertibility.	
unchangeability	immutabilitas, -atis, f.	193, 208, 210, 214.	
	incommutabilitas, -atis, f.	187, 188, 189, 193, 208.	
unchangeable	immutabilis, -e	189, 192, 210, 211, 213, 214.	
	incommutabilis, -e	189, 191, 192, 193, 210.	
undergo	patior, patî, passus	191 (cf. *passive).	
understand	intelligo, -ere, -êxî, -ectum	187, 188, 191, 202, 203, 207, 212. See also *intellect.	
understanding	intelligere (infinitive of intelligo)		195, 212.
	intelligendi (gerund of I.)	196.	
understanding	intellectus, -ûs, m.	196, 199, 200, 209. See also *intellect.	
unique	unicus, -a, -um	227.	
universal	universalis, -e	213, 215, 227.	
universally	universaliter	217.	
univocally	univoce	198	q. 1, a. 2, sol.
		222	q. 4, a. 2, ad 1.
		225	q. 4, a. 3, ad 1.
		See also *equivocally and *analogously.	
unknowing	ignorantia, -ae, f.	197	q. 1, a. 1, ad 4.
	ignoro, -are, -avi, -atum	not know: 222.	
various	diversus, -a, -um	188, 232. See *diverse.	
verb	verbum, -î, n.	188, 201, 206, 207, 208. Cf. *word.	
	verbum substantivum	188	The verb "to be" (*esse*).
vertibility	vertibilitas, -atis, f.	213, 214.	See *Damascene, note to p. 213.
way, in a certain	aliquo modo	198, 204, 210. q. 2, a. 2, sol.: in some fashion or other. For other citations, see *manner.	
wayfarer(s), as	in statû viae	194, 195.	
what (he/she/it) is	quid est	194, 195, 196, 201, 222. Contrast with "*that He is."	
Who Is	qui est	187, 192, 194, 195, 196, 199, 209, 231, 235, 236.	

whole	totus, -a, -um	190, 191, 192, 195, 201, 202, 203, 204, 205, 209, 213, 214, 225, 229, 231, 232, 233, 234, 235, 236.
with		
regard to what	secundum quod	207.
respect to <the fact> that		216.
word	verbum, -i, n.	187, 193, 194, 195, 199, 206 (the Word). See also *verb.

Appendix: A Conspectus of Book One of Peter Lombard's Sentences Tabulated in 210 Chapter-Headings and 48 Distinctions

Since, unlike some of his later, more personal works, the structure of St. Thomas' *Scriptum super libros Sententiarum* is largely determined by that of the text he is commenting, let us paraphrase the 210 chapter headings of Book I, superimposing the later break-down according to 48 *Distinctiones*, so that the context within which he is operating will be clearer. The chapters of Distinction VIII, the target of the present translation, are set in bold type.

Distinctio I

Ch 1.	Every teaching is either about things or about signs
Ch. 2.	That some things that are to be enjoyed, others to be used; and still others, both enjoyed and used.
Ch. 3	What enjoying and using are.

Distinctio II

Ch. 4.	On trinity and unity
Ch. 5.	The intention of writers on the Trinity
Ch. 6.	The order to be preserved when dealing with the Trinity
Ch. 7.	The testimony of the Old Testament for the mystery of the Trinity
Ch. 8.	The corresponding testimony of the New Testament.

Distinctio III

Ch. 9.	Knowing the Creator through creatures in which a trace of the Trinity appears.
Ch. 10.	The image and likeness of the Trinity in the human soul.
Ch. 11.	The likeness of the creating and the created trinity.
Ch. 12.	The unity of the Trinity.

Distinctio IV

Ch. 13.	Did God the Father generate God Himself?
Ch. 14.	Is the trinity predicated of the one God, as one God is of the three Persons?

Distinctio V

Ch. 15. Did the divine essence generate the Son or was it generated by the Father, or was the Son born of or the Holy Spirit proceeding from it?

Ch. 16. That is Son is not from nothing but from something, but not matter; so too the Holy Spirit.

Ch. 17. Why the Word of the Father is called Son of <the same> nature.

Distinctio VI

Ch. 18. Did the Father generate the Son by will or by necessity, and is He God willy-nilly?

Distinctio VII

Ch. 19. Could or would the Father generate the Son?

Ch. 20. Is the power to generate the Son a power in the Father that is not in the Son?

Distinctio VIII

Ch. 21. The truth and propriety of the divine essence.

Ch. 22. Its incommutability.

Ch. 23. Its simplicity.

Ch. 24. How a bodily or spiritual creature is multiple and not simple.

Ch. 25. That though God is simple, He is spoken of in many ways.

Ch. 26. That God's simplicity is not subject to any of the categories.

Ch. 27. That God is called a substance by abuse of language.

Ch. 28. That there is nothing in God which is not God.

Distinctio IX

Ch. 29. The distinction of the three persons.

Ch. 30. The coeternity of the Father and the Son.

Ch. 31. The ineffable and incomprehensible manner of generation.

Ch. 32. Ought one to say 'the Son is always being generated' or 'the Son was always generated'?

Ch. 33. The objections of heretics trying to prove that the Son is not coeternal with the Father.

Distinctio X

Ch. 34. On the Holy Spirit: that the love of the Father and of the Son is spoken of properly, since the love which is the Trinity is in the Trinity; just as the Word is properly called wisdom and yet the whole Trinity is called wisdom.

Ch. 35. That the same names are taken properly and universally.

Ch. 36. That the Holy Spirit, just as He is common to Father and Son, so does the common name have <something> proper.

Distinctio XI

Ch. 37. That the Holy Spirit proceeds from the Father and the Son, even though the Greeks disagree that He proceeds from the Son.

Ch. 38. The agreement of the Latins and the Greeks in meaning and their difference in words.

Distinctio XII

Ch. 39. Does the Holy Spirit more properly or more fully proceed from the Father than from the Son?

Ch. 40. That the Holy Spirit principally and properly is said to proceed from the Father.

Distinctio XIII

Ch. 41. Why, though the Holy Spirit is of the substance of the Father, He is not said to be generated but only proceeding.

Ch. 42. Why the Son is said to proceed, though the Holy Spirit is not said to be generated.

Ch. 43. That a mortal cannot distinguish between the generation of the Son and the procession of the Holy Spirit.

Ch. 44. Ought the Holy Spirit be called ungenerated, since He is not generated?

Distinctio XIV

Ch. 45. The twin procession of the Holy Spirit, temporal and eternal.

Ch. 46. That not only the gifts of the Holy Spirit but even God the Holy Spirit Himself is given and sent to human beings.

Ch. 47. Can saints give the Holy Spirit?

Distinctio XV

Ch. 48. That the Holy Spirit is given by Himself and the Son is sent by Himself.

Ch. 49. How their being sent (*missio*) is to be understood.

Ch. 50. That the Son is also sent by the Holy Spirit.

Ch. 51. That the Son is also given by Himself.

Ch. 52. How 'I did not come of Myself' is to be understood.

Ch. 53. Was the Son sent only once or several times?

Ch. 54. The two types of the Son's mission.

Ch. 55. That according to the one type, He was sent once, according to the other several times; and according to the one, He is said to have been sent into the world, but not according to the other.

Ch. 56. That the Father is not said to have been sent.

Ch. 57. That the Son and the Holy Spirit are not in any way less than the Father for having been sent.

Distinctio XVI

Ch. 58. The mission of the Holy Spirit, which comes about in two ways: visibly and invisibly.

Ch. 59. That the Son, as man, is not only less than the Father, but also to the Holy Spirit and even Himself.

Distinctio XVII

Ch. 60. That the Holy Spirit is the charity by which we love God and neighbor.

Ch. 61. That fraternal love is not God the Father or the Son but only God the Holy Spirit.

Ch. 62. The expression 'God is love' is not said causally, like 'You are my patience and my hope'.
Ch. 63. How the Holy Spirit is sent or given to us.
Ch. 64. Is the Holy Spirit increased in man, or had or given to a lesser or greater degree, and is it given to one who has and to one who has it not?
Ch. 65. That some people say that the love of God and neighbor is not the Holy Spirit.

Distinctio XVIII

Ch. 66. Should it be admitted that gifts are given by gift?
Ch. 67. Is the Holy Spirit called a gift for the same reason, whether He is something given (*datum*) or donated (*donatum*)?
Ch. 68. That just as the Son by being begotten gets not only to be Son but also to be essence, so too does the Holy Spirit by proceeding get not only to be a gift but also to be essence.
Ch. 69. That the Holy Spirit is called a gift and something donated with respect to these two modes of procession: as gift, He is referred to the Father; as given, to Him who gives and to those to whom He is given.
Ch. 70. Can the Son, when He is given to us, be, as is the Holy Spirit, called 'our'.
Ch. 71. Is the Holy Spirit related to Himself?

Distinctio XIX

Ch. 72. The equality of the three Persons.
Ch. 73. That eternity, magnitude, and power in God is one, even if they seem diverse.
Ch. 74. That one person does not exceed another in magnitude, since one person is not greater than another, nor is any pair greater than one, nor any three than two or one.
Ch. 75. How the Father is said to be in the Son and the Son in the Father and the Holy Spirit in both.
Ch. 76. That there is no part of the persons in the Trinity.
Ch. 77. Why the three persons are said to be one in the highest degree.
Ch. 78. When we say that the three persons are one essence, this is not the case in the way that we predicate a genus of its species nor as we predicate a species of its individuals, since the essence is not the genus and the person the species nor the essence a species and the persons the individuals.
Ch. 79. Neither are the three persons one essence according to material cause.
Ch. 80. Nor are the three persons said to be one essence they way three men are one nature.
Ch. 81. Do the three persons, which are distinct by their proprieties, differ in number?

Ch. 82. Why the three persons together are not any greater than one.
Ch. 83. That God is not to be called triple but trine.

Distinctio XX

Ch. 84. None of the persons exceeds any other in power.
Ch. 85. The Son cannot be less than the Father.
Ch. 86. Concerning the heretical objections against this point and the Catholic answers.

Distinctio XXI

Ch. 87. How it is possible to speak of 'only the Father' or 'only the Son' or 'only the Holy Spirit' when they are inseparable.
Ch. 88. Ought one to say that 'only the Father is God' or 'only the Son is God' or 'only the Holy Spirit is God', or 'the Father is the only God', 'the Son is the only God' 'the Holy Spirit is the only God'?
Ch. 89. How 'the Trinity is the only God' is said, given that it is with the spirits and souls of the saints.

Distinctio XXII

Ch. 90. The differences of the names we use when speaking about God.
Ch. 91. Things that belong to God temporally and are spoken of relatively.
Ch. 92. The name 'trinity'.
Ch. 93. Things that belong to God temporally but are not spoken of relatively.
Ch. 94. Things that pertain properly to the single persons and those that signify unity of essence.

Distinctio XXIII

Ch. 95. The name 'person': that when it is predicated substantially is nevertheless predicated as a plural and not as a singular of the trinity.
Ch. 96. Why the Latins have to say 'three persons' and the Greeks 'three hypostases or substances'.
Ch. 97. Why we do not say that Father, Son, and Holy Spirit, as three persons, are three gods.
Ch. 98. Why we do not say that as three persons they are three essences.
Ch. 99. That there is not diversity, singularity, or solitude in the Trinity, but only unity and trinity, and distinction and identity.
Ch. 100. That God ought not to be called multiple.

Distinctio XXIV

Ch. 101. What is signified by the names one, two (duo vel duae), three (tres vel tria), trine or trinity, many or plurality, distinction or distinct, when we use them to speak about God.

Distinctio XXV

Ch. 102. What is signified by the name 'person' in the plural, when we speak of 'persons'?
Ch. 103. The three ways of taking the name 'person' in the Trinity.

Distinctio XXX

Ch. 129. The things that are predicated temporally of God and relatively (i.e. accidentally) are accidental not to God but to creatures.

Ch. 130. May the Holy Spirit be said to be given or donated relatively to Himself when He is given by Himself?

Distinctio XXXI

Ch. 131. May the Son be called equal to or similar to the Father with respect to substance?

Ch. 132. St. Hilary's opinion on the proper features of the persons in the Trinity.

Ch. 133. Why unity is attributed to the Father.

Ch. 134. Why Father and Son are said to be one (unum) or one God (unus Deus), but not one (unus).

Ch. 135. Why there is said to be equality in the Son.

Ch. 136. Why the concord or connection of them both is said to be in the Holy Spirit.

Distinctio XXXII

Ch. 137. Does the Father or the Son love with that love which proceeds from them both, i.e. with the Holy Spirit?

Ch. 138. Is the Father wise by the wisdom that He has begotten?

Ch. 139. Is the Son wise by Himself or through Himself?

Ch. 140. Is the Father's wisdom the only one?

Ch. 141. Just as there is in the Trinity a love which is the Trinity and yet the Holy Spirit is a love which is not the Trinity, and yet there are not two loves, so too in the case of wisdom.

Ch. 142. Why the Father is not called wise by the begotten wisdom, any more than that he is called loving by the love that proceeds from Him.

Distinctio XXXIII

Ch. 143. Are the proprieties of the persons the persons themselves or the divine usia?

Ch. 144. How can the proprieties be in God's nature and yet not determine it?

Distinctio XXXIV

Ch. 145. On the words of Hilary by which he seems to say, according to the understanding of the depraved, that the divine nature and a thing belonging to that nature are not identical, and that God and what is of God are not identical.

Ch. 146. Is it the same thing to say 'one God of three persons' as 'one essence of three persons', and 'three persons of one God' as 'three persons of one essence'?

Ch. 147. That in Scripture, power, wisdom, and goodness are sometimes referred to the persons distinctly.

Ch. 148. Why power is attributed to the Father, wisdom to the Son, and

goodness to the Holy Spirit, even though there is one power, wisdom, and goodness belonging to the three.

Ch. 149. When the name 'homousion' was received as authoritative and what it signifies.

Distinctio XXXV

Ch. 150. God's knowledge and his foreknowledge, providence, disposition and predestination.
Ch. 151. What God's foreknowledge and foresight are about.
Ch. 152. The objects of His disposition.
Ch. 153. The objects of His predestination.
Ch. 154. The objects of His providence.
Ch. 155. The objects of His wisdom or knowledge.
Ch. 156. Whether God's foreknowledge, disposition, or predestination could have existed if there were no future things.
Ch. 157. That God's knowledge is of temporal and eternal things.
Ch. 158. How all things are said to be in God, and life <is said to be> in Him.

Distinctio XXXVI

Ch. 159. Ought all things to be said to be in God's essence as they are said to be in God's cognition or presence?
Ch. 160. Why are good things said to be in God and not bad ones?
Ch. 161. Is it the same for all things to be from God and through Him and in Him?
Ch. 162. That all things in any of the three are both through Him and in Him.
Ch. 163. That not all things that are from God are also of Him.

Distinctio XXXVII

Ch. 164. In what ways God is said to be in things.
Ch. 165. God does not dwell wherever He is, but wherever He dwells He is.
Ch. 166. Where God was before there was a creature.
Ch. 167. That though God is in all things essentially, He is nevertheless not contaminated by their defects.
Ch. 168. Though God is everywhere and always, nevertheless He is not confined to a place nor is He moved in place nor in time.
Ch. 169. In what ways is something said to be in a place or circumscribable?
Ch. 170. What is it to be changed (mutari) with respect to time>?
Ch. 171. Are created spirits in place and circumscribable?
Ch. 172. That God is everywhere without local motion.

Distinctio XXXVIII

Ch. 173. Is God's knowledge or foreknowledge the cause of things or is it the other way around?
Ch. 174. Can God's foreknowledge fail?

Distinctio XXXIX

Ch. 175. Can God's knowledge be increased or diminished or changed in any way?

Ch. 176. Can God get knowledge or foreknowledge of anything in a new way or from time?

Ch. 177. Is God able to know more than He does?

Ch. 178. That God knows all things both always and simultaneously.

Distinctio XL

Ch. 179. Can anyone predestined be damned or anyone reprobate be saved?

Ch. 180. What is God's reprobation and in whom is it considered, and what is the effect of predestination?

Distinctio XLI

Ch. 181. Is there any merit for obduracy or mercy?

Ch. 182. Various opinions of carnal people on this issue.

Ch. 183. Whether God always knows and preknows and always will know and preknow what he once knows or preknows.

Distinctio XLII

Ch. 184. God's omnipotence: why He is called omnipotent though we can do many things He cannot.

Ch. 185. How God is said to be omnipotent.

Ch. 186. That God's omnipotence is considered in two ways.

Distinctio XLIII

Ch. 187. Attack against those who claim that God can do nothing but what He wills and does.

Distinctio XLIV

Ch. 188. Can God make anything better than He does, or in any other, better way?

Ch. 189. Is God always able to do what He could have?

Distinctio XLV

Ch. 190. God's will, which is God's essence, and the signs of it.

Ch. 191. Although for God willing is the same as being, still God cannot be said to be all that He wills.

Ch. 192. Understanding the expressions 'God knows' or 'God wills', 'God knows all things' or 'He wills something'.

Ch. 193. God's will is the highest good, the cause of all things that naturally exist, <a cause> whose cause is not to be sought after, since it is the first and highest cause of all.

Ch. 194. The ways in which God's will can be taken.

Ch. 195. That preception, prohibition, permission, counsel, operation are <all> sometimes understood by the will.

Ch. 196. Does God will that what He orders should be done, or that what he forbids should not be done by all?

Distinctio XLVI

- Ch. 197. God's will, which is Himself, cannot fail in anything.
- Ch. 198. How one ought to understand 'I willed to gather your sons and you were unwilling' and 'He who wills that all men be saved'?
- Ch. 199. Do bad things come about whether God wills them or not?
- Ch. 200. How to understand Augustine's <remark> 'It is good for bad things to come about'.
- Ch. 201. On the multiple meaning of the good.
- Ch. 202. That bad things are prevalent in the universe but yet are beneficial to the elect who do their own or who suffer those of others.
- Ch. 203. That the cause that a man be worse does not exist in God.

Distinctio XLVII

- Ch. 204. How God's will is fulfilled in the case of a human being, whichever way he turns.
- Ch. 205. In what sense certain things are said to come about against the will of God.
- Ch. 206. Why does God order everyone to do good things and avoid evil, if He does not will that it be fulfilled by everyone?

Distinctio XLVIII

- Ch. 207. That man sometimes with a good will wills something other than what God does, and sometimes with a bad will he wills the same thing as God does.
- Ch. 208. That God's will is fulfilled through the bad wills of men.
- Ch. 209. Would the saints want Christ to suffer and die?
- Ch. 210. Ought we to will the sufferings of the saints?